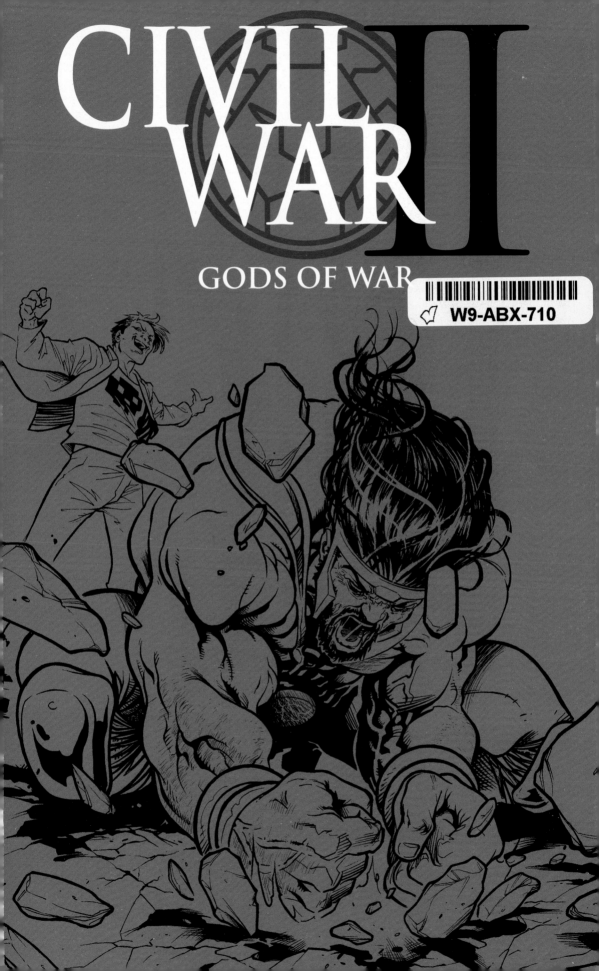

CIVIL WAR II

GODS OF WAR

IN ANCIENT DAYS, HERCULES WAS THE GREATEST HERO OF ALL. BUT IN THE MODERN WORLD, IMMORTAL HERCULES HAS DONE LITTLE BUT ENJOY HIS CELEBRITY. HIS DESTINY, IT SEEMED, WAS SEEMED, WAS TO FADE INTO OBSCURITY AND SCANDAL. BUT HERCULES DEFIED HIS FATE AND HAS STARTED TO RECLAIM HIS REPUTATION AS A TRUE HERO.

WHILE GETTING HIS LIFE BACK ON TRACK, HERCULES DISCOVERS THE UPRISING STORM: A PANTHEON OF NEW GODS BORN OF THE MODERN AGE, SEEKING TO DESTROY THEIR ANCIENT COUNTERPARTS.

TOGETHER WITH FELLOW GODS GILGAMESH AND IRE, HERCULES BATTLED THE UPRISING STORM, WHERE HE WAS MARKED BY A BRAND LACED WITH STRANGE TECHNOLOGY. SHUNNED BY THE HERO COMMUNITY, HERCULES IS MORE ISOLATED THAN EVER, AND SOON ENOUGH THE STORM WILL COME LOOKING FOR ROUND TWO...

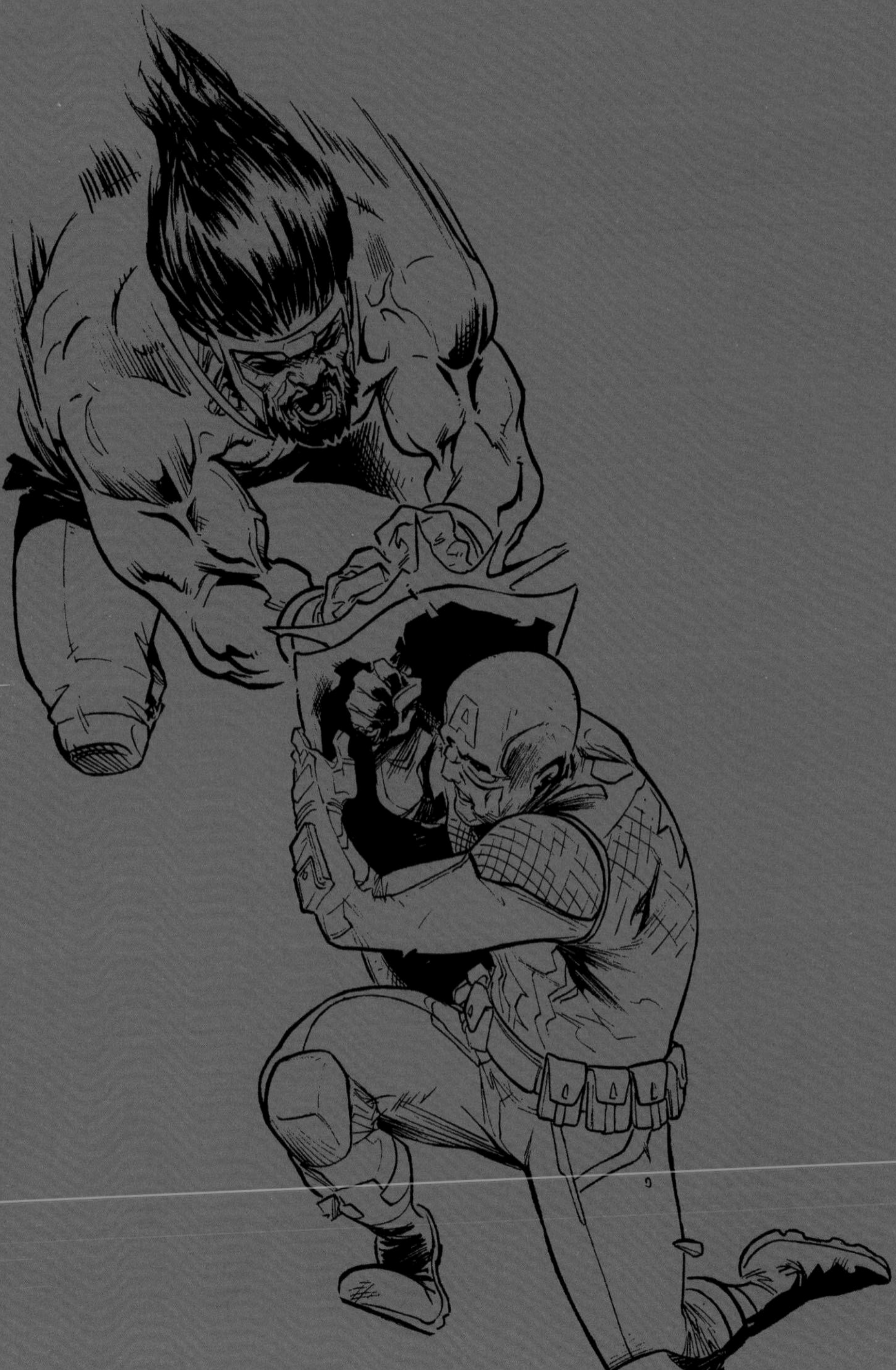

CIVIL WAR II

GODS OF WAR

WRITER
DAN ABNETT

ARTIST
EMILIO LAISO

COLOR ARTIST
GURU-eFX

LETTERER
VC's JOE SABINO

COVER ARTISTS
JAY ANACLETO & ROMULO FAJARDO JR.

ASSISTANT EDITOR
CHRISTINA HARRINGTON

EDITOR
KATIE KUBERT

EXECUTIVE EDITOR
TOM BREVOORT

HERCULES CREATED BY
STAN LEE AND **JACK KIRBY**

COLLECTION EDITOR
SARAH BRUNSTAD
ASSOCIATE MANAGING EDITOR
KATERI WOODY
SENIOR EDITOR, SPECIAL PROJECTS
JENNIFER GRÜNWALD
EDITOR, SPECIAL PROJECTS
MARK D. BEAZLEY
VP PRODUCTION & SPECIAL PROJECTS
JEFF YOUNGQUIST
SVP PRINT, SALES & MARKETING
DAVID GABRIEL

BOOK DESIGNER
ADAM DEL RE

EDITOR IN CHIEF
AXEL ALONSO
CHIEF CREATIVE OFFICER
JOE QUESADA
PUBLISHER
DAN BUCKLEY
EXECUTIVE PRODUCER
ALAN FINE

CIVIL WAR II: GODS OF WAR. Contains material originally published in magazine form as CIVIL WAR II: GODS OF WAR #1-4 and JOURNEY INTO MYSTERY ANNUAL #1. First printing 2016. ISBN# 978-1-302-90034-2. Published by MARVEL WORLDWIDE, INC., a subsidiary of MARVEL ENTERTAINMENT, LLC. OFFICE OF PUBLICATION: 135 West 50th Street, New York, NY 10020. Copyright © 2016 MARVEL No similarity between any of the names, characters, persons, and/or institutions in this magazine with those of any living or dead person or institution is intended, and any such similarity which may exist is purely coincidental. **Printed in Canada.** ALAN FINE, President, Marvel Entertainment; DAN BUCKLEY, President, TV, Publishing & Brand Management; JOE QUESADA, Chief Creative Officer; TOM BREVOORT, SVP of Publishing; DAVID BOGART, SVP of Business Affairs & Operations, Publishing & Partnership; C.B. CEBULSKI, VP of Brand Management & Development, Asia; DAVID GABRIEL, SVP of Sales & Marketing, Publishing; JEFF YOUNGQUIST, VP of Production & Special Projects; DAN CARR, Executive Director of Publishing Technology; ALEX MORALES, Director of Publishing Operations; SUSAN CRESPI, Production Manager; STAN LEE, Chairman Emeritus. For information regarding advertising in Marvel Comics or on Marvel.com, please contact Vit DeBellis, Integrated Sales Manager, at vdebellis@marvel.com. For Marvel subscription inquiries, please call 888-511-5480. **Manufactured between 9/16/2016 and 10/24/2016 by SOLISCO PRINTERS, SCOTT, QC, CANADA.**

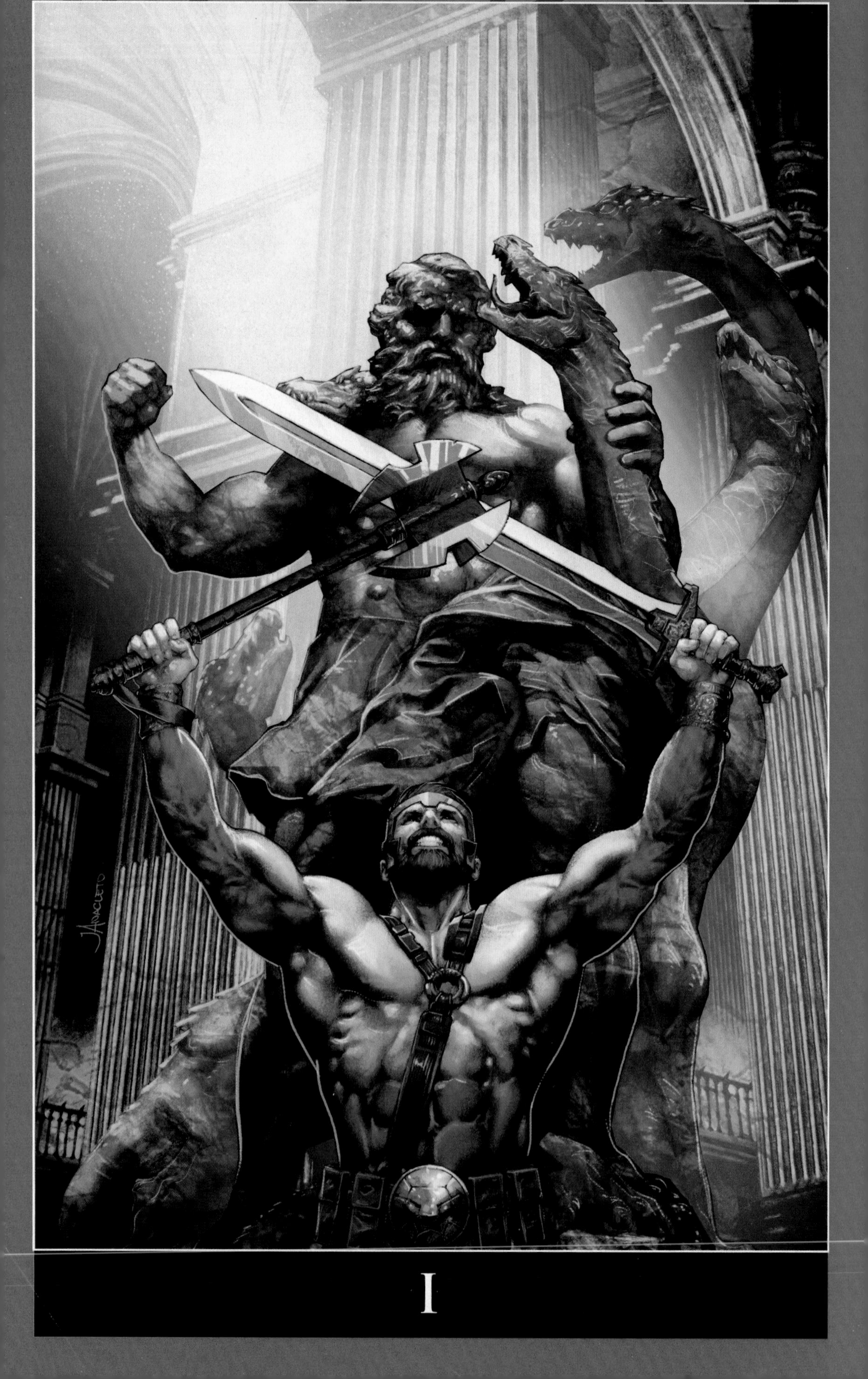

I

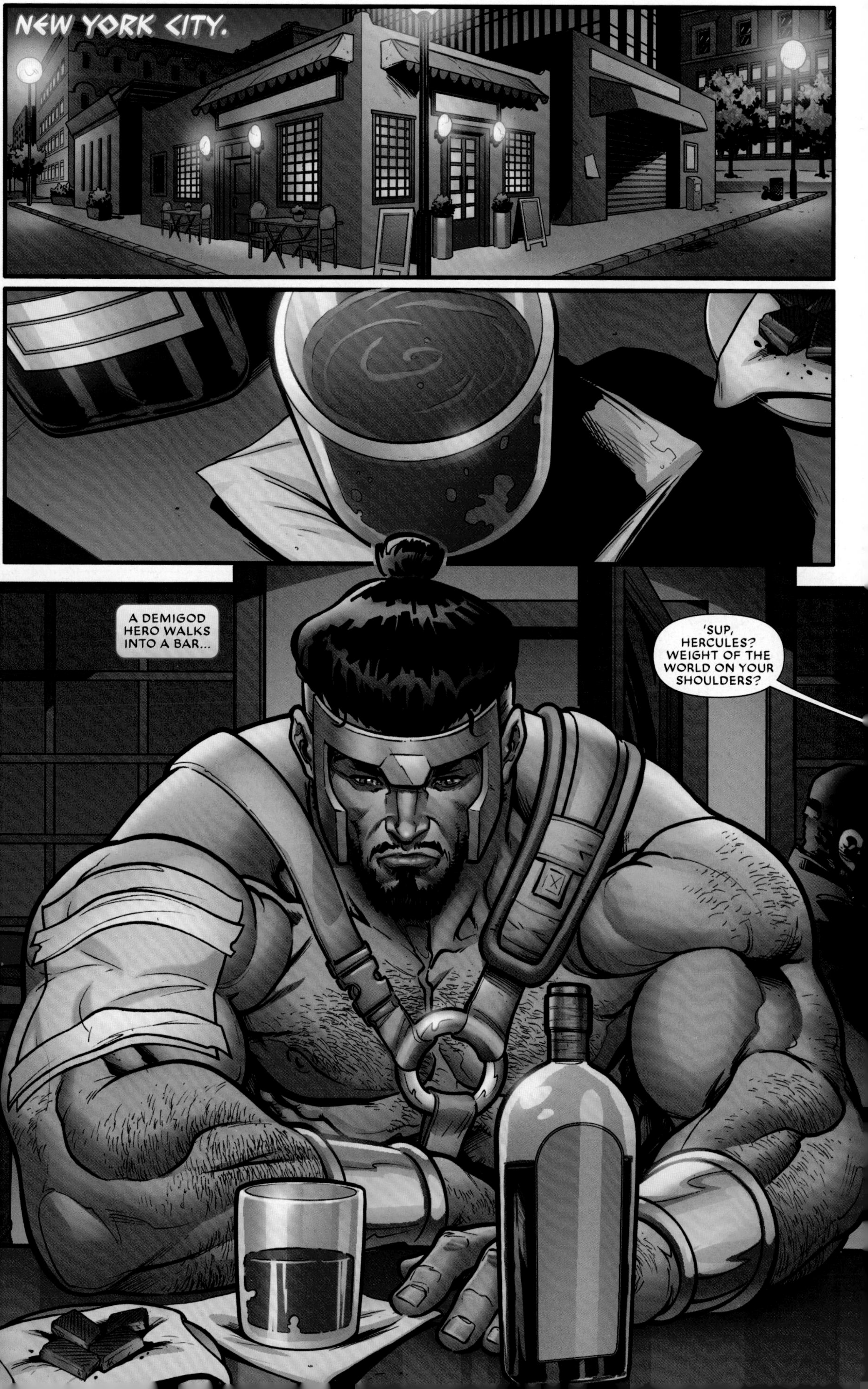
NEW YORK CITY.
A DEMIGOD HERO WALKS INTO A BAR...
'SUP, HERCULES? WEIGHT OF THE WORLD ON YOUR SHOULDERS?

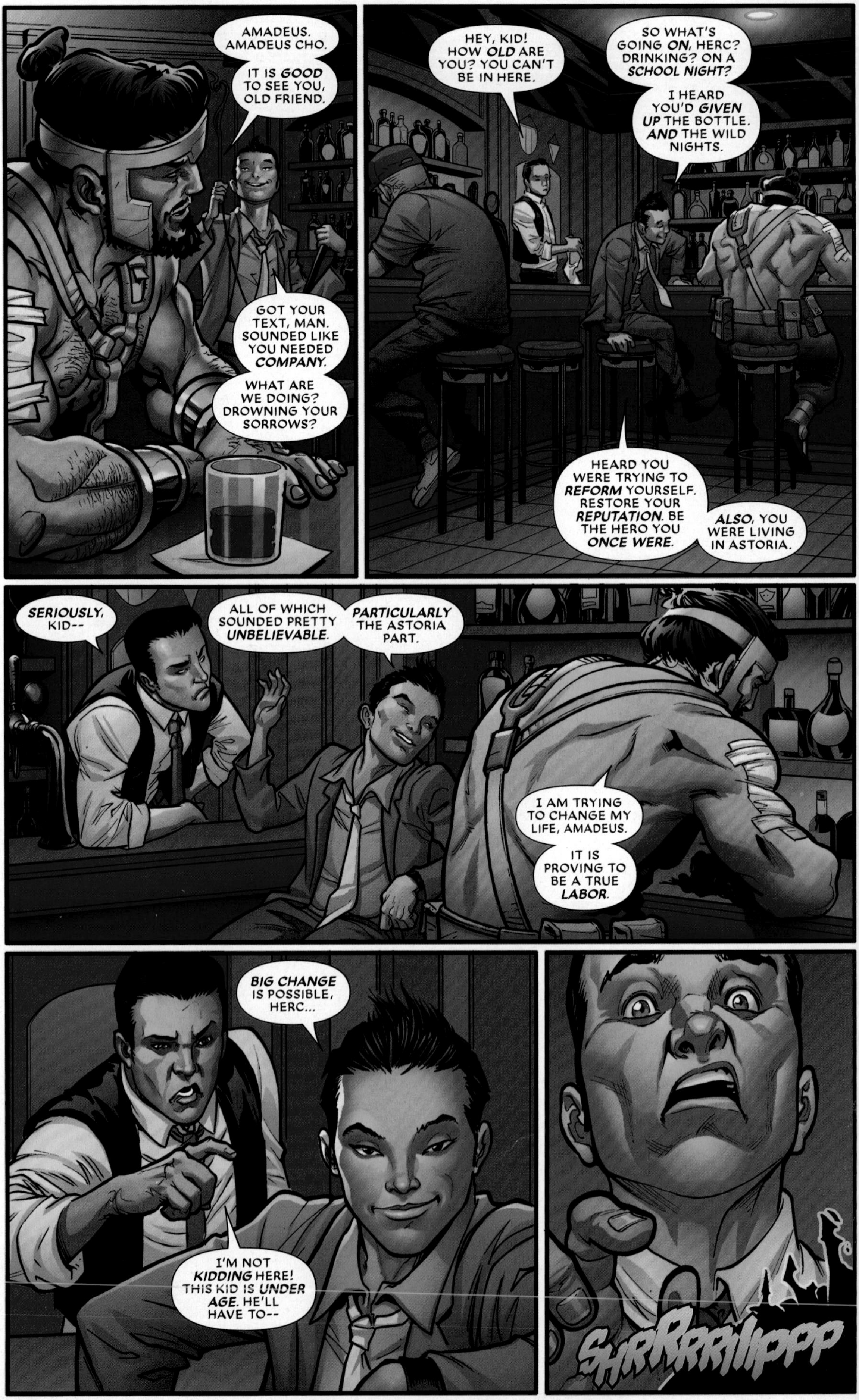

AMADEUS. AMADEUS CHO.
IT IS GOOD TO SEE YOU, OLD FRIEND.
GOT YOUR TEXT, MAN. SOUNDED LIKE YOU NEEDED COMPANY.
WHAT ARE WE DOING? DROWNING YOUR SORROWS?
HEY, KID! HOW OLD ARE YOU? YOU CAN'T BE IN HERE.
SO WHAT'S GOING ON, HERC? DRINKING? ON A SCHOOL NIGHT?
I HEARD YOU'D GIVEN UP THE BOTTLE. AND THE WILD NIGHTS.
HEARD YOU WERE TRYING TO REFORM YOURSELF. RESTORE YOUR REPUTATION. BE THE HERO YOU ONCE WERE.
ALSO, YOU WERE LIVING IN ASTORIA.
SERIOUSLY, KID--
ALL OF WHICH SOUNDED PRETTY UNBELIEVABLE.
PARTICULARLY THE ASTORIA PART.
I AM TRYING TO CHANGE MY LIFE, AMADEUS.
IT IS PROVING TO BE A TRUE LABOR.
BIG CHANGE IS POSSIBLE, HERC...
I'M NOT KIDDING HERE! THIS KID IS UNDER AGE. HE'LL HAVE TO--
SHRRRRIIIPPP

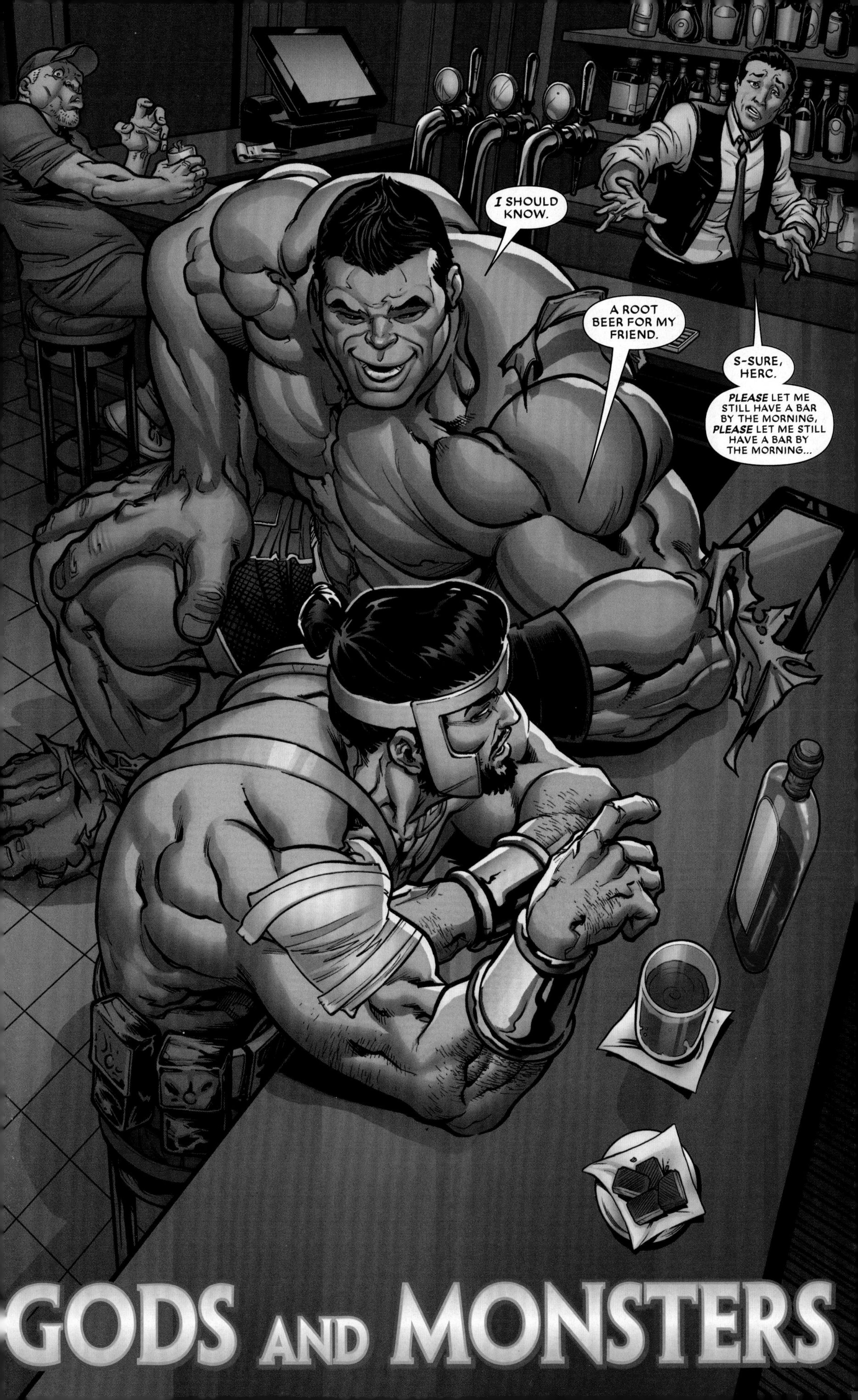
I SHOULD KNOW.
A ROOT BEER FOR MY FRIEND.
S-SURE, HERC.
PLEASE LET ME STILL HAVE A BAR BY THE MORNING, PLEASE LET ME STILL HAVE A BAR BY THE MORNING...
GODS AND MONSTERS

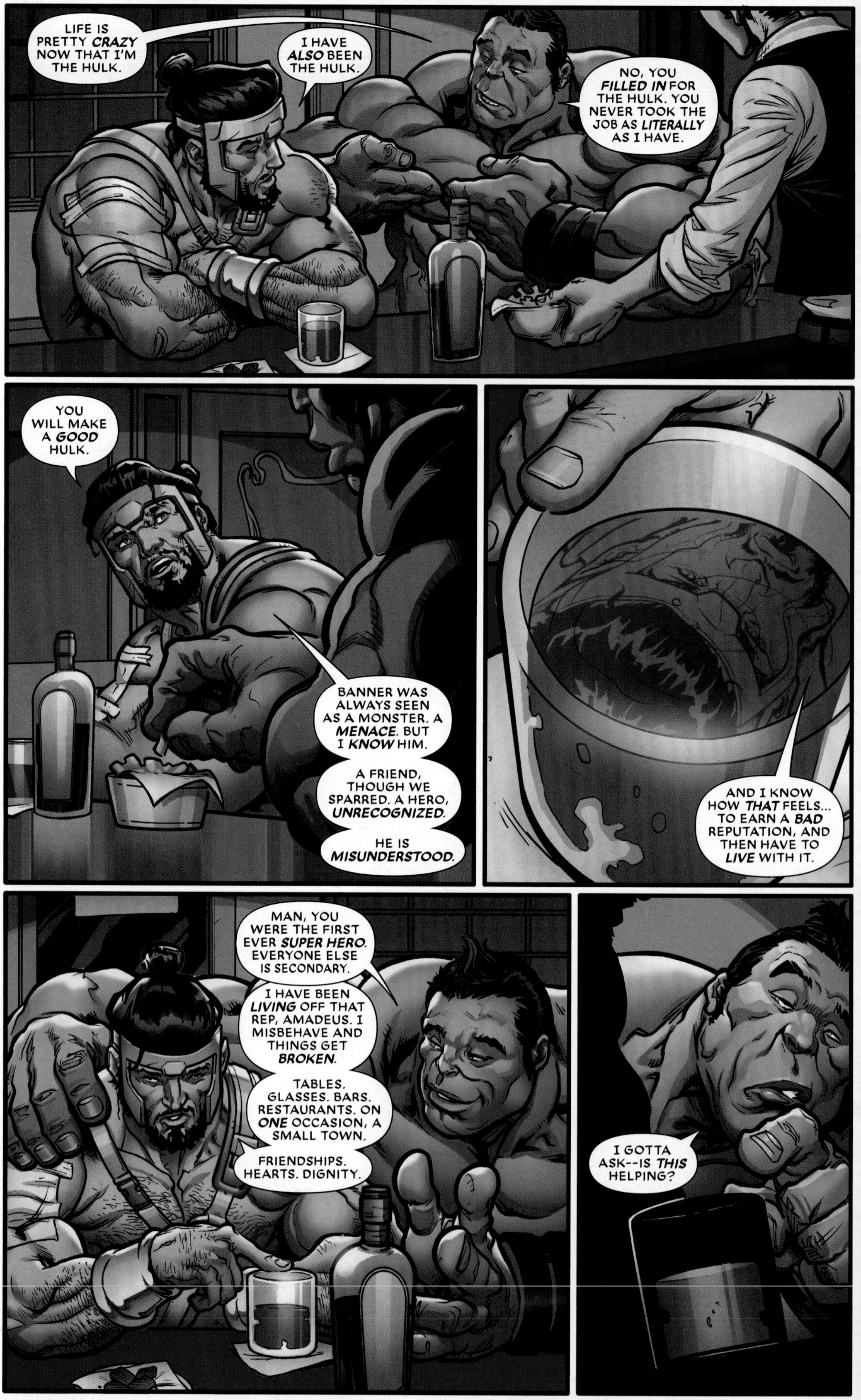
LIFE IS PRETTY *CRAZY* NOW THAT I'M THE HULK.
I HAVE *ALSO* BEEN THE HULK.
NO, YOU *FILLED IN* FOR THE HULK. YOU NEVER TOOK THE JOB AS *LITERALLY* AS I HAVE.
YOU WILL MAKE A *GOOD* HULK.
BANNER WAS ALWAYS SEEN AS A MONSTER. A *MENACE*. BUT I *KNOW* HIM.
A FRIEND, THOUGH WE SPARRED. A HERO, *UNRECOGNIZED*.
HE IS *MISUNDERSTOOD*.
AND I KNOW HOW *THAT* FEELS... TO EARN A *BAD* REPUTATION, AND THEN HAVE TO *LIVE* WITH IT.
MAN, YOU WERE THE FIRST EVER *SUPER HERO*. EVERYONE ELSE IS SECONDARY.
I HAVE BEEN *LIVING* OFF THAT REP, AMADEUS. I MISBEHAVE AND THINGS GET *BROKEN*.
TABLES. GLASSES. BARS. RESTAURANTS. ON *ONE* OCCASION, A SMALL TOWN.
FRIENDSHIPS. HEARTS. DIGNITY.
I GOTTA ASK--IS *THIS* HELPING?

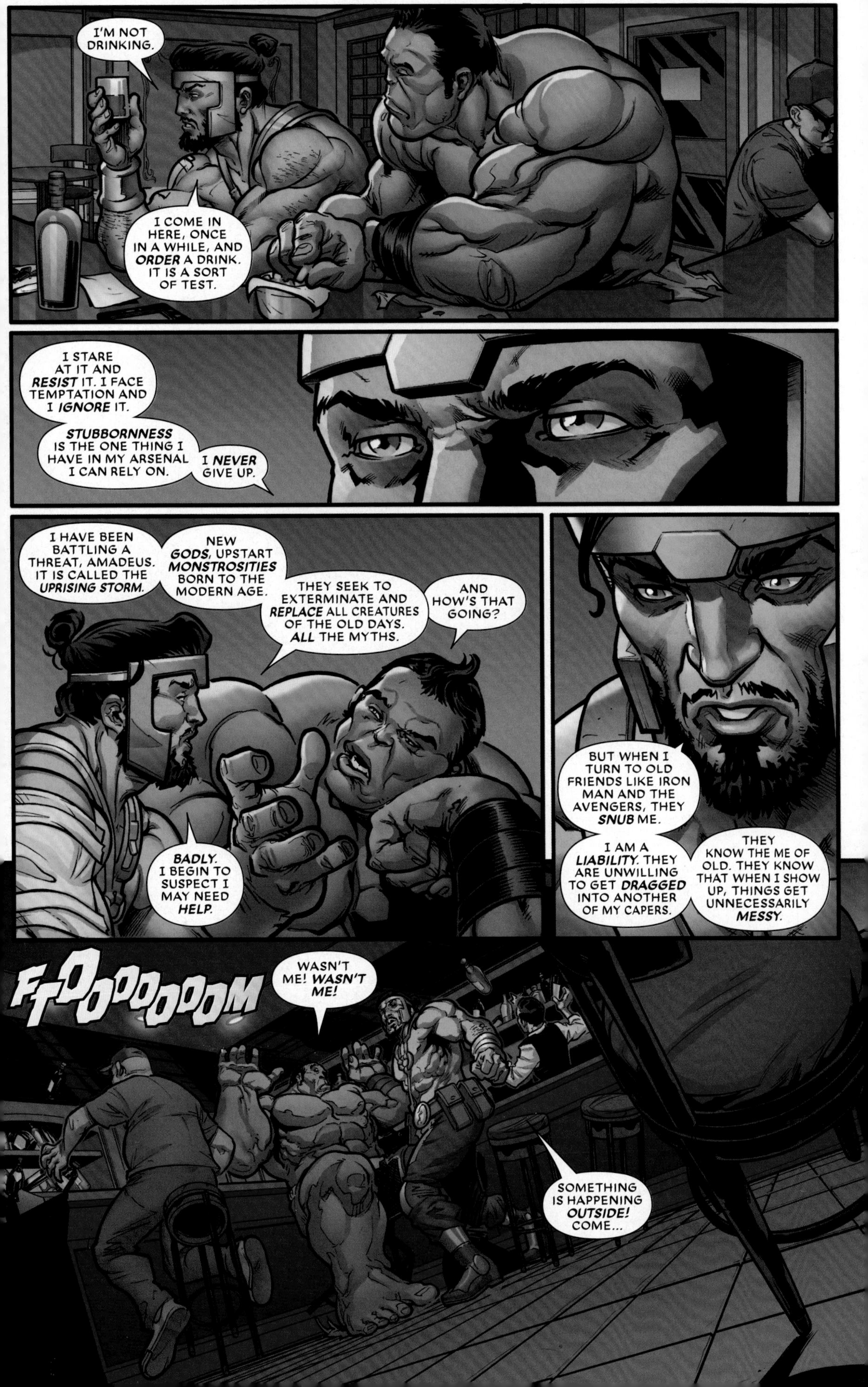
I'M NOT DRINKING.
I COME IN HERE, ONCE IN A WHILE, AND ORDER A DRINK. IT IS A SORT OF TEST.
I STARE AT IT AND RESIST IT. I FACE TEMPTATION AND I IGNORE IT.
STUBBORNNESS IS THE ONE THING I HAVE IN MY ARSENAL I CAN RELY ON.
I NEVER GIVE UP.
I HAVE BEEN BATTLING A THREAT, AMADEUS. IT IS CALLED THE UPRISING STORM.
NEW GODS, UPSTART MONSTROSITIES BORN TO THE MODERN AGE.
THEY SEEK TO EXTERMINATE AND REPLACE ALL CREATURES OF THE OLD DAYS. ALL THE MYTHS.
AND HOW'S THAT GOING?
BADLY. I BEGIN TO SUSPECT I MAY NEED HELP.
BUT WHEN I TURN TO OLD FRIENDS LIKE IRON MAN AND THE AVENGERS, THEY SNUB ME.
I AM A LIABILITY. THEY ARE UNWILLING TO GET DRAGGED INTO ANOTHER OF MY CAPERS.
THEY KNOW THE ME OF OLD. THEY KNOW THAT WHEN I SHOW UP, THINGS GET UNNECESSARILY MESSY.
FTOOOOOOOOM
WASN'T ME! WASN'T ME!
SOMETHING IS HAPPENING OUTSIDE! COME...

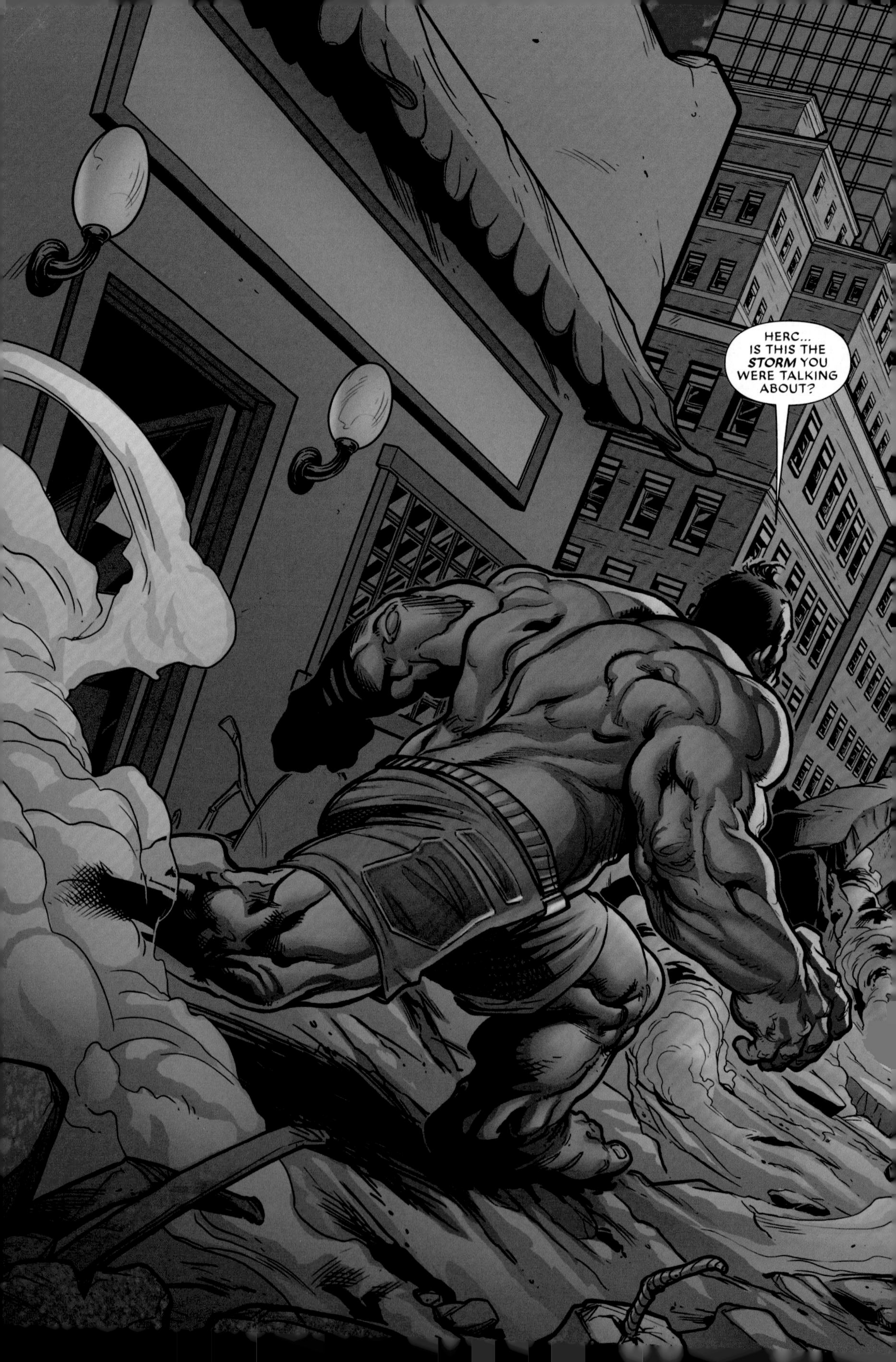
HERC...
IS THIS THE
STORM YOU
WERE TALKING
ABOUT?

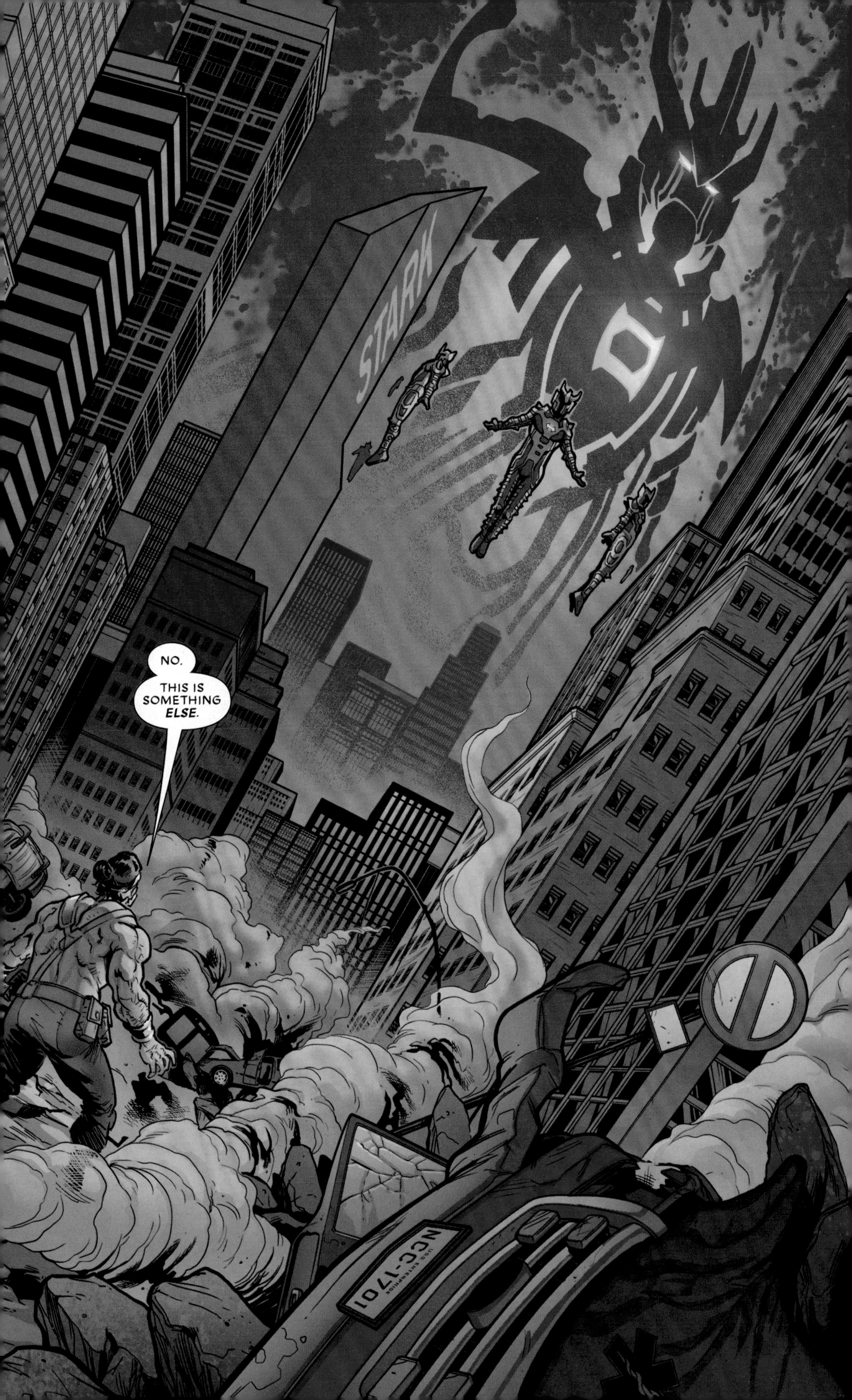
NO.
THIS IS SOMETHING *ELSE*.
STARK
NCC-1701

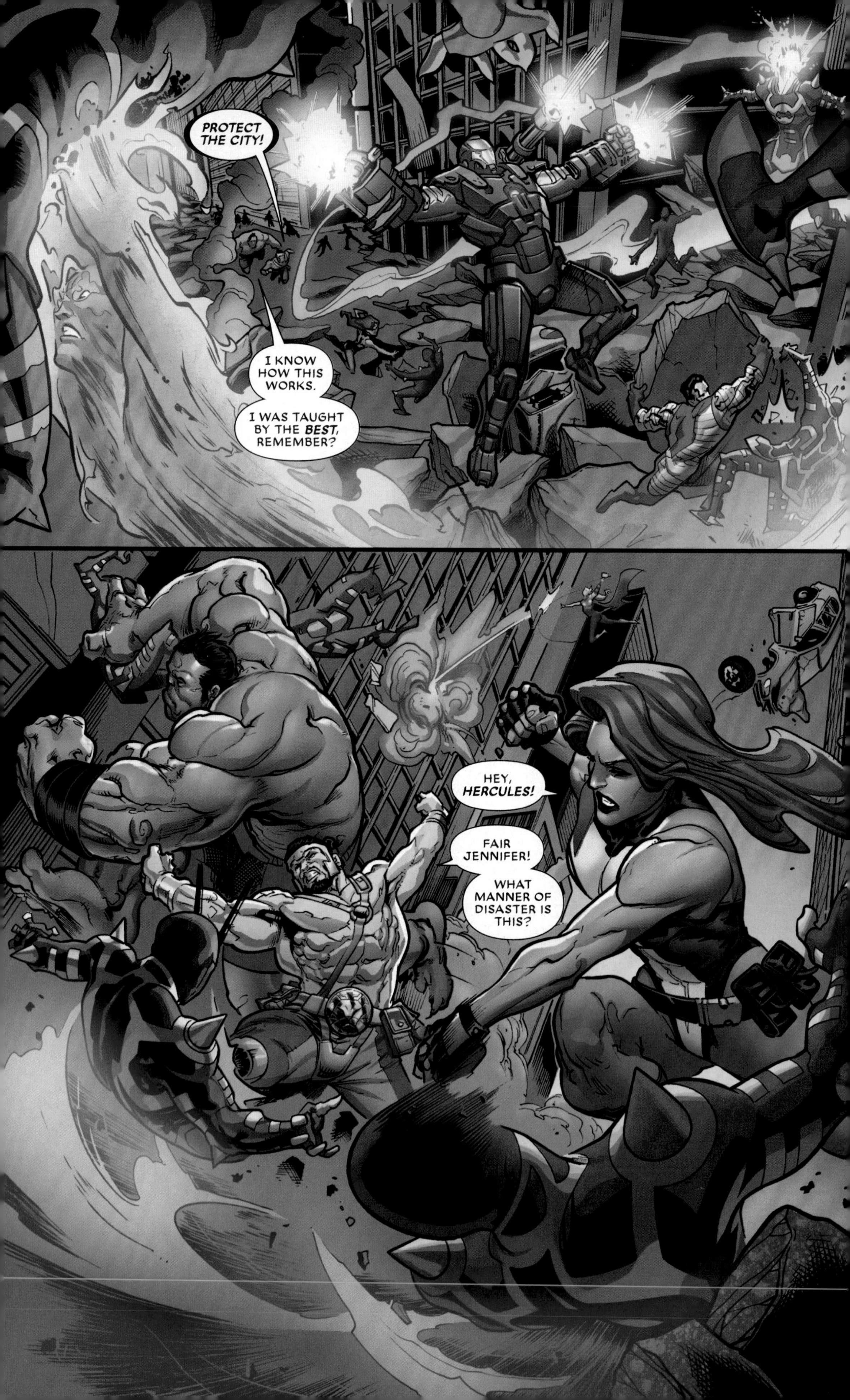
PROTECT THE CITY!
I KNOW HOW THIS WORKS.
I WAS TAUGHT BY THE BEST, REMEMBER?
HEY, HERCULES!
FAIR JENNIFER!
WHAT MANNER OF DISASTER IS THIS?

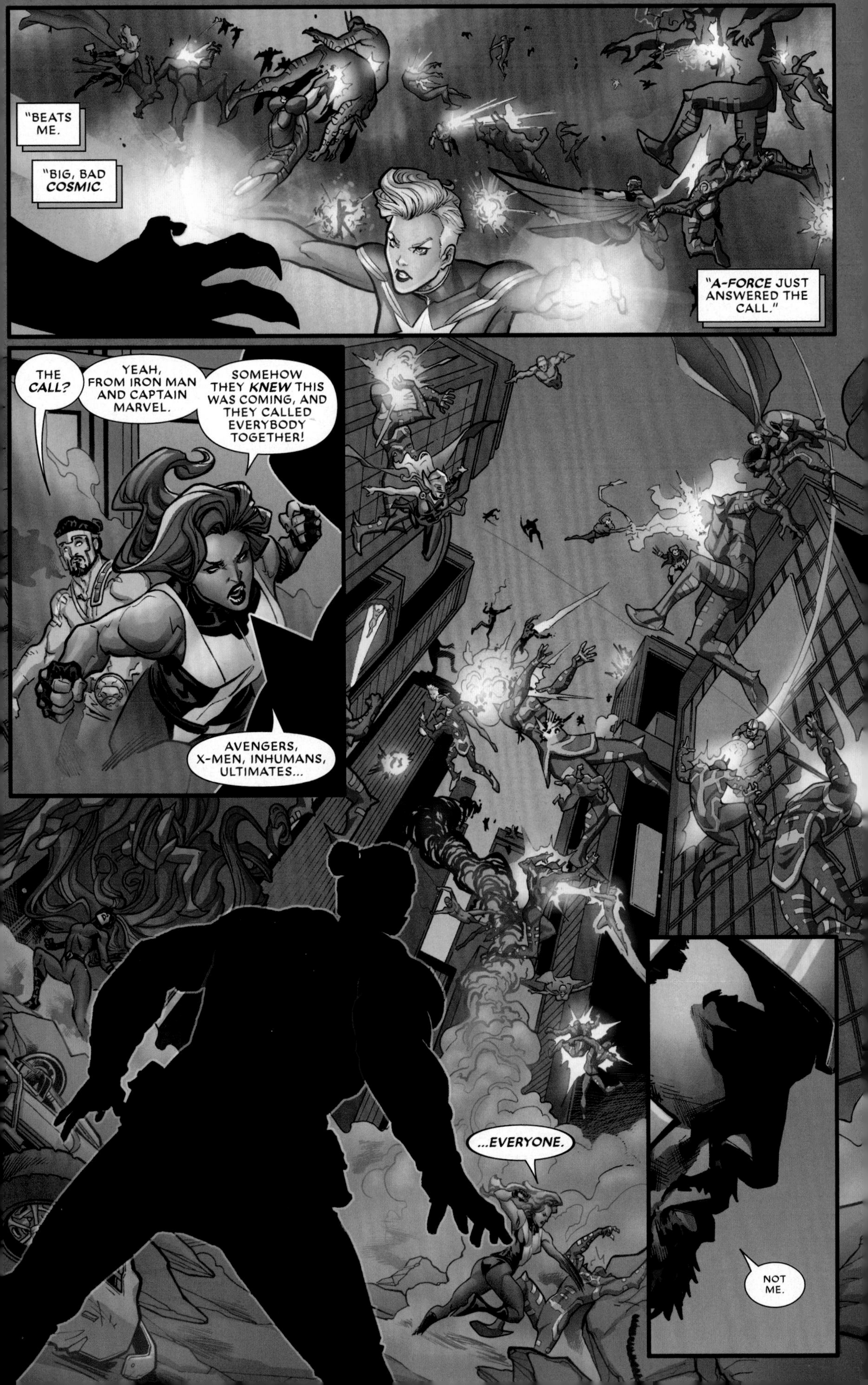
"BEATS ME.
"BIG, BAD COSMIC.
"A-FORCE JUST ANSWERED THE CALL."
THE CALL?
YEAH, FROM IRON MAN AND CAPTAIN MARVEL.
SOMEHOW THEY KNEW THIS WAS COMING, AND THEY CALLED EVERYBODY TOGETHER!
AVENGERS, X-MEN, INHUMANS, ULTIMATES...
...EVERYONE.
NOT ME.

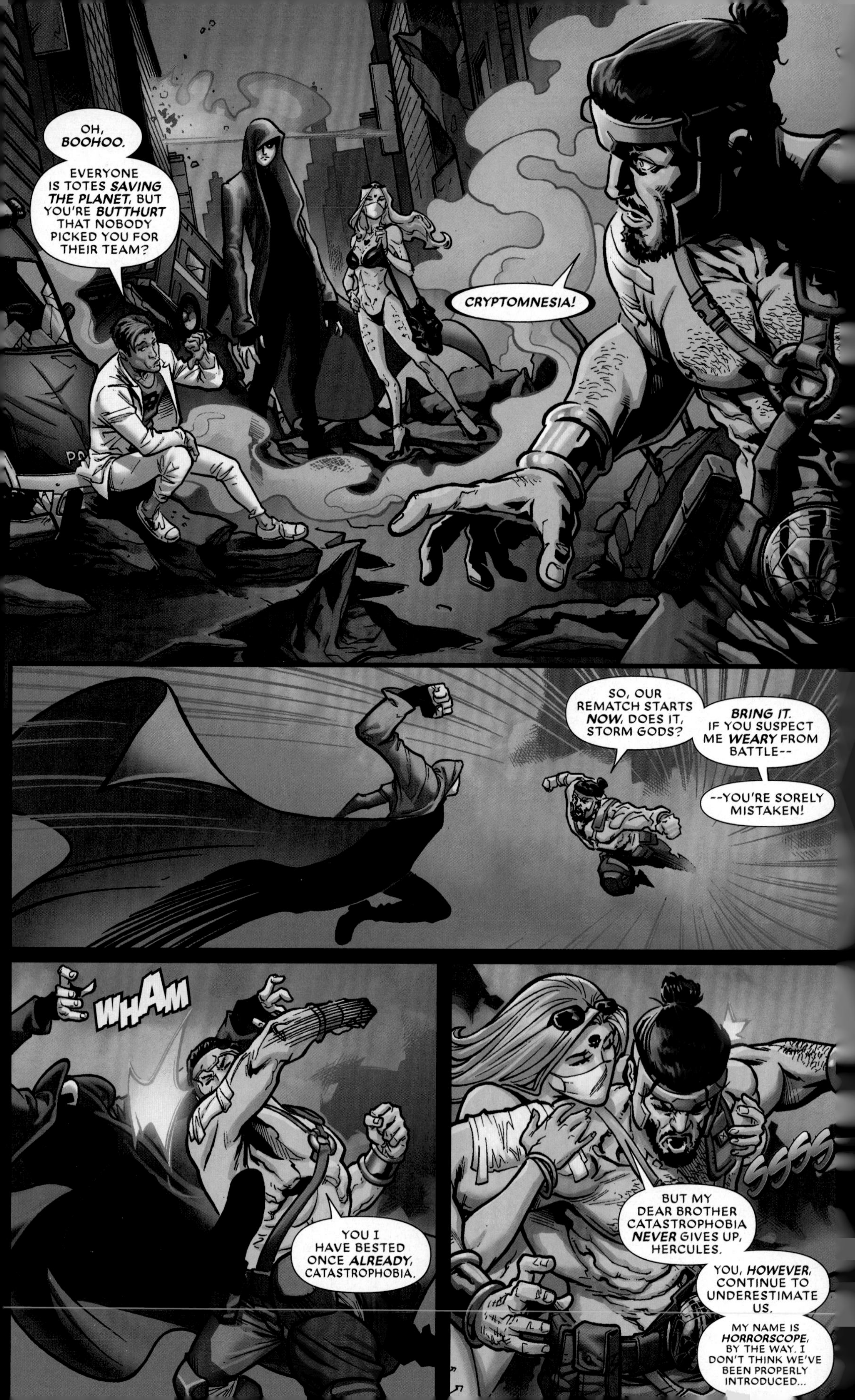
OH, BOOHOO.
EVERYONE IS TOTES SAVING THE PLANET, BUT YOU'RE BUTTHURT THAT NOBODY PICKED YOU FOR THEIR TEAM?
CRYPTOMNESIA!
SO, OUR REMATCH STARTS NOW, DOES IT, STORM GODS?
BRING IT. IF YOU SUSPECT ME WEARY FROM BATTLE--
--YOU'RE SORELY MISTAKEN!
WHAM
YOU I HAVE BESTED ONCE ALREADY, CATASTROPHOBIA.
SSSS
BUT MY DEAR BROTHER CATASTROPHOBIA NEVER GIVES UP, HERCULES.
YOU, HOWEVER, CONTINUE TO UNDERESTIMATE US.
MY NAME IS HORRORSCOPE, BY THE WAY. I DON'T THINK WE'VE BEEN PROPERLY INTRODUCED...

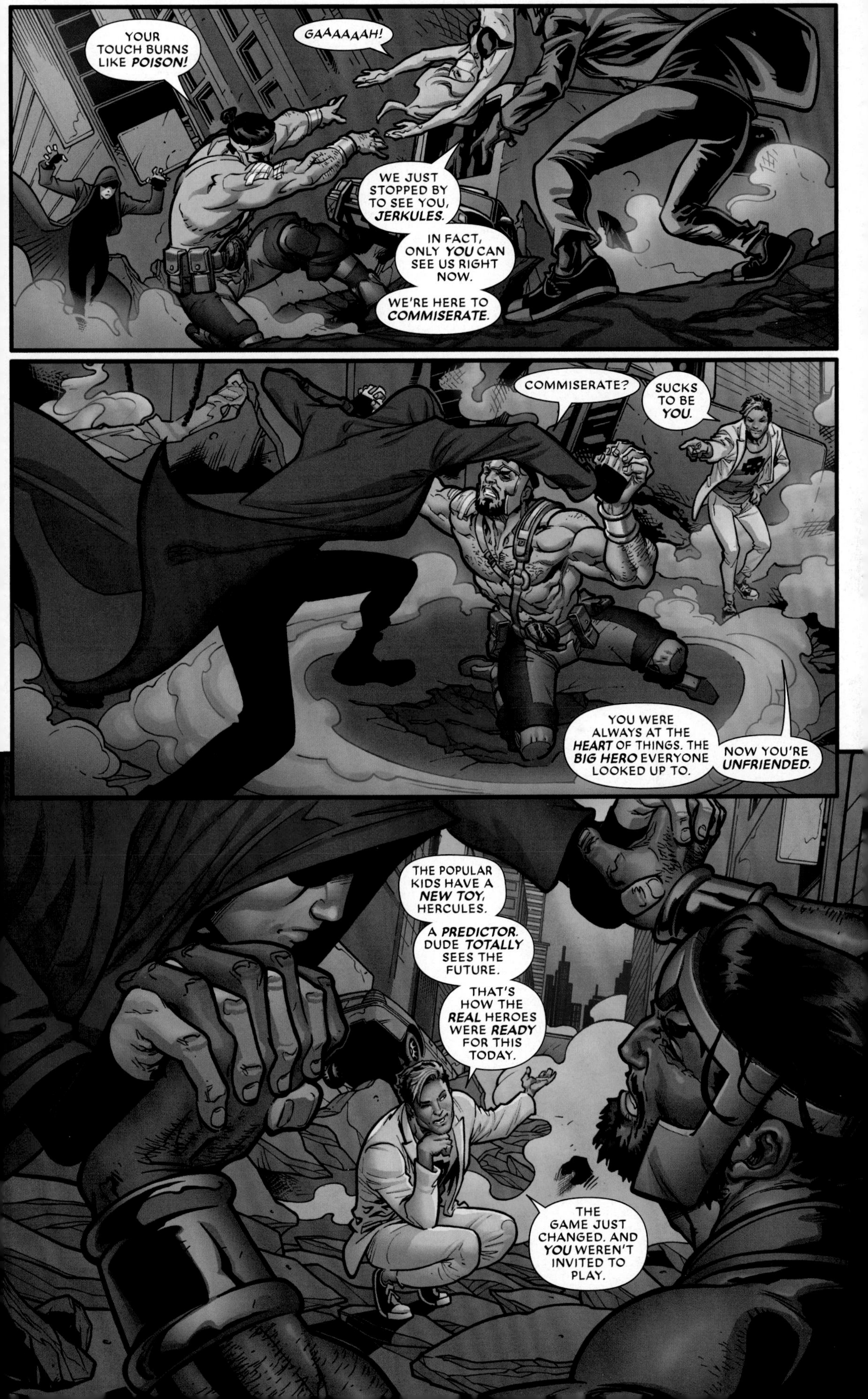
YOUR TOUCH BURNS LIKE *POISON!*
GAAAAAAH!
WE JUST STOPPED BY TO SEE YOU, *JERKULES*.
IN FACT, ONLY *YOU* CAN SEE US RIGHT NOW.
WE'RE HERE TO *COMMISERATE*.
COMMISERATE?
SUCKS TO BE *YOU*.
YOU WERE ALWAYS AT THE *HEART* OF THINGS. THE *BIG HERO* EVERYONE LOOKED UP TO.
NOW YOU'RE *UNFRIENDED*.
THE POPULAR KIDS HAVE A *NEW TOY*, HERCULES.
A *PREDICTOR*. DUDE *TOTALLY* SEES THE FUTURE.
THAT'S HOW THE *REAL* HEROES WERE *READY* FOR THIS TODAY.
THE GAME JUST CHANGED. AND *YOU* WEREN'T INVITED TO PLAY.

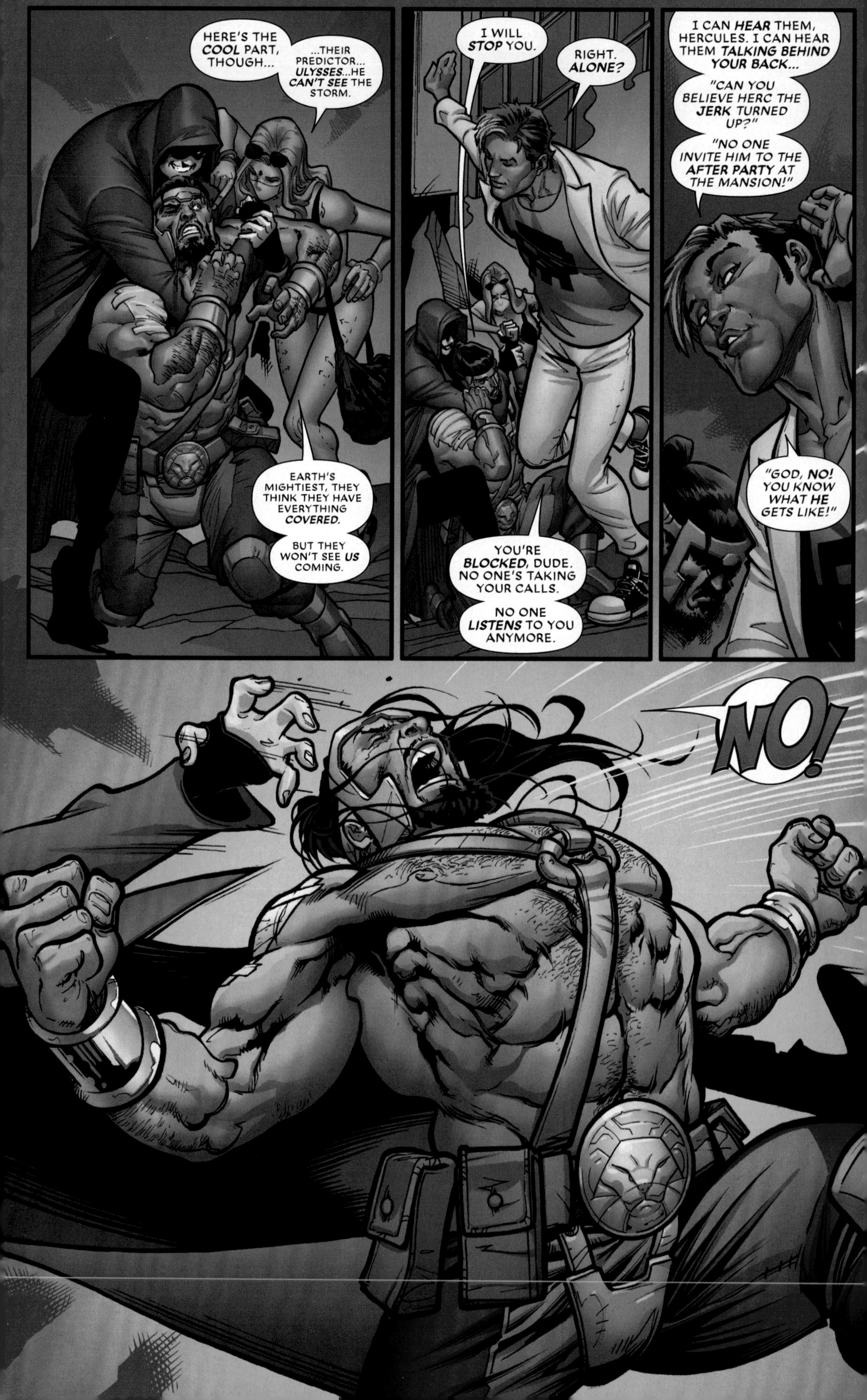
HERE'S THE COOL PART, THOUGH...
...THEIR PREDICTOR... ULYSSES...HE CAN'T SEE THE STORM.
EARTH'S MIGHTIEST, THEY THINK THEY HAVE EVERYTHING COVERED.
BUT THEY WON'T SEE US COMING.
I WILL STOP YOU.
RIGHT. ALONE?
YOU'RE BLOCKED, DUDE. NO ONE'S TAKING YOUR CALLS.
NO ONE LISTENS TO YOU ANYMORE.
I CAN HEAR THEM, HERCULES. I CAN HEAR THEM TALKING BEHIND YOUR BACK...
"CAN YOU BELIEVE HERC THE JERK TURNED UP?"
"NO ONE INVITE HIM TO THE AFTER PARTY AT THE MANSION!"
"GOD, NO! YOU KNOW WHAT HE GETS LIKE!"
NO!

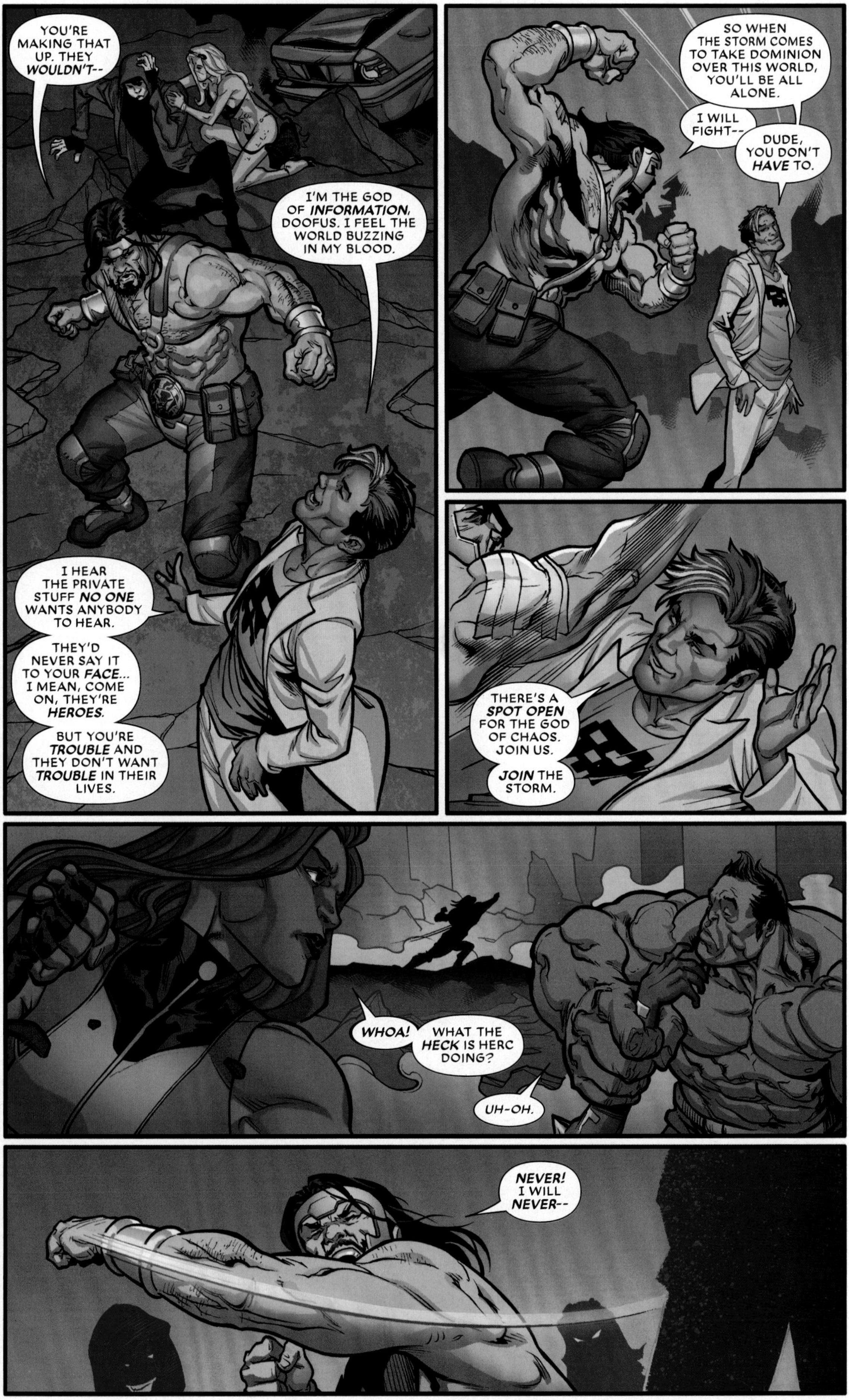
YOU'RE MAKING THAT UP. THEY WOULDN'T--
I'M THE GOD OF INFORMATION, DOOFUS. I FEEL THE WORLD BUZZING IN MY BLOOD.
I HEAR THE PRIVATE STUFF NO ONE WANTS ANYBODY TO HEAR.
THEY'D NEVER SAY IT TO YOUR FACE... I MEAN, COME ON, THEY'RE HEROES.
BUT YOU'RE TROUBLE AND THEY DON'T WANT TROUBLE IN THEIR LIVES.
SO WHEN THE STORM COMES TO TAKE DOMINION OVER THIS WORLD, YOU'LL BE ALL ALONE.
I WILL FIGHT--
DUDE, YOU DON'T HAVE TO.
THERE'S A SPOT OPEN FOR THE GOD OF CHAOS. JOIN US.
JOIN THE STORM.
WHOA!
WHAT THE HECK IS HERC DOING?
UH-OH.
NEVER! I WILL NEVER--

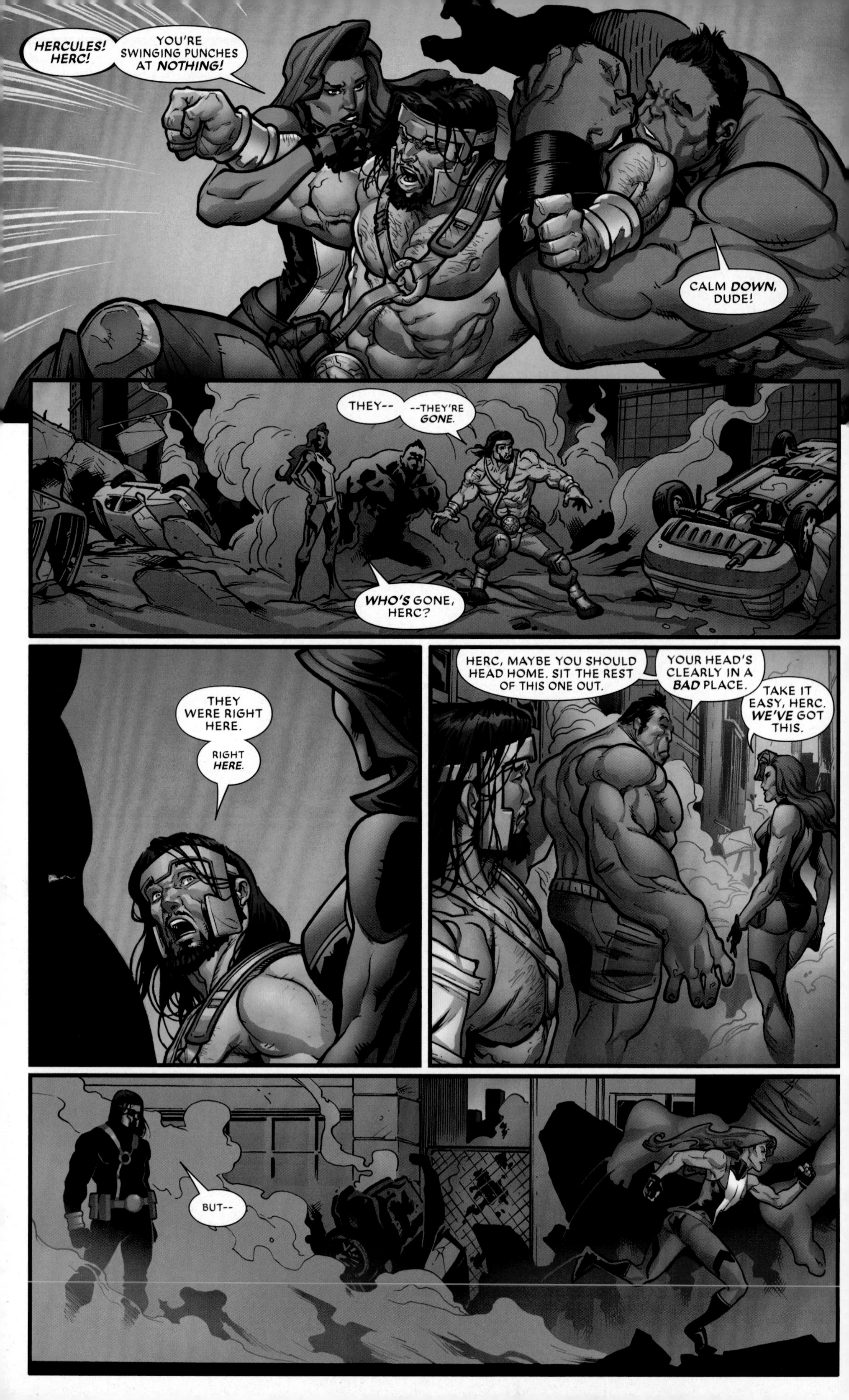
HERCULES! HERC!
YOU'RE SWINGING PUNCHES AT NOTHING!
CALM DOWN, DUDE!
THEY--
--THEY'RE GONE.
WHO'S GONE, HERC?
THEY WERE RIGHT HERE.
RIGHT HERE.
HERC, MAYBE YOU SHOULD HEAD HOME. SIT THE REST OF THIS ONE OUT.
YOUR HEAD'S CLEARLY IN A BAD PLACE.
TAKE IT EASY, HERC. WE'VE GOT THIS.
BUT--

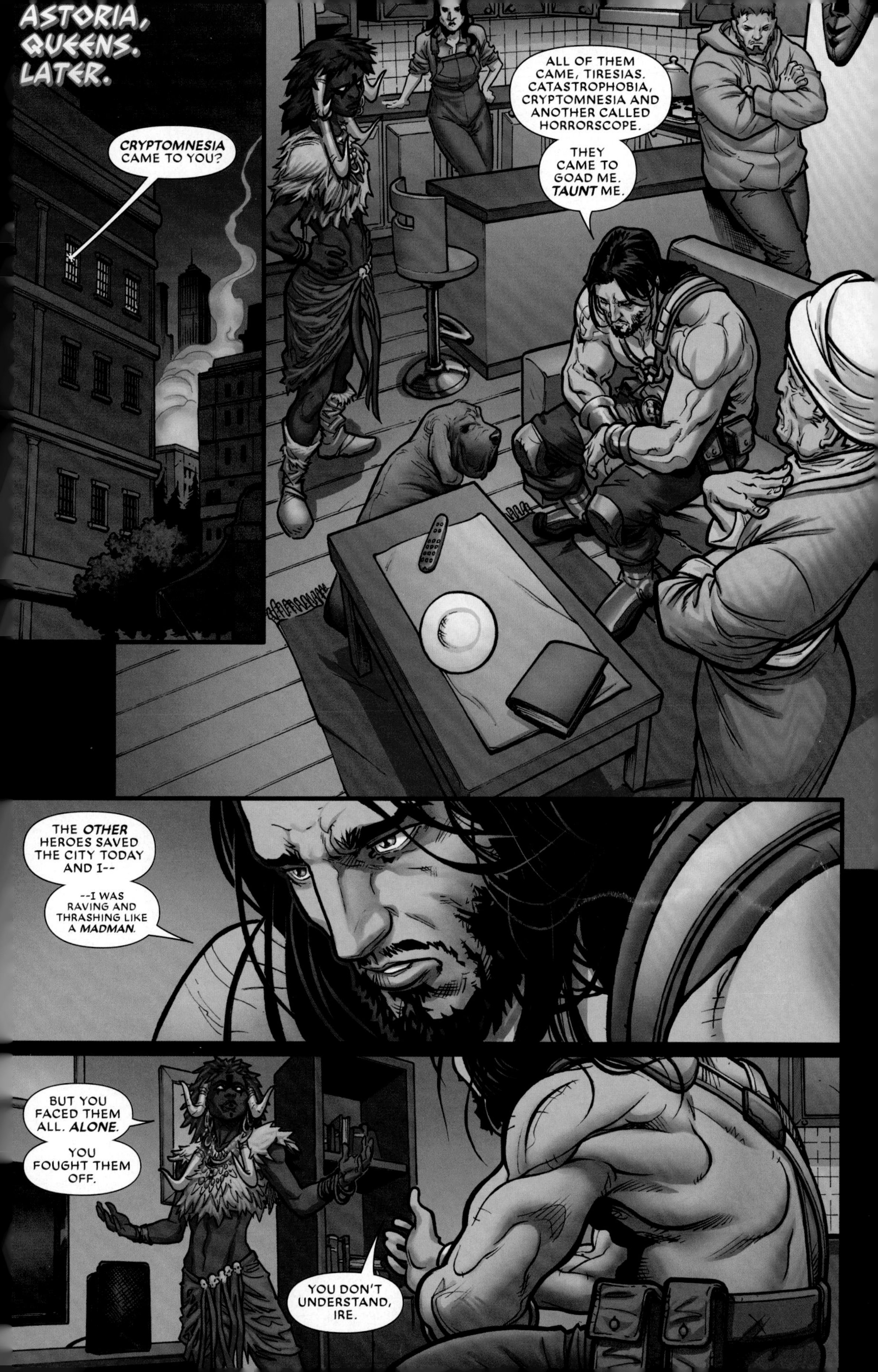
ASTORIA, QUEENS. LATER.
CRYPTOMNESIA CAME TO YOU?
ALL OF THEM CAME, TIRESIAS. CATASTROPHOBIA, CRYPTOMNESIA AND ANOTHER CALLED HORRORSCOPE.
THEY CAME TO GOAD ME. TAUNT ME.
THE OTHER HEROES SAVED THE CITY TODAY AND I--
--I WAS RAVING AND THRASHING LIKE A MADMAN.
BUT YOU FACED THEM ALL. ALONE.
YOU FOUGHT THEM OFF.
YOU DON'T UNDERSTAND, IRE.

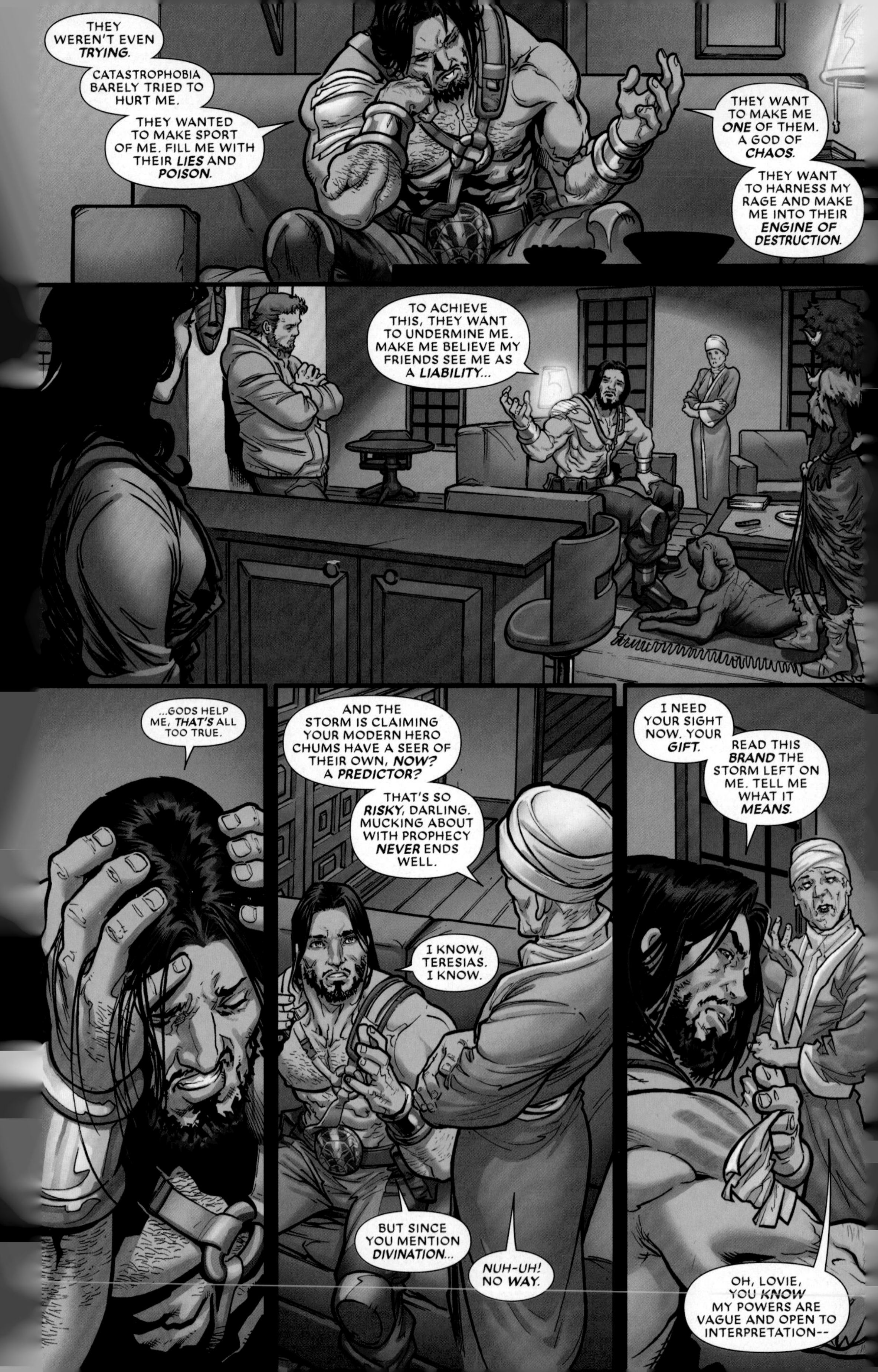
THEY WEREN'T EVEN TRYING.
CATASTROPHOBIA BARELY TRIED TO HURT ME.
THEY WANTED TO MAKE SPORT OF ME. FILL ME WITH THEIR LIES AND POISON.
THEY WANT TO MAKE ME ONE OF THEM. A GOD OF CHAOS.
THEY WANT TO HARNESS MY RAGE AND MAKE ME INTO THEIR ENGINE OF DESTRUCTION.
TO ACHIEVE THIS, THEY WANT TO UNDERMINE ME. MAKE ME BELIEVE MY FRIENDS SEE ME AS A LIABILITY...
...GODS HELP ME, THAT'S ALL TOO TRUE.
AND THE STORM IS CLAIMING YOUR MODERN HERO CHUMS HAVE A SEER OF THEIR OWN, NOW? A PREDICTOR?
THAT'S SO RISKY, DARLING. MUCKING ABOUT WITH PROPHECY NEVER ENDS WELL.
I KNOW, TERESIAS. I KNOW.
BUT SINCE YOU MENTION DIVINATION...
NUH-UH! NO WAY.
I NEED YOUR SIGHT NOW. YOUR GIFT.
READ THIS BRAND THE STORM LEFT ON ME. TELL ME WHAT IT MEANS.
OH, LOVIE, YOU KNOW MY POWERS ARE VAGUE AND OPEN TO INTERPRETATION--

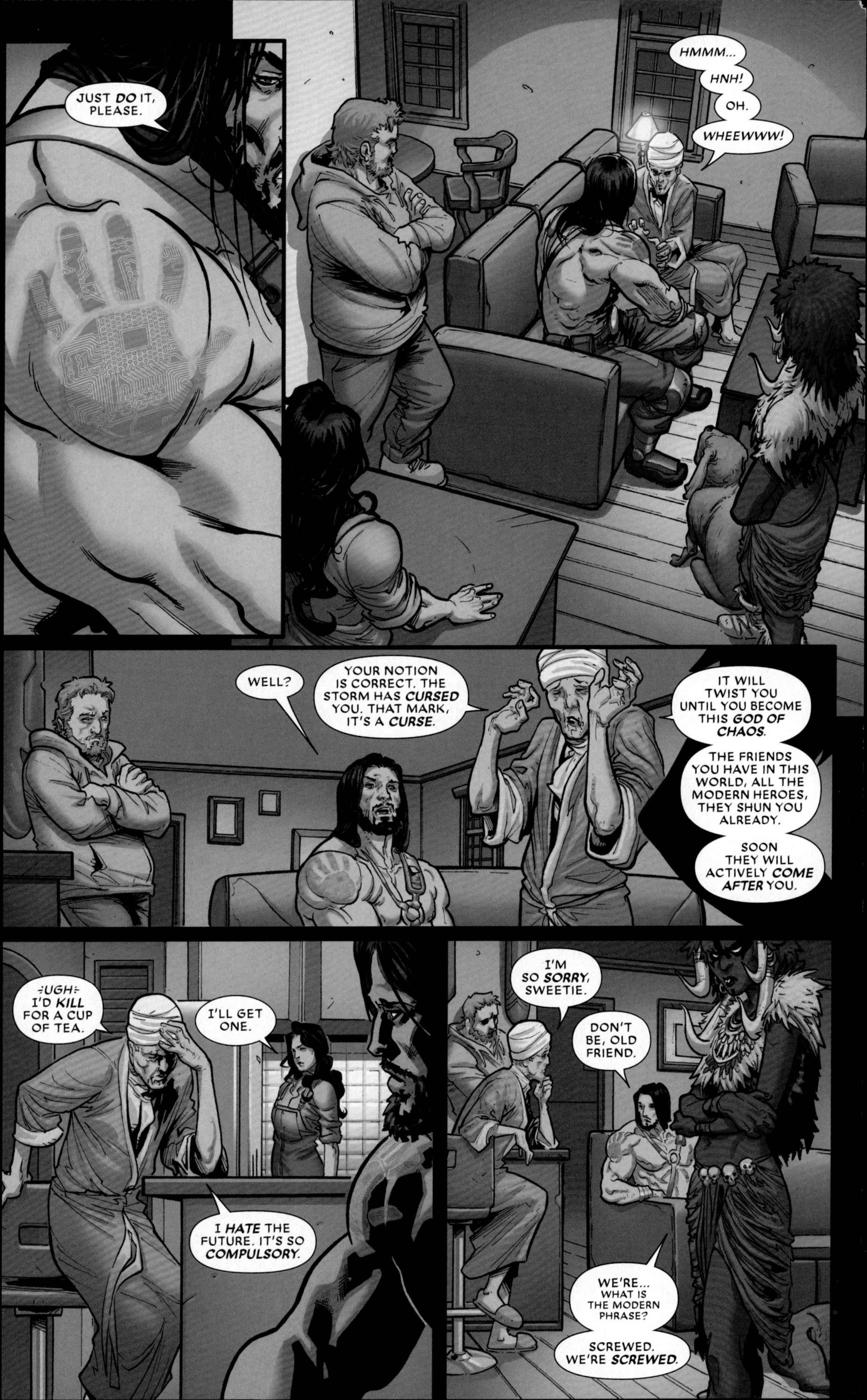
JUST DO IT, PLEASE.
HMMM...
HNH!
OH.
WHEEWWW!
WELL?
YOUR NOTION IS CORRECT. THE STORM HAS CURSED YOU. THAT MARK, IT'S A CURSE.
IT WILL TWIST YOU UNTIL YOU BECOME THIS GOD OF CHAOS.
THE FRIENDS YOU HAVE IN THIS WORLD, ALL THE MODERN HEROES, THEY SHUN YOU ALREADY.
SOON THEY WILL ACTIVELY COME AFTER YOU.
UGH
I'D KILL FOR A CUP OF TEA.
I'LL GET ONE.
I HATE THE FUTURE. IT'S SO COMPULSORY.
I'M SO SORRY, SWEETIE.
DON'T BE, OLD FRIEND.
WE'RE... WHAT IS THE MODERN PHRASE?
SCREWED. WE'RE SCREWED.

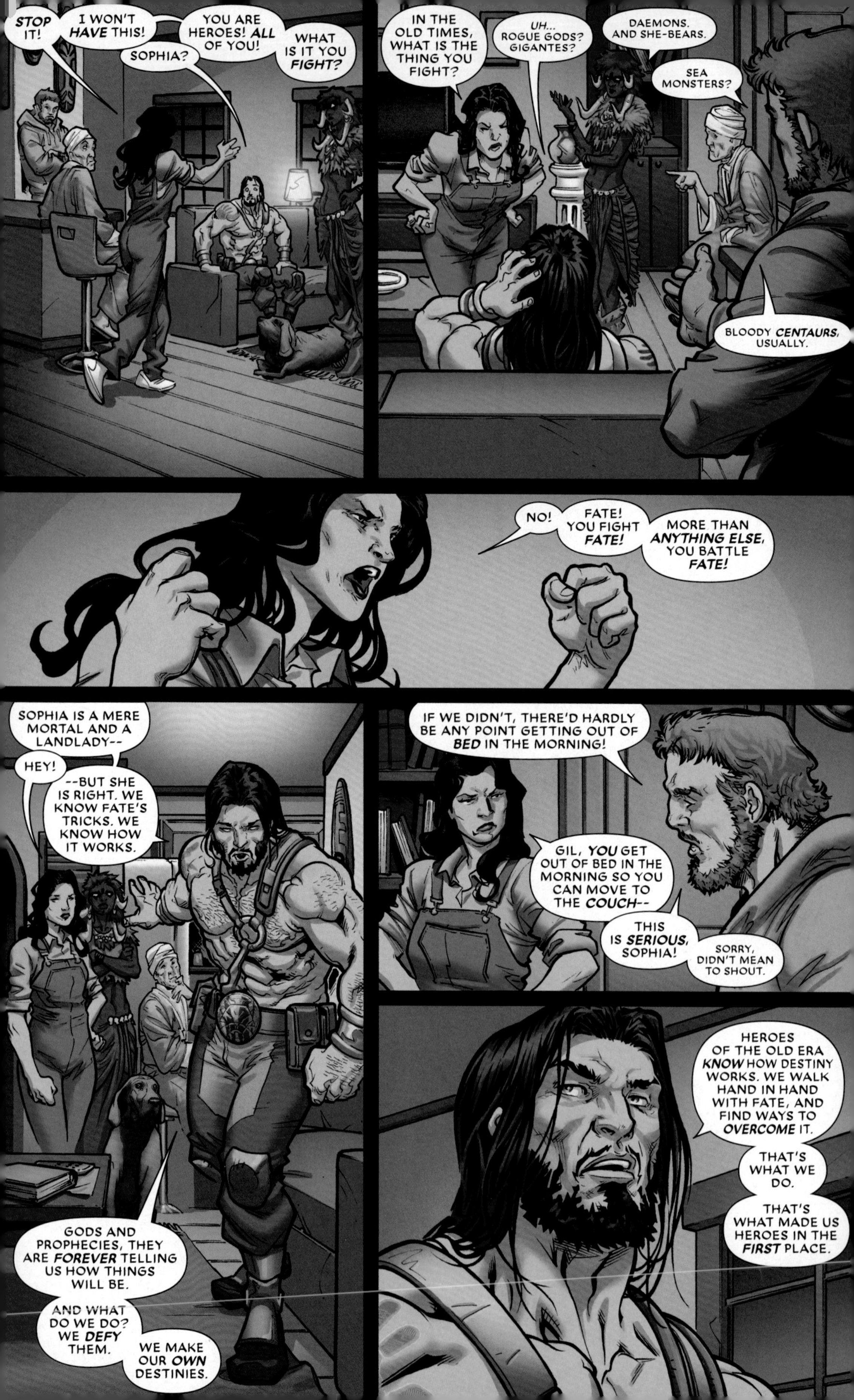

STOP IT!
I WON'T HAVE THIS!
YOU ARE HEROES! ALL OF YOU!
SOPHIA?
WHAT IS IT YOU FIGHT?
IN THE OLD TIMES, WHAT IS THE THING YOU FIGHT?
UH... ROGUE GODS? GIGANTES?
DAEMONS. AND SHE-BEARS.
SEA MONSTERS?
BLOODY CENTAURS, USUALLY.
NO!
FATE! YOU FIGHT FATE!
MORE THAN ANYTHING ELSE, YOU BATTLE FATE!
SOPHIA IS A MERE MORTAL AND A LANDLADY--
HEY!
--BUT SHE IS RIGHT. WE KNOW FATE'S TRICKS. WE KNOW HOW IT WORKS.
GODS AND PROPHECIES, THEY ARE FOREVER TELLING US HOW THINGS WILL BE.
AND WHAT DO WE DO? WE DEFY THEM.
WE MAKE OUR OWN DESTINIES.
IF WE DIDN'T, THERE'D HARDLY BE ANY POINT GETTING OUT OF BED IN THE MORNING!
GIL, YOU GET OUT OF BED IN THE MORNING SO YOU CAN MOVE TO THE COUCH--
THIS IS SERIOUS, SOPHIA!
SORRY, DIDN'T MEAN TO SHOUT.
HEROES OF THE OLD ERA KNOW HOW DESTINY WORKS. WE WALK HAND IN HAND WITH FATE, AND FIND WAYS TO OVERCOME IT.
THAT'S WHAT WE DO.
THAT'S WHAT MADE US HEROES IN THE FIRST PLACE.

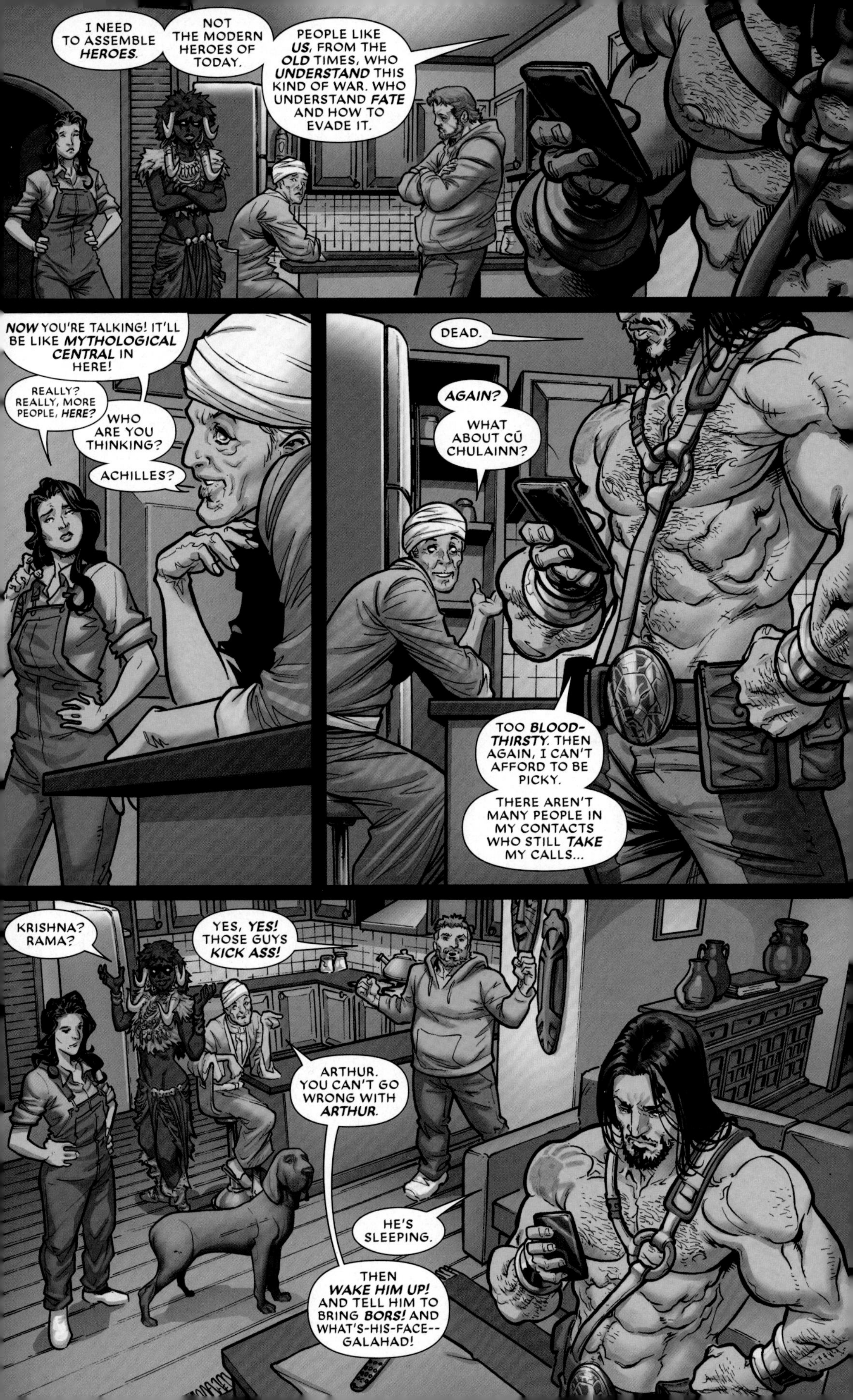
I NEED TO ASSEMBLE *HEROES*.
NOT THE MODERN HEROES OF TODAY.
PEOPLE LIKE *US*, FROM THE *OLD* TIMES, WHO *UNDERSTAND* THIS KIND OF WAR. WHO UNDERSTAND *FATE* AND HOW TO EVADE IT.
NOW YOU'RE TALKING! IT'LL BE LIKE *MYTHOLOGICAL CENTRAL* IN HERE!
REALLY? REALLY, MORE PEOPLE, *HERE?*
WHO ARE YOU THINKING?
ACHILLES?
DEAD.
AGAIN?
WHAT ABOUT CÚ CHULAINN?
TOO *BLOOD-THIRSTY*. THEN AGAIN, I CAN'T AFFORD TO BE PICKY.
THERE AREN'T MANY PEOPLE IN MY CONTACTS WHO STILL *TAKE* MY CALLS...
KRISHNA? RAMA?
YES, *YES!* THOSE GUYS *KICK ASS!*
ARTHUR. YOU CAN'T GO WRONG WITH *ARTHUR*.
HE'S SLEEPING.
THEN *WAKE HIM UP!* AND TELL HIM TO BRING *BORS!* AND WHAT'S-HIS-FACE-- GALAHAD!

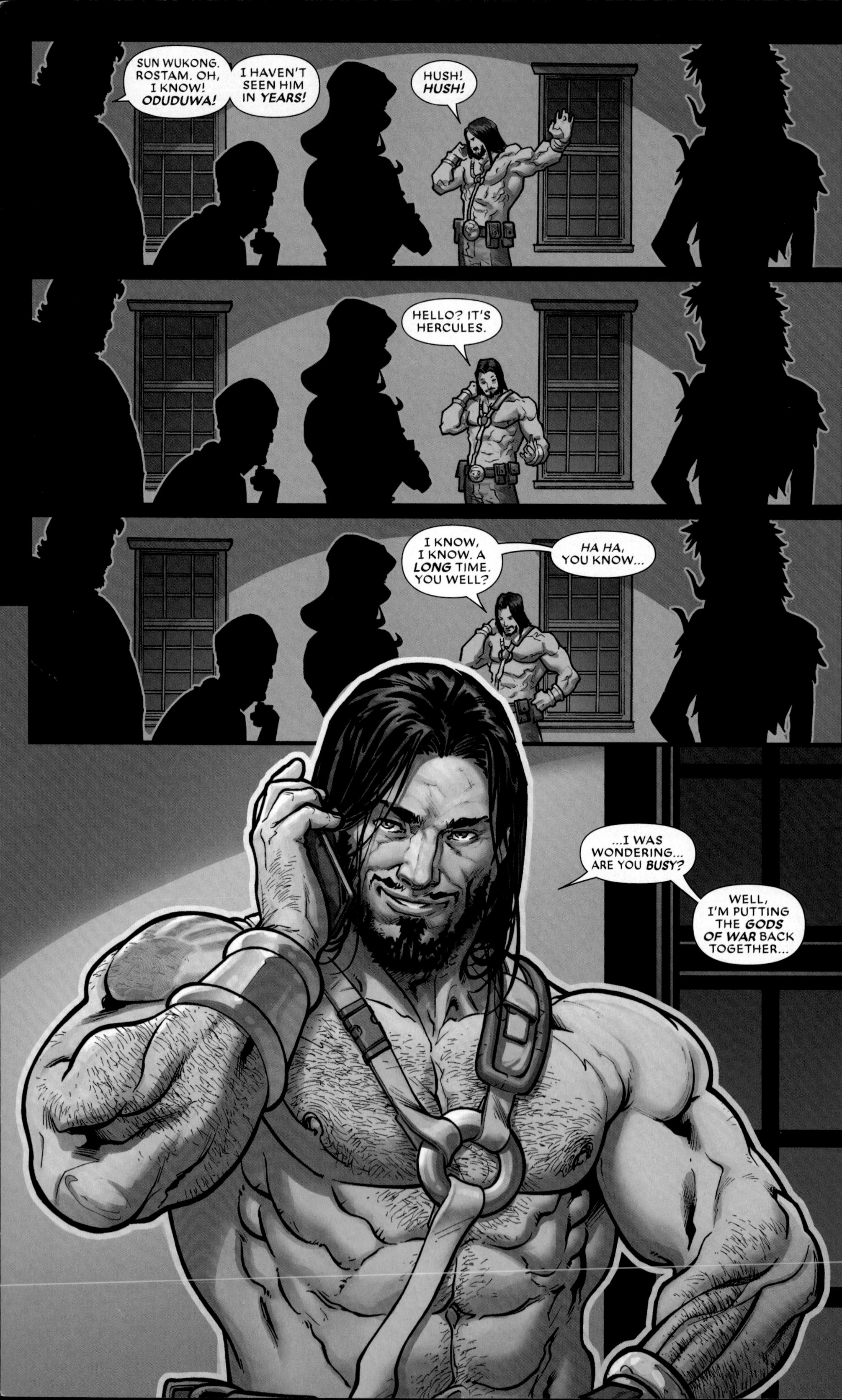
SUN WUKONG. ROSTAM. OH, I KNOW! ODUDUWA!
I HAVEN'T SEEN HIM IN YEARS!
HUSH! HUSH!
HELLO? IT'S HERCULES.
I KNOW, I KNOW. A LONG TIME. YOU WELL?
HA HA, YOU KNOW...
...I WAS WONDERING... ARE YOU BUSY?
WELL, I'M PUTTING THE GODS OF WAR BACK TOGETHER...

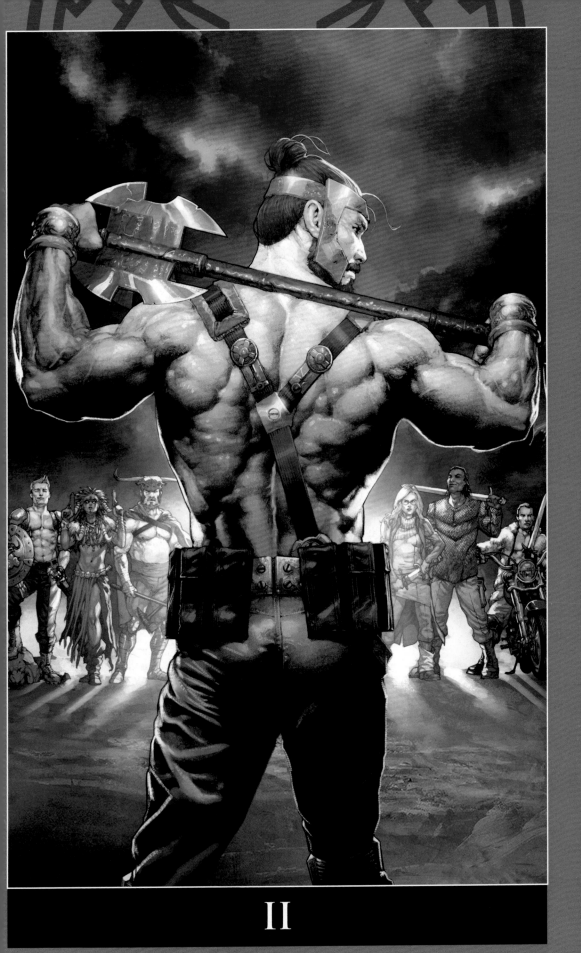

II

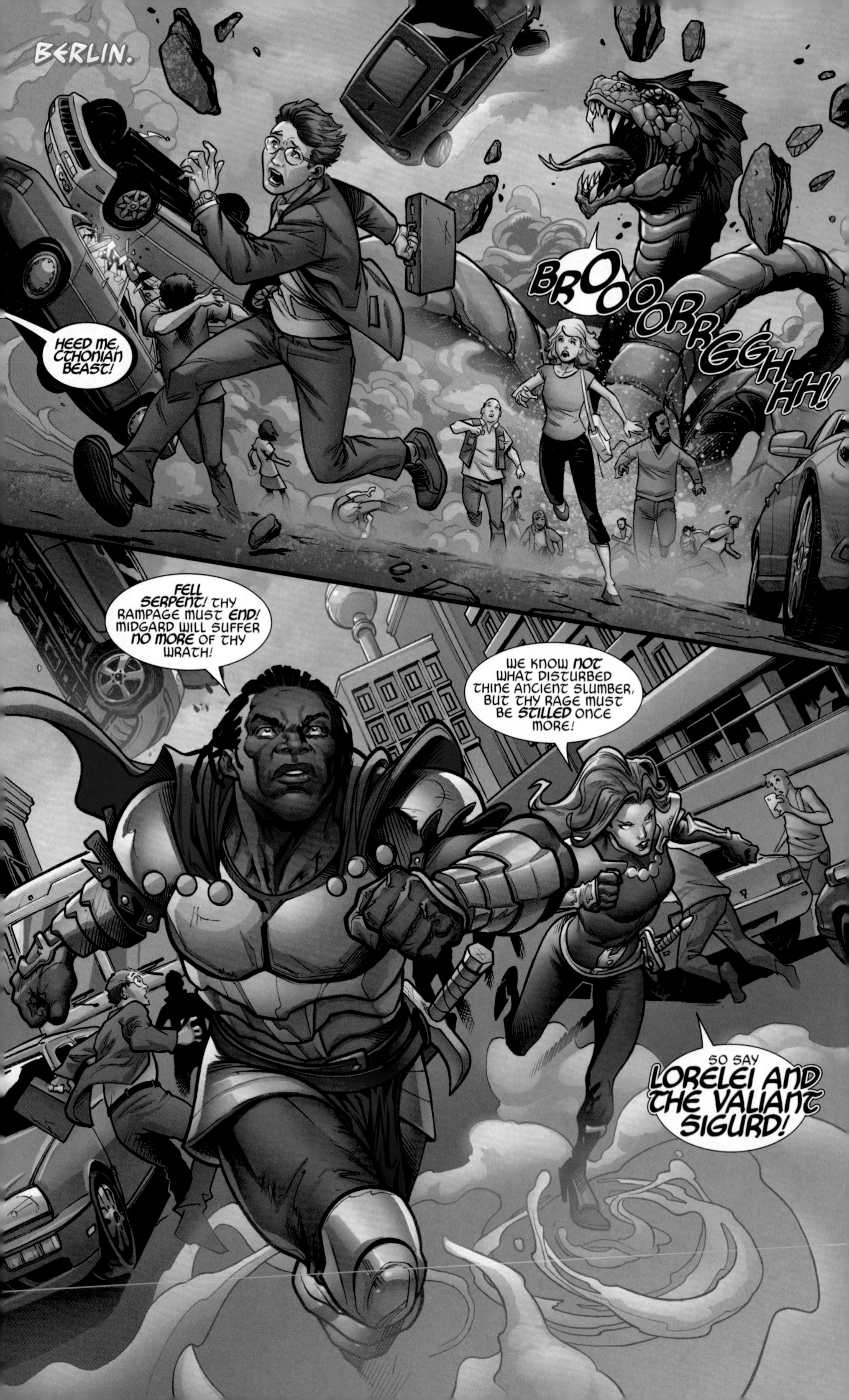
BERLIN.
BROOOORRGGHHH!
HEED ME, CTHONIAN BEAST!
FELL SERPENT! THY RAMPAGE MUST END! MIDGARD WILL SUFFER NO MORE OF THY WRATH!
WE KNOW NOT WHAT DISTURBED THINE ANCIENT SLUMBER, BUT THY RAGE MUST BE STILLED ONCE MORE!
SO SAY LORELEI AND THE VALIANT SIGURD!

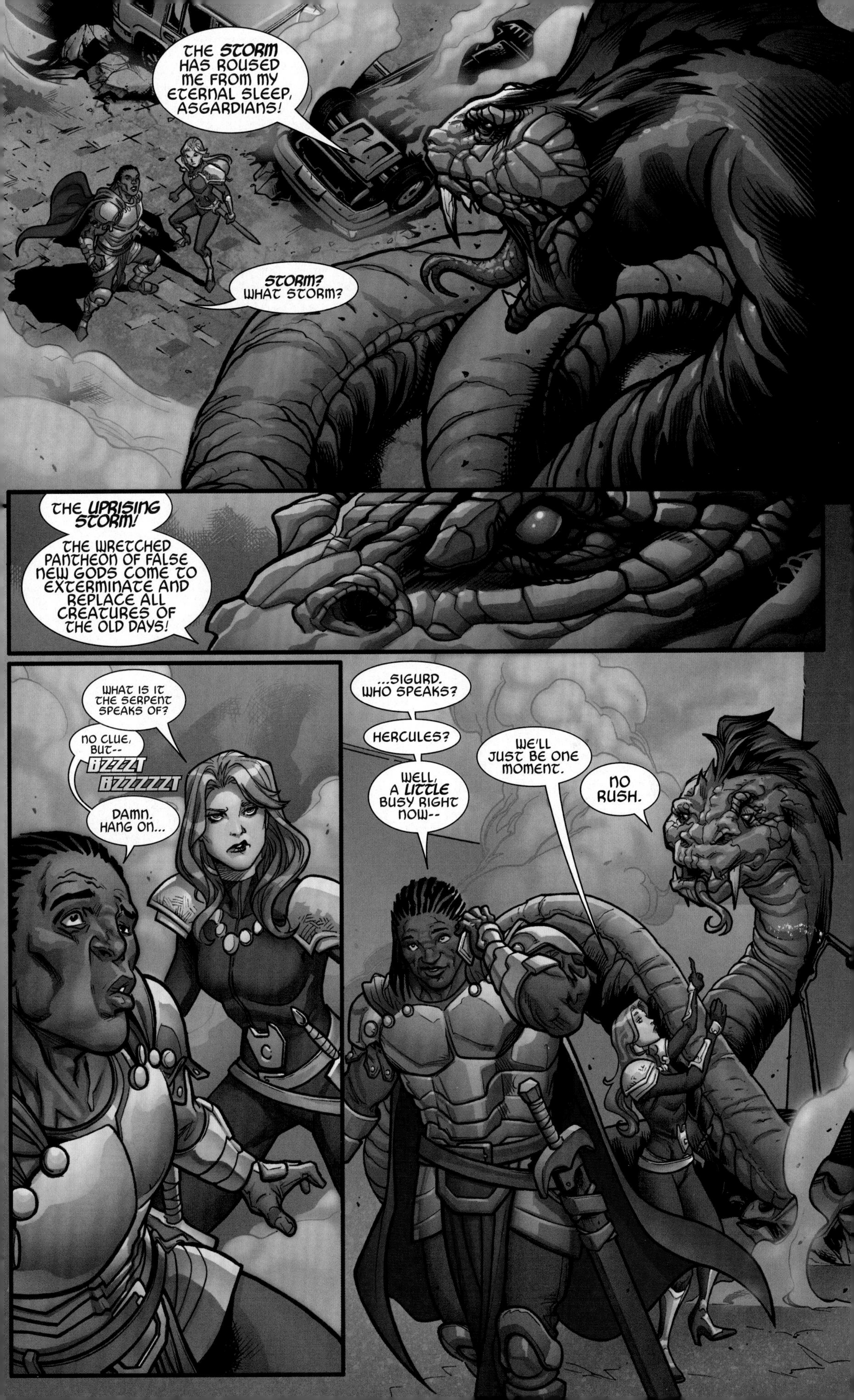
THE STORM HAS ROUSED ME FROM MY ETERNAL SLEEP, ASGARDIANS!
STORM? WHAT STORM?
THE UPRISING STORM!
THE WRETCHED PANTHEON OF FALSE NEW GODS COME TO EXTERMINATE AND REPLACE ALL CREATURES OF THE OLD DAYS!
WHAT IS IT THE SERPENT SPEAKS OF?
NO CLUE, BUT--
BZZZZT
BZZZZZZT
DAMN. HANG ON...
...SIGURD. WHO SPEAKS?
HERCULES?
WELL, A LITTLE BUSY RIGHT NOW--
WE'LL JUST BE ONE MOMENT.
NO RUSH.

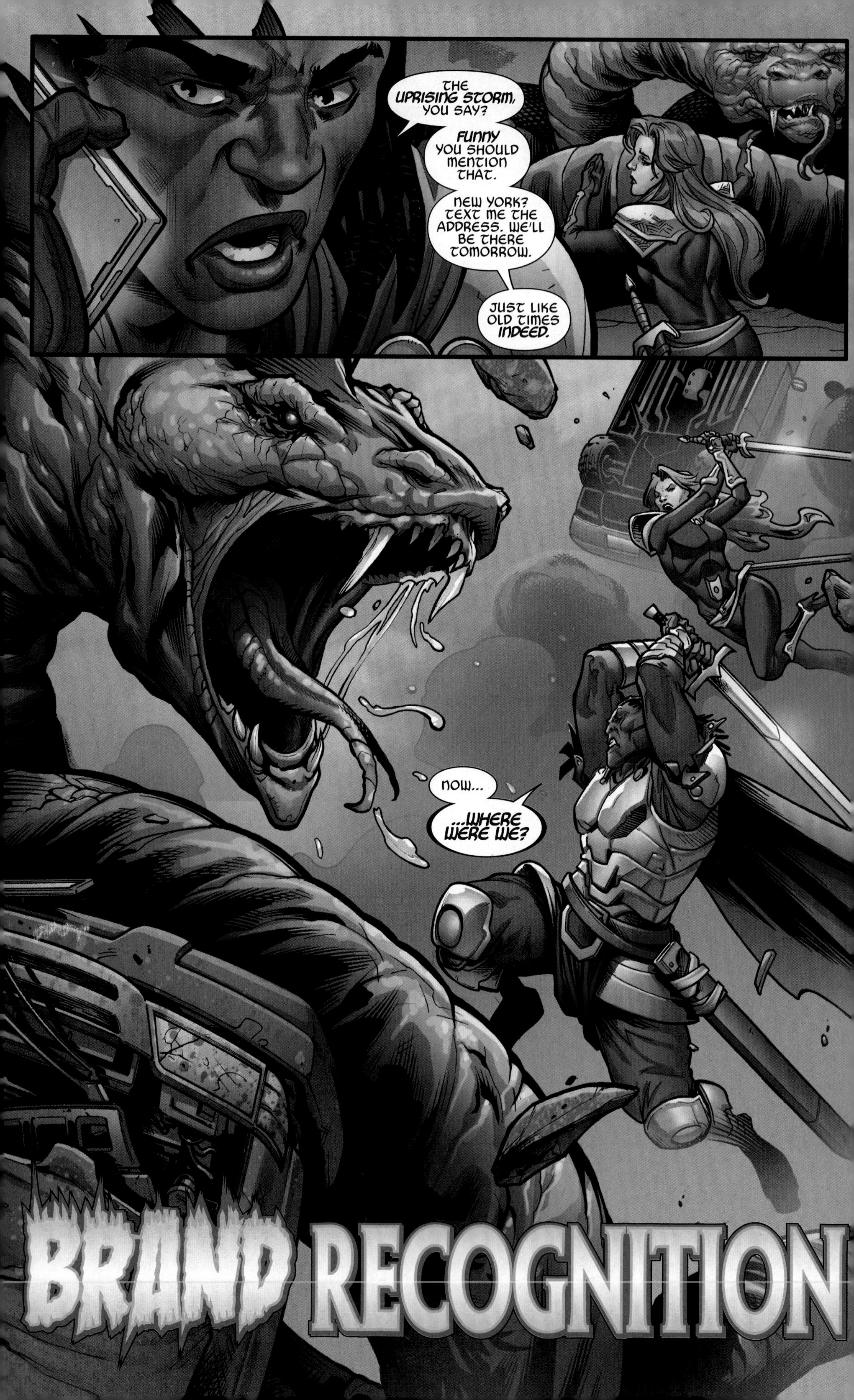
THE UPRISING STORM, YOU SAY?
FUNNY YOU SHOULD MENTION THAT.
NEW YORK? TEXT ME THE ADDRESS. WE'LL BE THERE TOMORROW.
JUST LIKE OLD TIMES INDEED.
NOW...
...WHERE WERE WE?
BRAND RECOGNITION

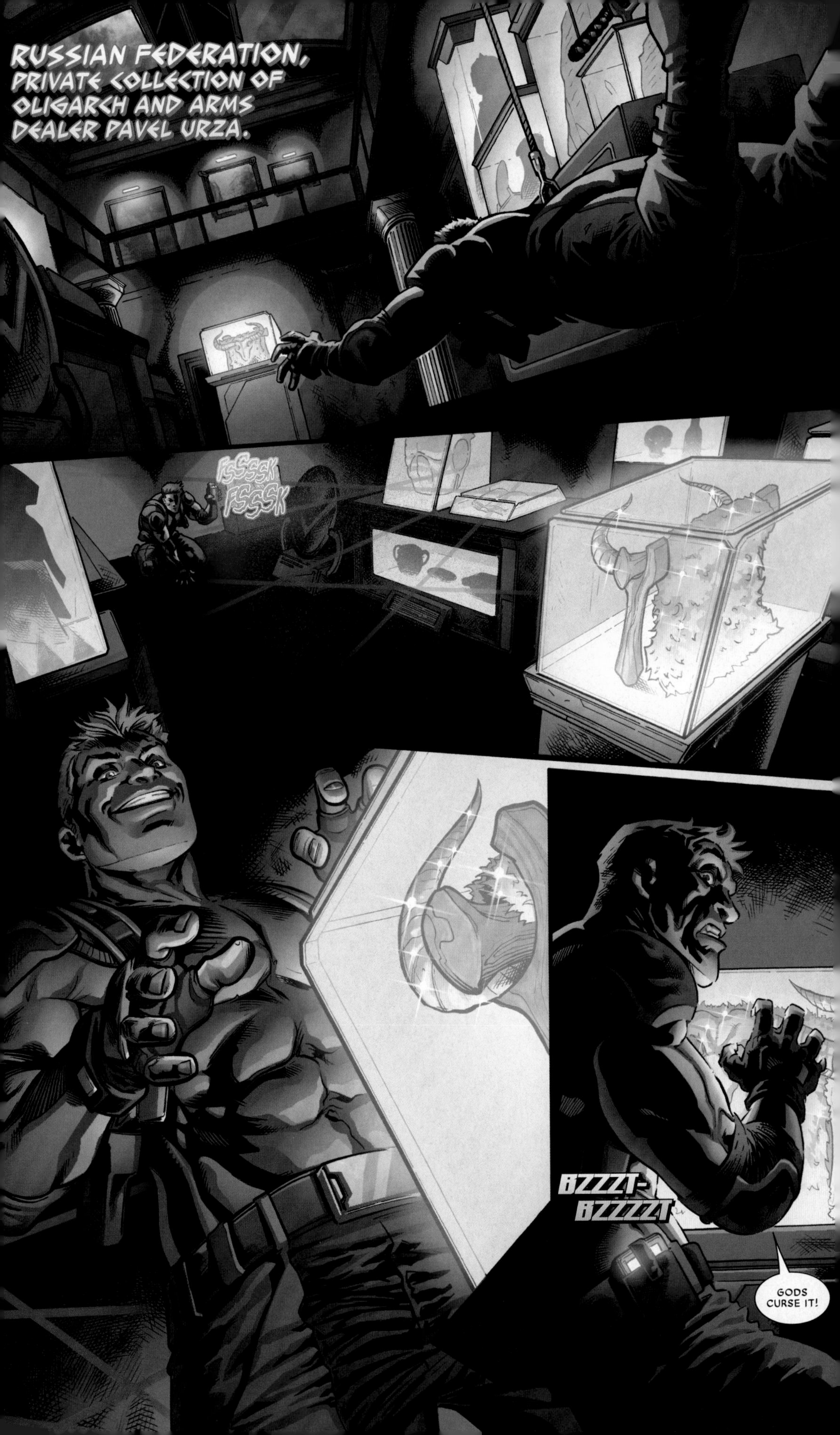
RUSSIAN FEDERATION,
PRIVATE COLLECTION OF OLIGARCH AND ARMS DEALER PAVEL URZA.
FSSSSK
FSSSK
BZZZZT-
BZZZZZT
GODS CURSE IT!

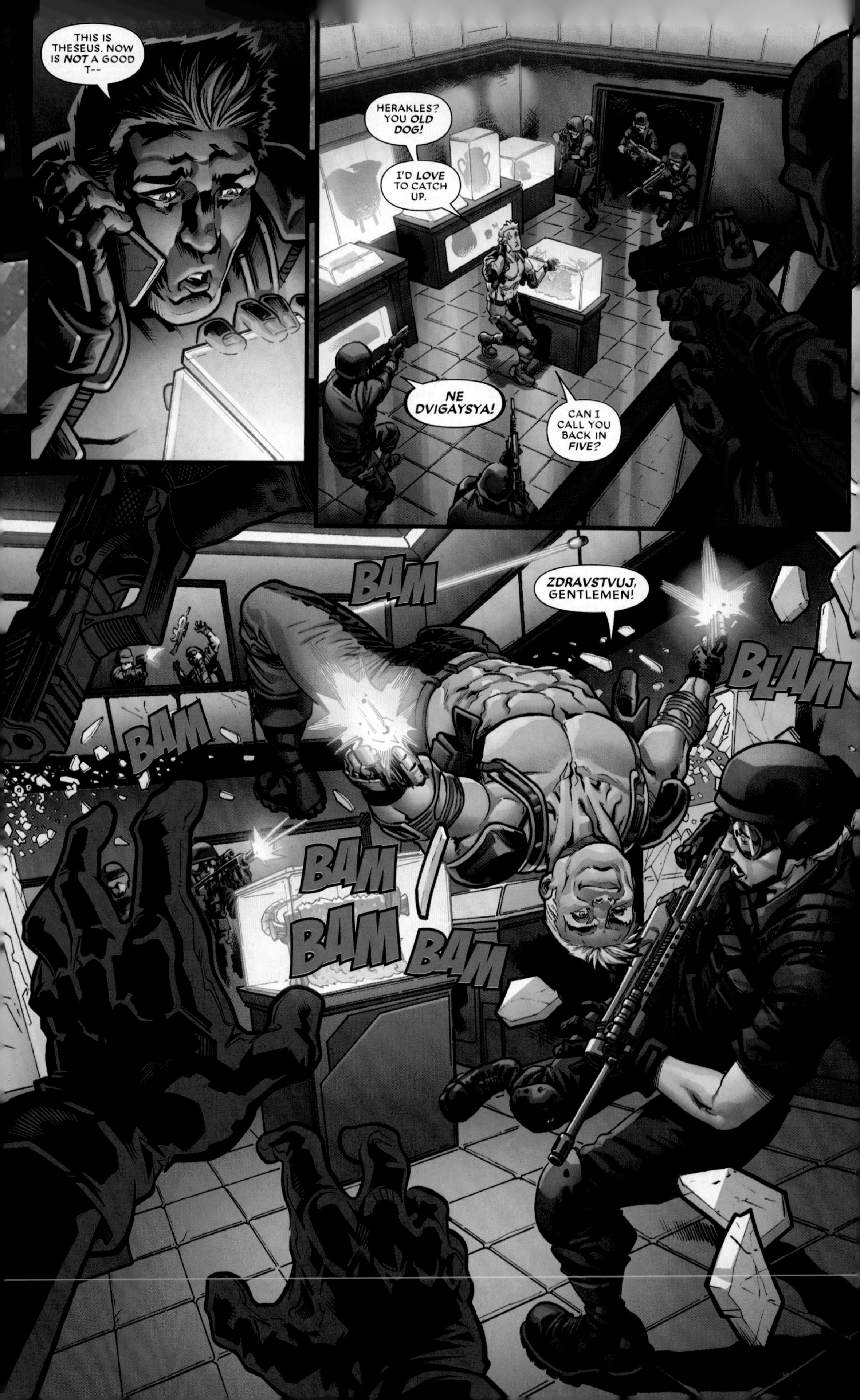
THIS IS THESEUS. NOW IS NOT A GOOD T--
HERAKLES? YOU OLD DOG!
I'D LOVE TO CATCH UP.
NE DVIGAYSYA!
CAN I CALL YOU BACK IN FIVE?
BAM
ZDRAVSTVUJ, GENTLEMEN!
BLAM
BAM
BAM
BAM
BAM

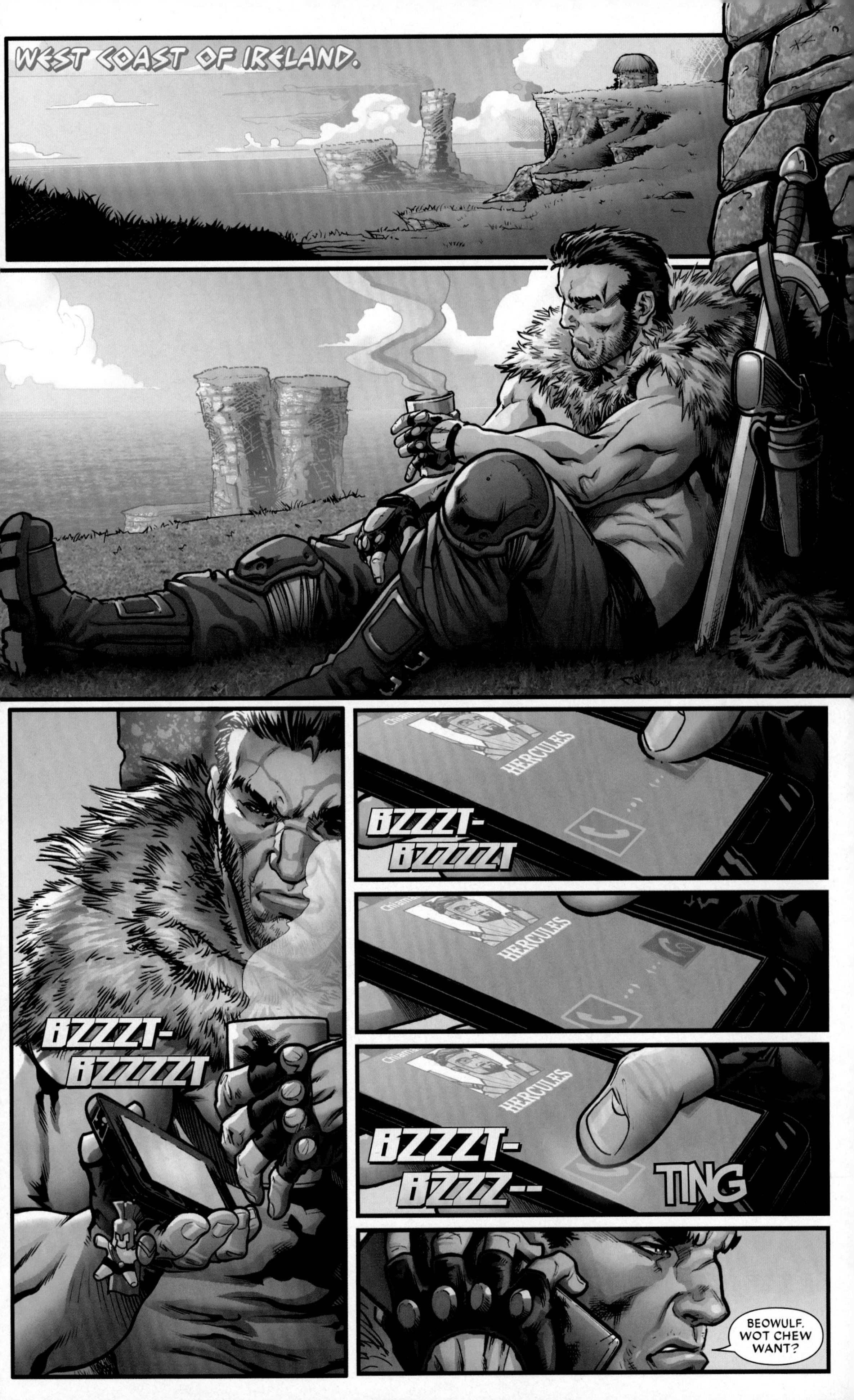
WEST COAST OF IRELAND.
BZZZT-
BZZZZZT
Chiama
HERCULES
BZZZT-
BZZZZZT
Chiama
HERCULES
Chiama
HERCULES
BZZZT-
BZZZ--
TING
BEOWULF. WOT CHEW WANT?

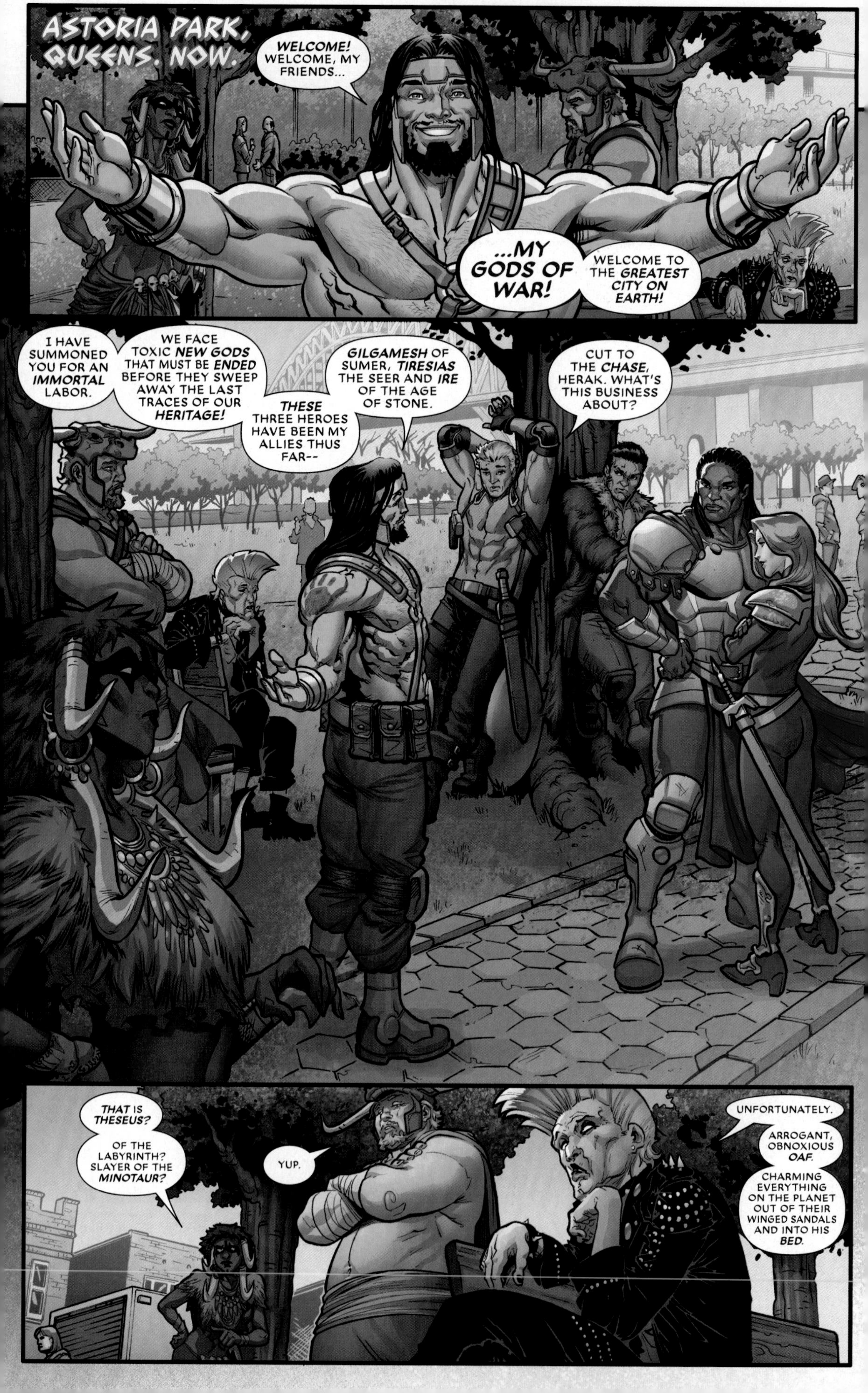
ASTORIA PARK, QUEENS. NOW.
WELCOME! WELCOME, MY FRIENDS...
...MY GODS OF WAR!
WELCOME TO THE GREATEST CITY ON EARTH!
I HAVE SUMMONED YOU FOR AN IMMORTAL LABOR.
WE FACE TOXIC NEW GODS THAT MUST BE ENDED BEFORE THEY SWEEP AWAY THE LAST TRACES OF OUR HERITAGE!
THESE THREE HEROES HAVE BEEN MY ALLIES THUS FAR--
GILGAMESH OF SUMER, TIRESIAS THE SEER AND IRE OF THE AGE OF STONE.
CUT TO THE CHASE, HERAK. WHAT'S THIS BUSINESS ABOUT?
THAT IS THESEUS?
OF THE LABYRINTH? SLAYER OF THE MINOTAUR?
YUP.
UNFORTUNATELY.
ARROGANT, OBNOXIOUS OAF.
CHARMING EVERYTHING ON THE PLANET OUT OF THEIR WINGED SANDALS AND INTO HIS BED.

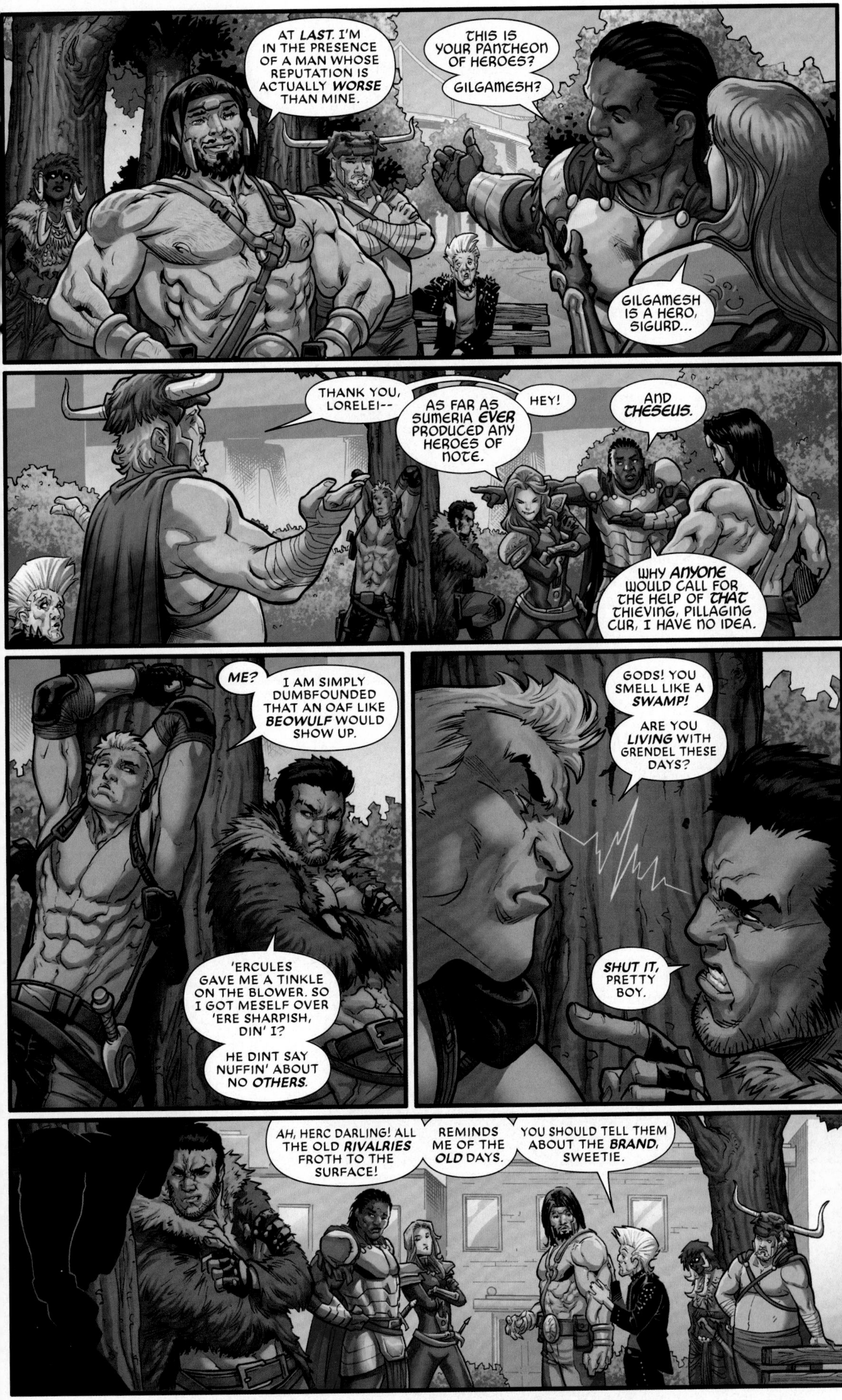
AT LAST. I'M IN THE PRESENCE OF A MAN WHOSE REPUTATION IS ACTUALLY WORSE THAN MINE.
THIS IS YOUR PANTHEON OF HEROES?
GILGAMESH?
GILGAMESH IS A HERO, SIGURD...
THANK YOU, LORELEI--
AS FAR AS SUMERIA EVER PRODUCED ANY HEROES OF NOTE.
HEY!
AND THESEUS.
WHY ANYONE WOULD CALL FOR THE HELP OF THAT THIEVING, PILLAGING CUR, I HAVE NO IDEA.
ME?
I AM SIMPLY DUMBFOUNDED THAT AN OAF LIKE BEOWULF WOULD SHOW UP.
'ERCULES GAVE ME A TINKLE ON THE BLOWER. SO I GOT MESELF OVER 'ERE SHARPISH, DIN' I?
HE DINT SAY NUFFIN' ABOUT NO OTHERS.
GODS! YOU SMELL LIKE A SWAMP!
ARE YOU LIVING WITH GRENDEL THESE DAYS?
SHUT IT, PRETTY BOY.
AH, HERC DARLING! ALL THE OLD RIVALRIES FROTH TO THE SURFACE!
REMINDS ME OF THE OLD DAYS.
YOU SHOULD TELL THEM ABOUT THE BRAND, SWEETIE.

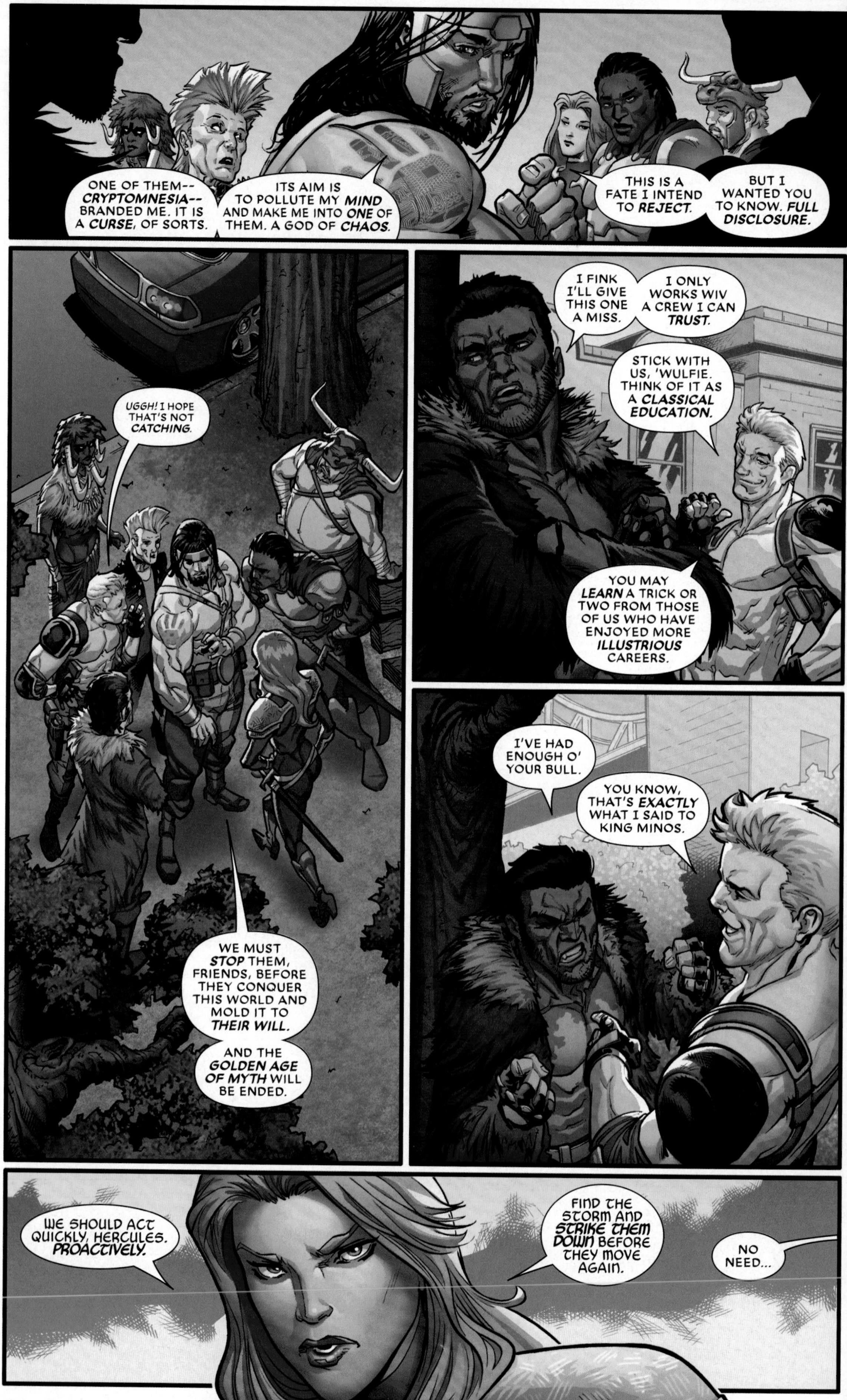
ONE OF THEM-- CRYPTOMNESIA-- BRANDED ME. IT IS A CURSE, OF SORTS.
ITS AIM IS TO POLLUTE MY MIND AND MAKE ME INTO ONE OF THEM. A GOD OF CHAOS.
THIS IS A FATE I INTEND TO REJECT.
BUT I WANTED YOU TO KNOW. FULL DISCLOSURE.
UGGH! I HOPE THAT'S NOT CATCHING.
WE MUST STOP THEM, FRIENDS, BEFORE THEY CONQUER THIS WORLD AND MOLD IT TO THEIR WILL.
AND THE GOLDEN AGE OF MYTH WILL BE ENDED.
I FINK I'LL GIVE THIS ONE A MISS.
I ONLY WORKS WIV A CREW I CAN TRUST.
STICK WITH US, 'WULFIE. THINK OF IT AS A CLASSICAL EDUCATION.
YOU MAY LEARN A TRICK OR TWO FROM THOSE OF US WHO HAVE ENJOYED MORE ILLUSTRIOUS CAREERS.
I'VE HAD ENOUGH O' YOUR BULL.
YOU KNOW, THAT'S EXACTLY WHAT I SAID TO KING MINOS.
WE SHOULD ACT QUICKLY, HERCULES. PROACTIVELY.
FIND THE STORM AND STRIKE THEM DOWN BEFORE THEY MOVE AGAIN.
NO NEED...

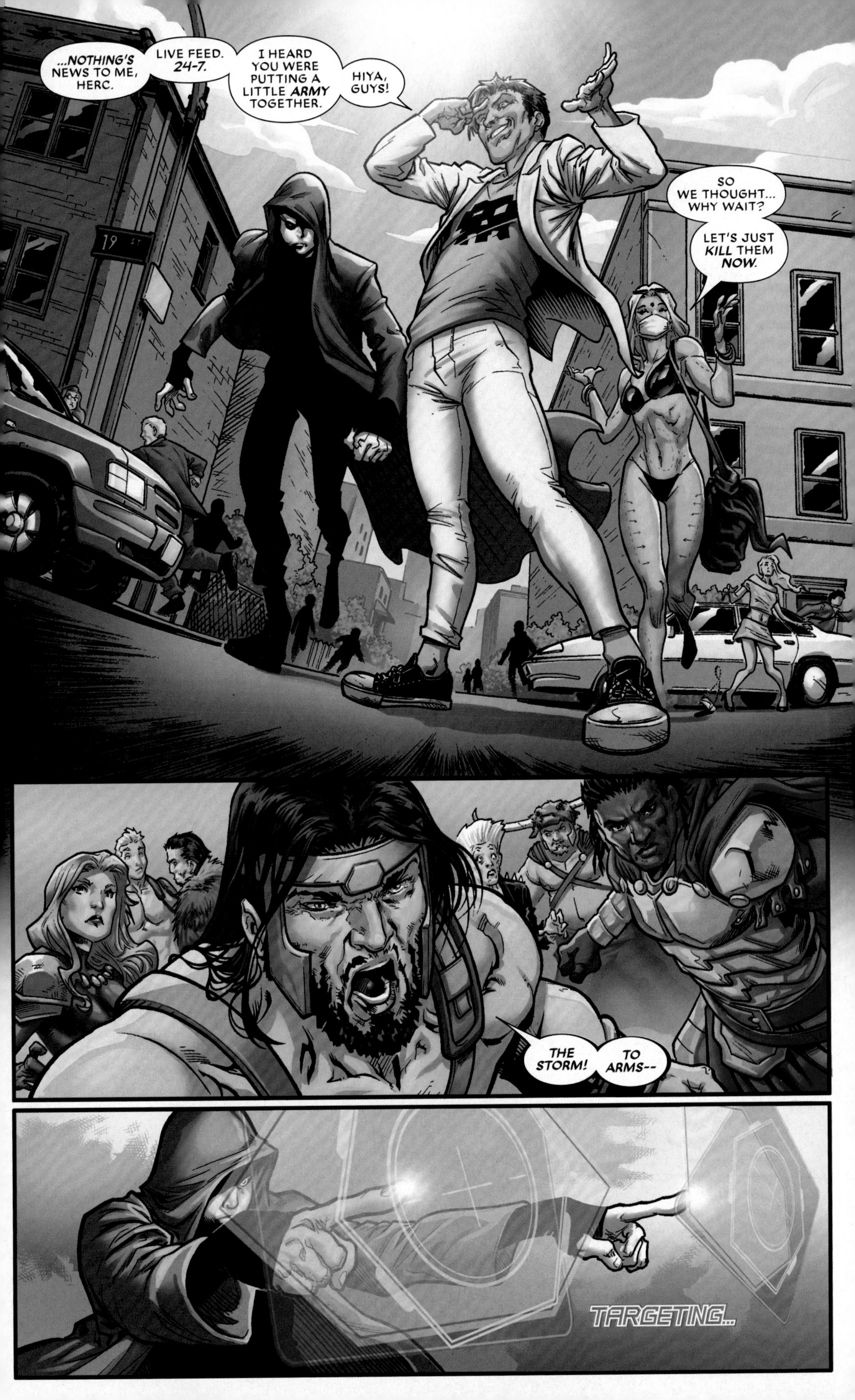
...NOTHING'S NEWS TO ME, HERC.
LIVE FEED. 24-7.
I HEARD YOU WERE PUTTING A LITTLE ARMY TOGETHER.
HIYA, GUYS!
19 ST
SO WE THOUGHT... WHY WAIT?
LET'S JUST KILL THEM NOW.
THE STORM!
TO ARMS--
TARGETING...

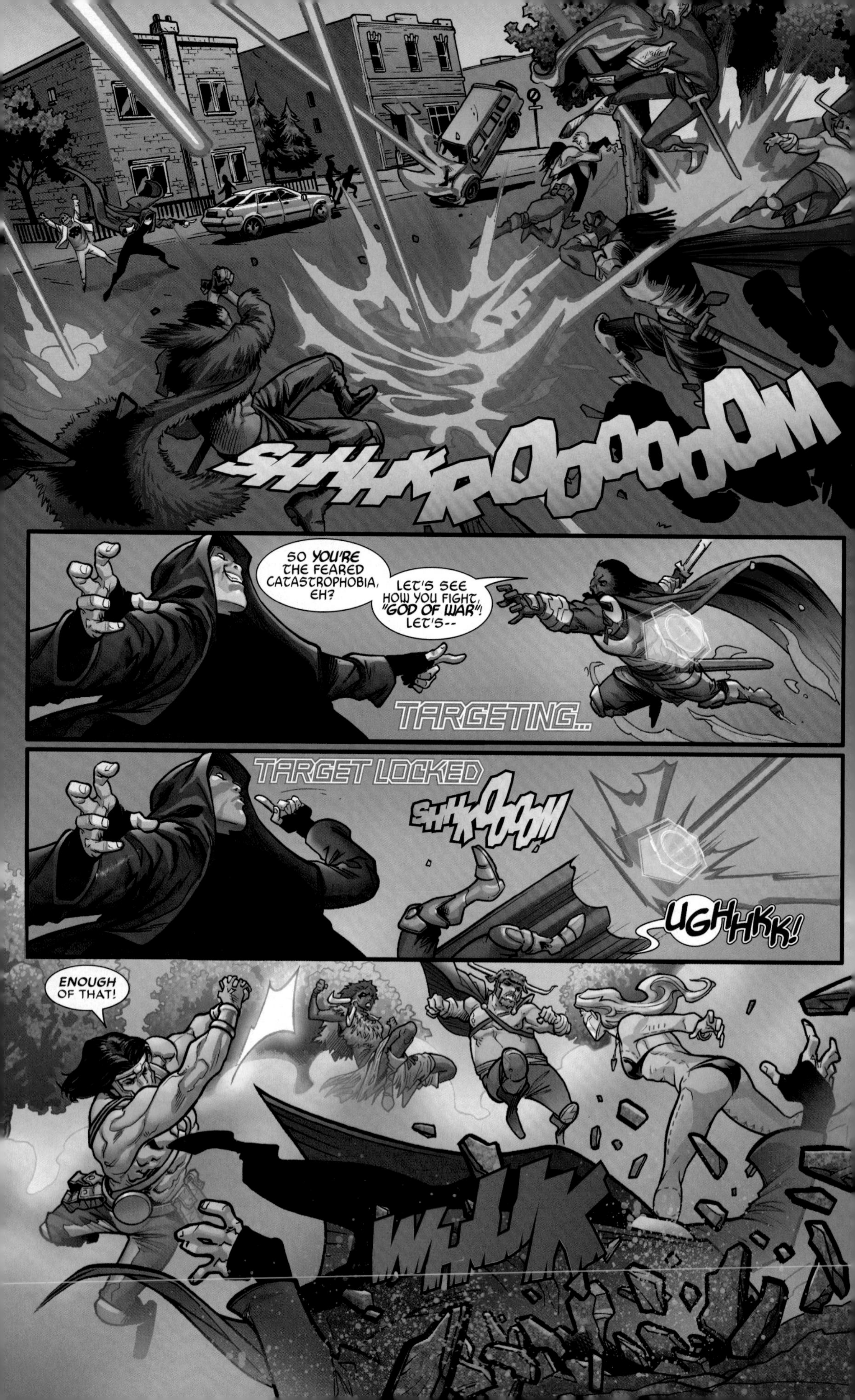
SHHHKROOOOOOOM
SO YOU'RE THE FEARED CATASTROPHOBIA, EH?
LET'S SEE HOW YOU FIGHT, "GOD OF WAR"! LET'S--
TARGETING...
TARGET LOCKED
SHHKOOOM
UGHHKK!
ENOUGH OF THAT!
WHUK

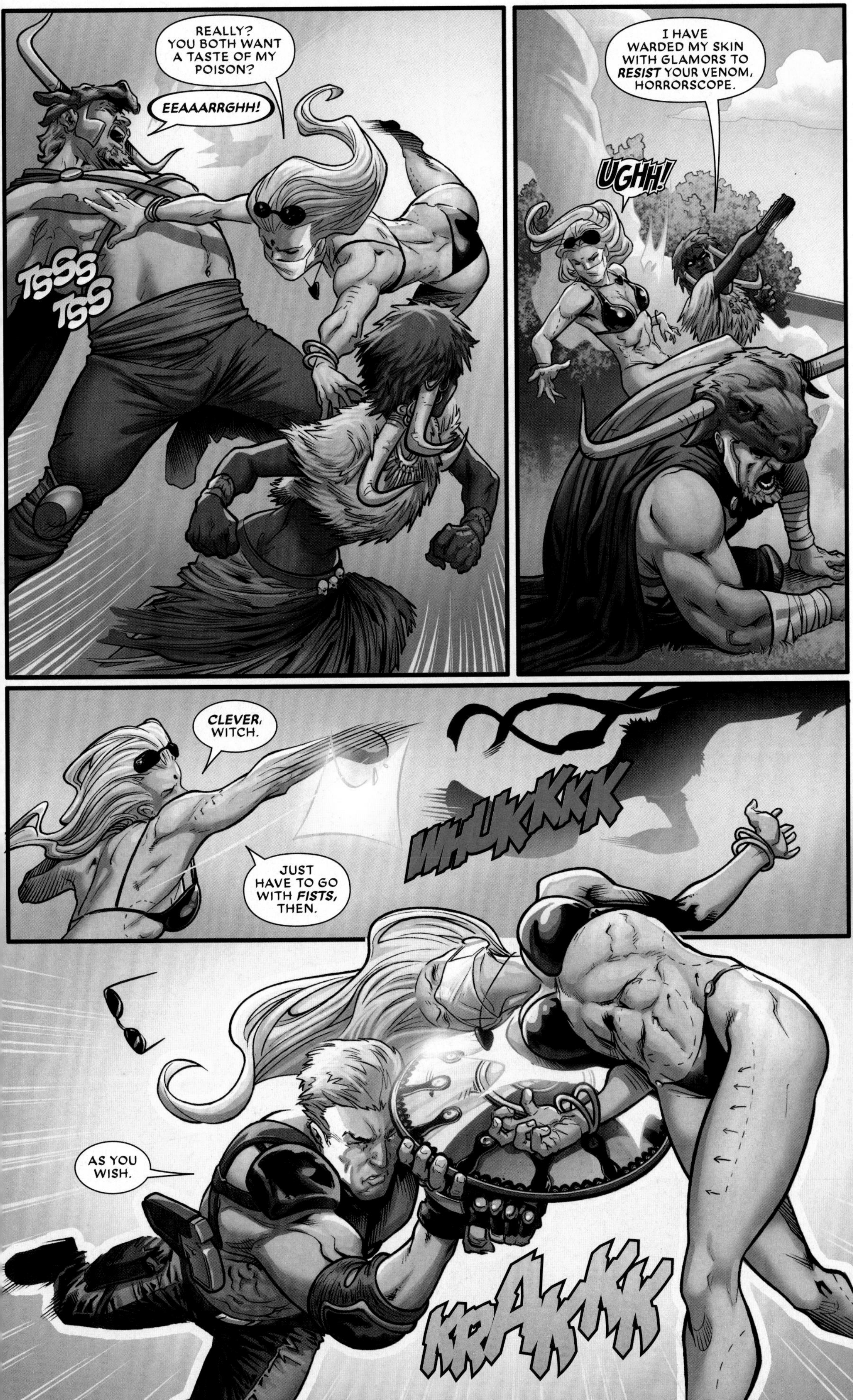
REALLY? YOU BOTH WANT A TASTE OF MY POISON?
EEAAARRGHH!
TSSS TSS
I HAVE WARDED MY SKIN WITH GLAMORS TO RESIST YOUR VENOM, HORRORSCOPE.
UGHH!
CLEVER, WITCH.
JUST HAVE TO GO WITH FISTS, THEN.
WHUKKKK
AS YOU WISH.
KRAKKK

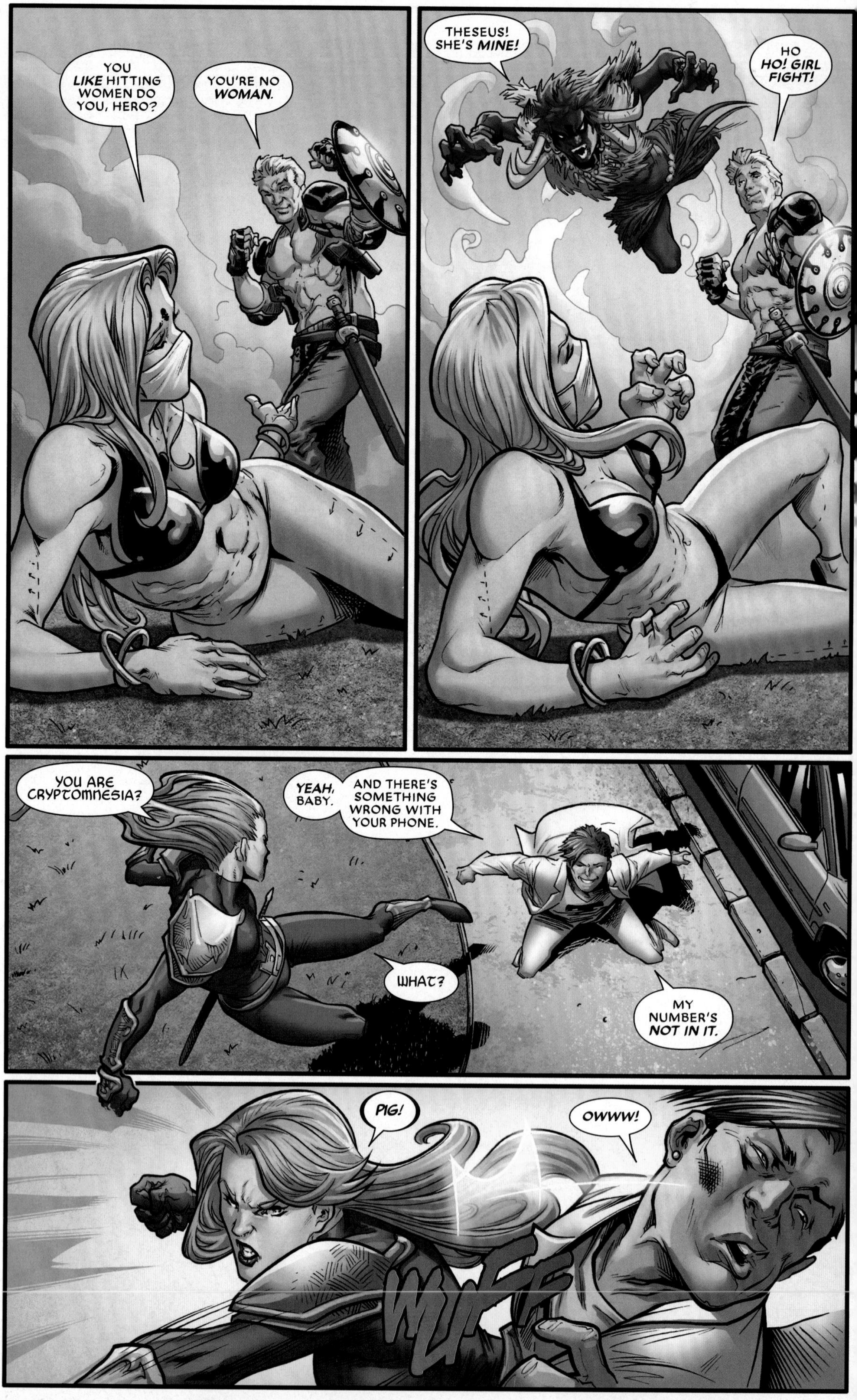
YOU LIKE HITTING WOMEN DO YOU, HERO?
YOU'RE NO WOMAN.
THESEUS! SHE'S MINE!
HO HO! GIRL FIGHT!
YOU ARE CRYPTOMNESIA?
YEAH, BABY.
AND THERE'S SOMETHING WRONG WITH YOUR PHONE.
WHAT?
MY NUMBER'S NOT IN IT.
PIG!
OWWW!
WUFF

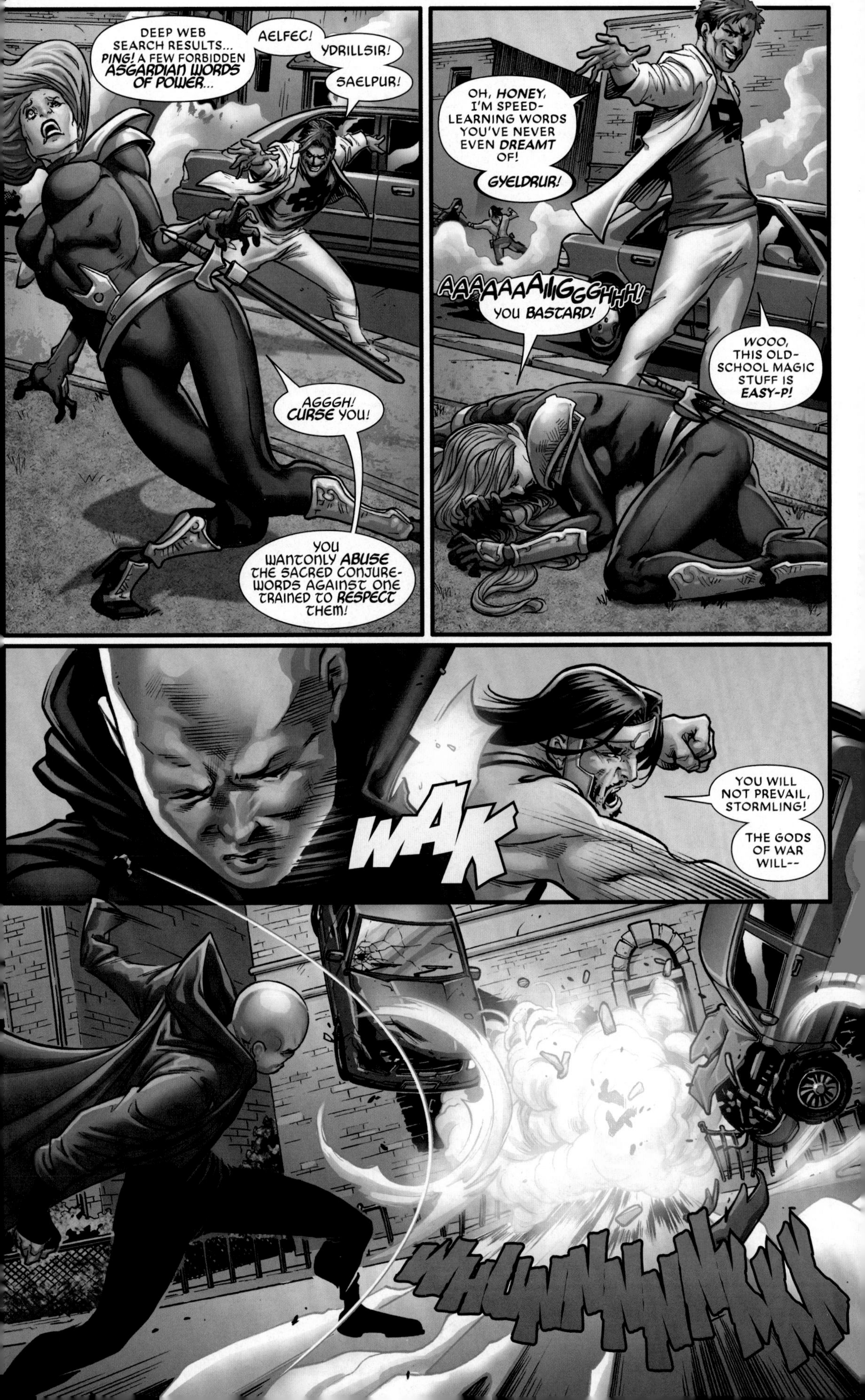
DEEP WEB SEARCH RESULTS... PING! A FEW FORBIDDEN ASGARDIAN WORDS OF POWER...
AELFEC!
YDRILLSIR!
SAELPUR!
AGGGH! CURSE YOU!
YOU WANTONLY ABUSE THE SACRED CONJURE-WORDS AGAINST ONE TRAINED TO RESPECT THEM!
OH, HONEY, I'M SPEED-LEARNING WORDS YOU'VE NEVER EVEN DREAMT OF!
GYELDRUR!
AAAAAAAIIIGGGHHH!
YOU BASTARD!
WOOO, THIS OLD-SCHOOL MAGIC STUFF IS EASY-P!
WAK
YOU WILL NOT PREVAIL, STORMLING!
THE GODS OF WAR WILL--
WHUMMMMMKKK

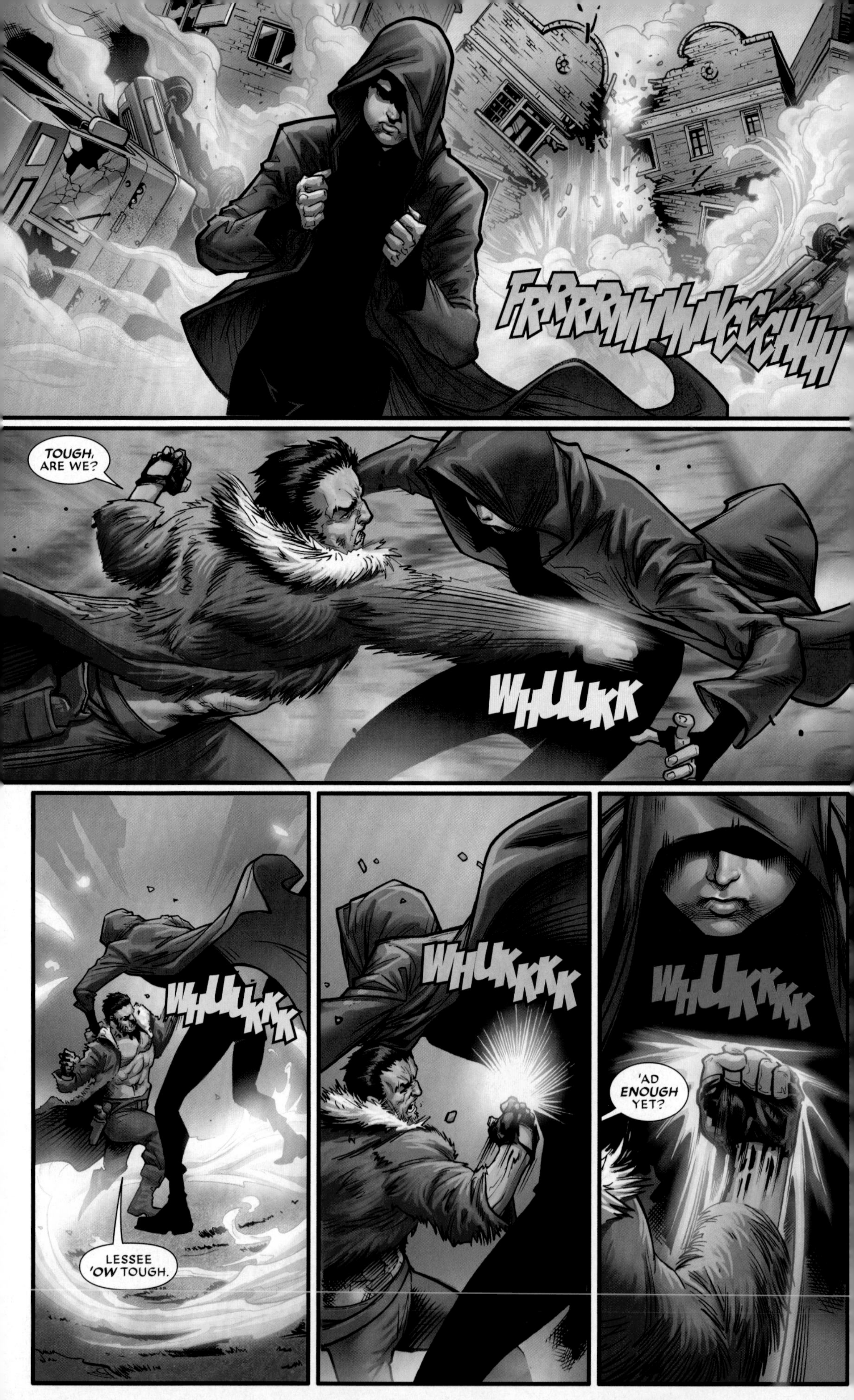
FRRRRMMMMNCCHHH
TOUGH, ARE WE?
WHUUKK
WHUUKKK
LESSEE 'OW TOUGH.
WHUKKKK
WHUKKKK
'AD ENOUGH YET?

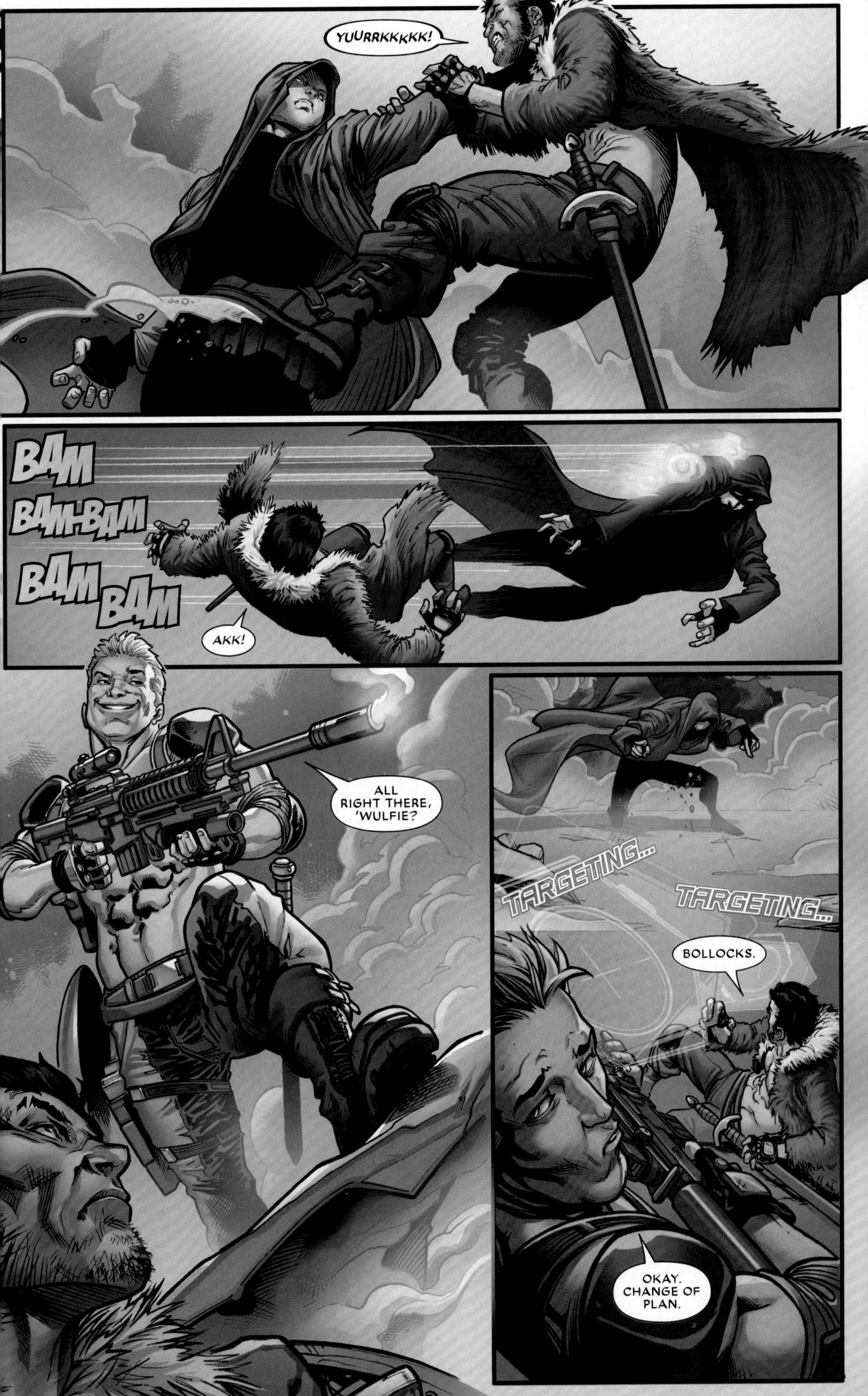
YUURRKKKKK!
BAM
BAM-BAM
BAM BAM
AKK!
ALL RIGHT THERE, 'WULFIE?
TARGETING...
TARGETING...
BOLLOCKS.
OKAY. CHANGE OF PLAN.

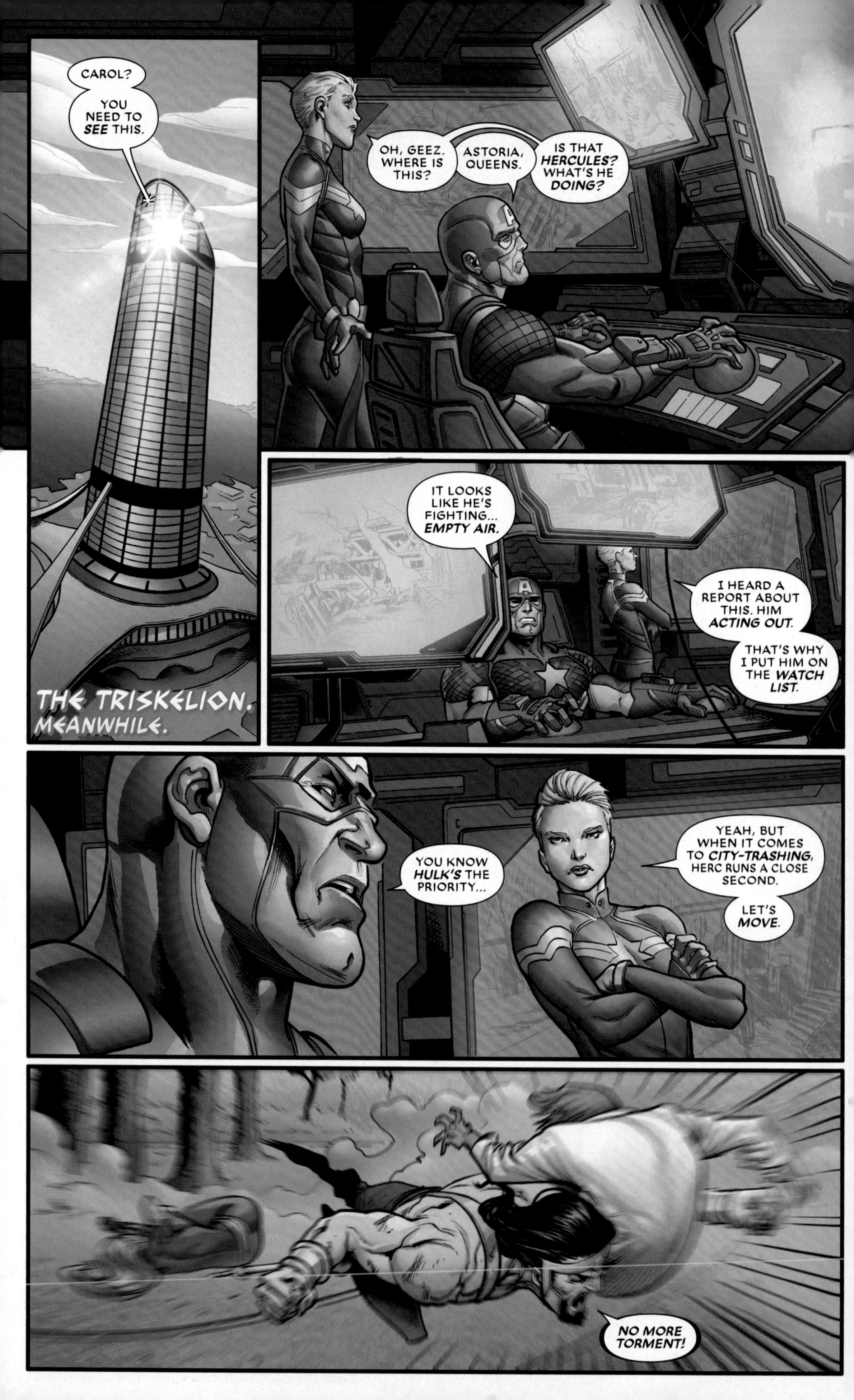
CAROL?
YOU NEED TO SEE THIS.
THE TRISKELION. MEANWHILE.
OH, GEEZ. WHERE IS THIS?
ASTORIA, QUEENS.
IS THAT HERCULES? WHAT'S HE DOING?
IT LOOKS LIKE HE'S FIGHTING... EMPTY AIR.
I HEARD A REPORT ABOUT THIS. HIM ACTING OUT.
THAT'S WHY I PUT HIM ON THE WATCH LIST.
YOU KNOW HULK'S THE PRIORITY...
YEAH, BUT WHEN IT COMES TO CITY-TRASHING, HERC RUNS A CLOSE SECOND.
LET'S MOVE.
NO MORE TORMENT!

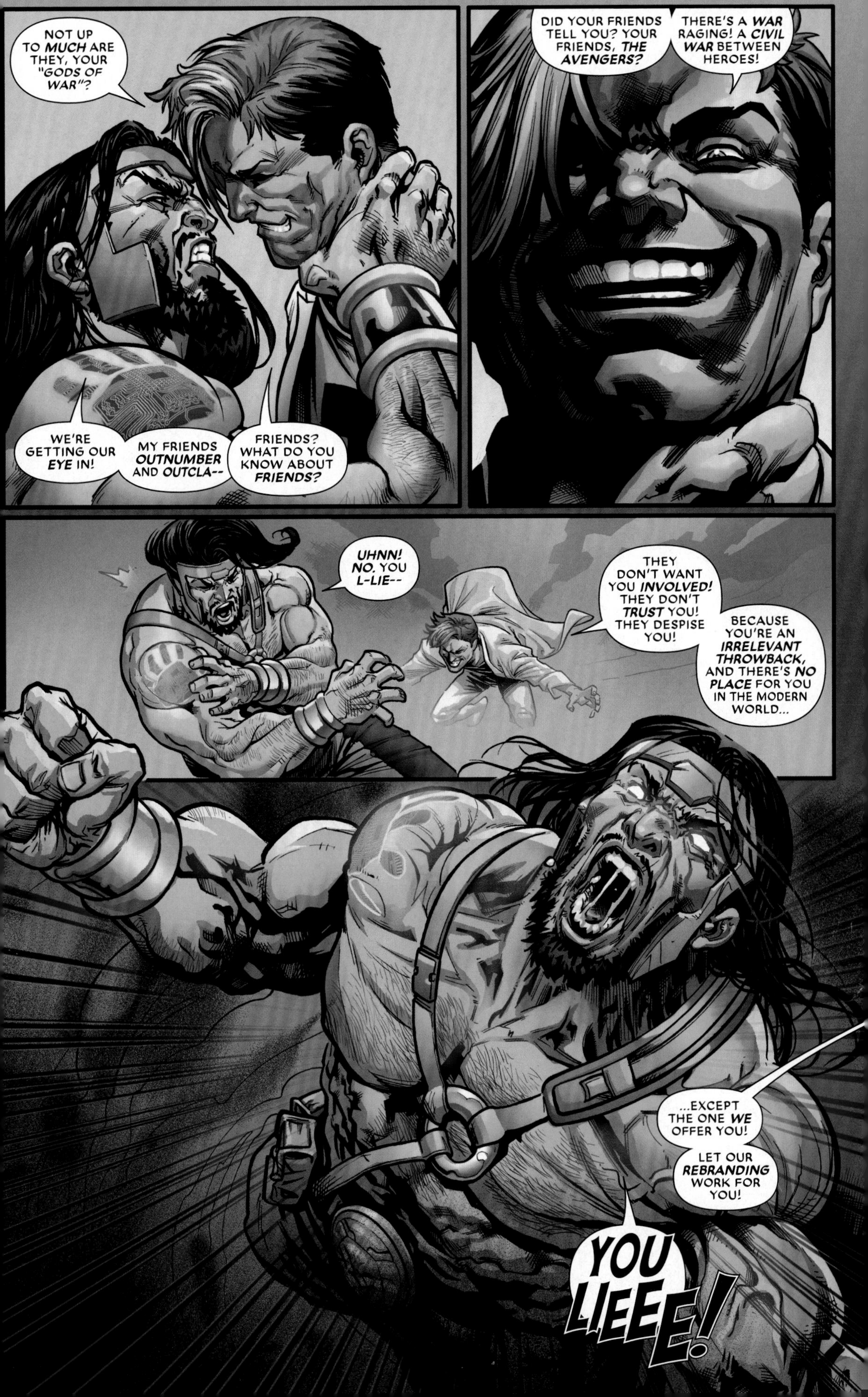
NOT UP TO *MUCH* ARE THEY, YOUR "*GODS OF WAR*"?
WE'RE GETTING OUR *EYE* IN!
MY FRIENDS *OUTNUMBER* AND *OUTCLA--*
FRIENDS? WHAT DO YOU KNOW ABOUT *FRIENDS?*
DID YOUR FRIENDS TELL YOU? YOUR FRIENDS, *THE AVENGERS?*
THERE'S A *WAR* RAGING! A *CIVIL WAR* BETWEEN HEROES!
UHNN! NO. YOU *L-LIE--*
THEY DON'T WANT YOU *INVOLVED!* THEY DON'T *TRUST* YOU! THEY DESPISE YOU!
BECAUSE YOU'RE AN *IRRELEVANT THROWBACK,* AND THERE'S *NO PLACE* FOR YOU IN THE MODERN WORLD...
...EXCEPT THE ONE *WE* OFFER YOU!
LET OUR *REBRANDING* WORK FOR YOU!
YOU LIEEE!

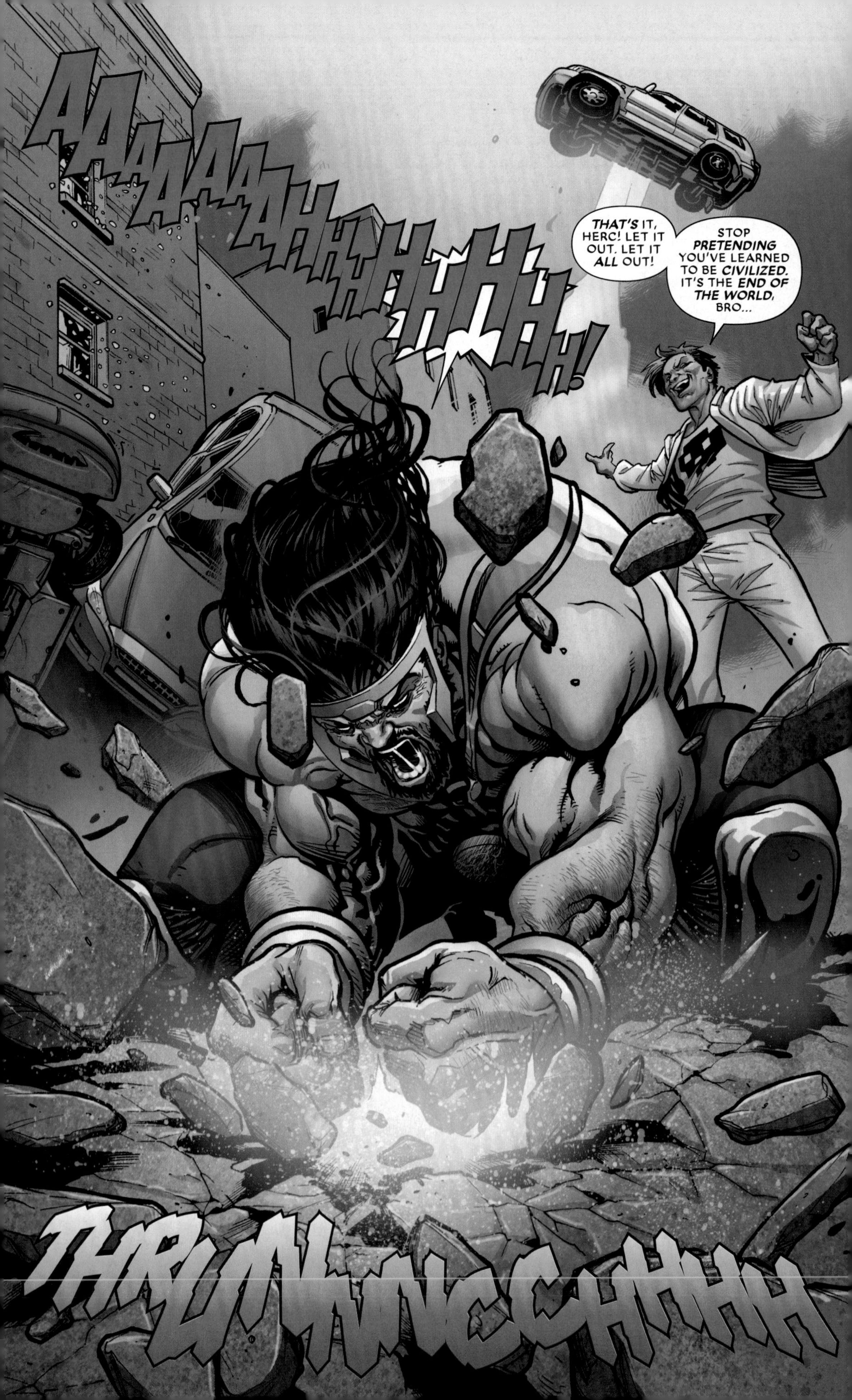
AAAAAAAAHHHHHHHHHH!
THAT'S IT, HERC! LET IT OUT. LET IT ALL OUT!
STOP PRETENDING YOU'VE LEARNED TO BE CIVILIZED. IT'S THE END OF THE WORLD, BRO...
THRUMMNCHHHH

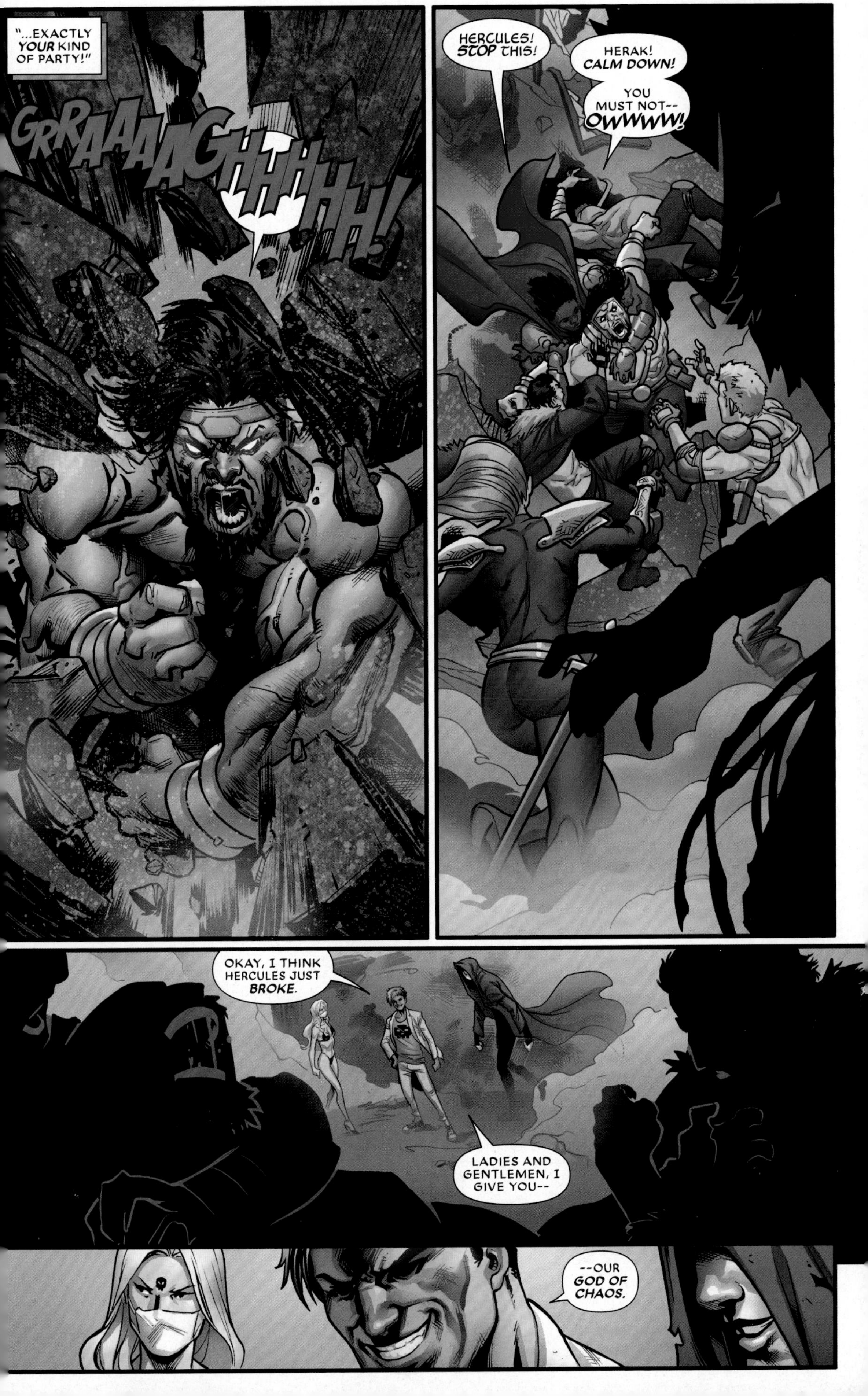
"...EXACTLY YOUR KIND OF PARTY!"
GRRAAAAGHHHHHH!
HERCULES! STOP THIS!
HERAK! CALM DOWN!
YOU MUST NOT-- OWWWW!
OKAY, I THINK HERCULES JUST BROKE.
LADIES AND GENTLEMEN, I GIVE YOU--
--OUR GOD OF CHAOS.

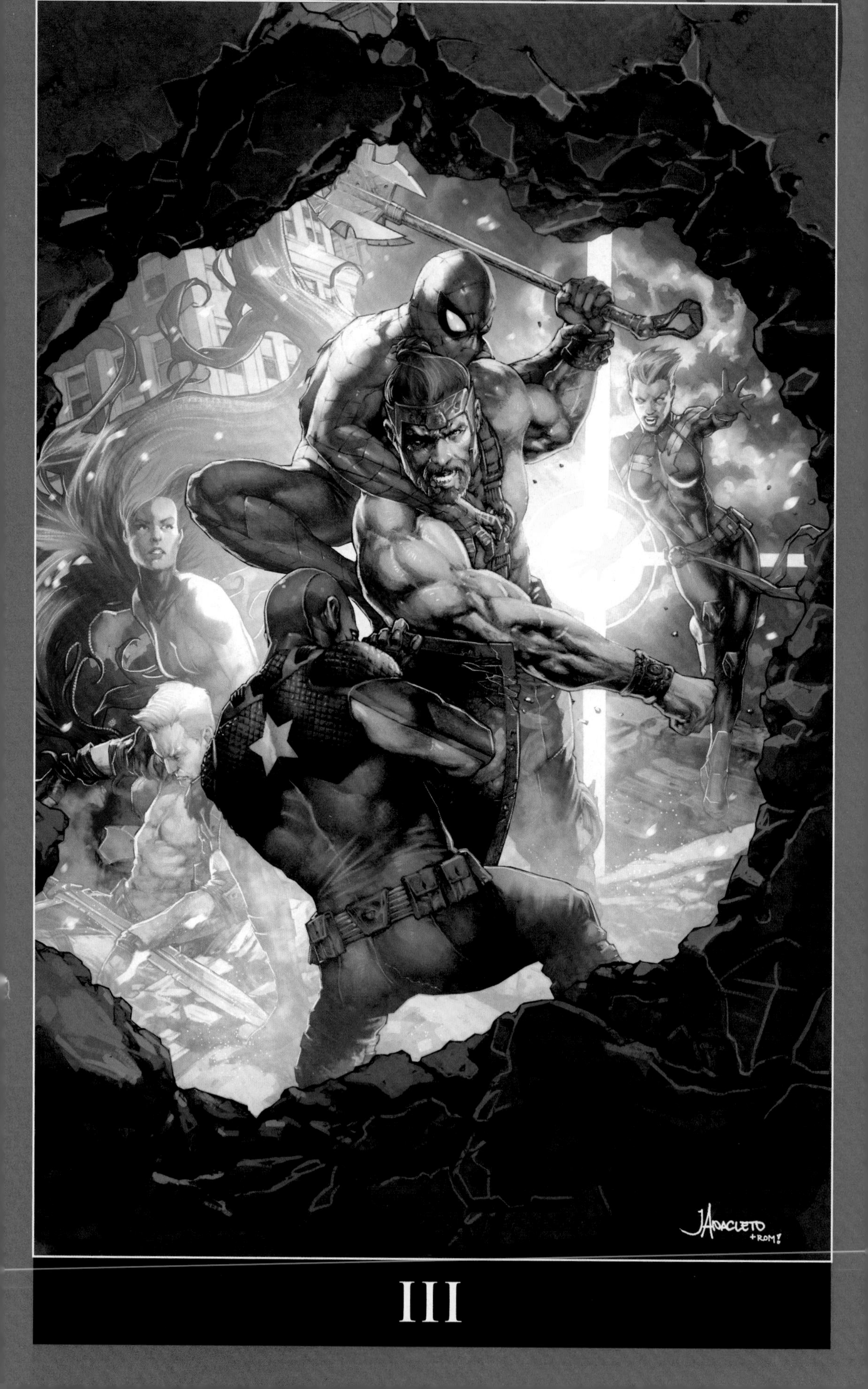

JAnacleto
+Rom!

III

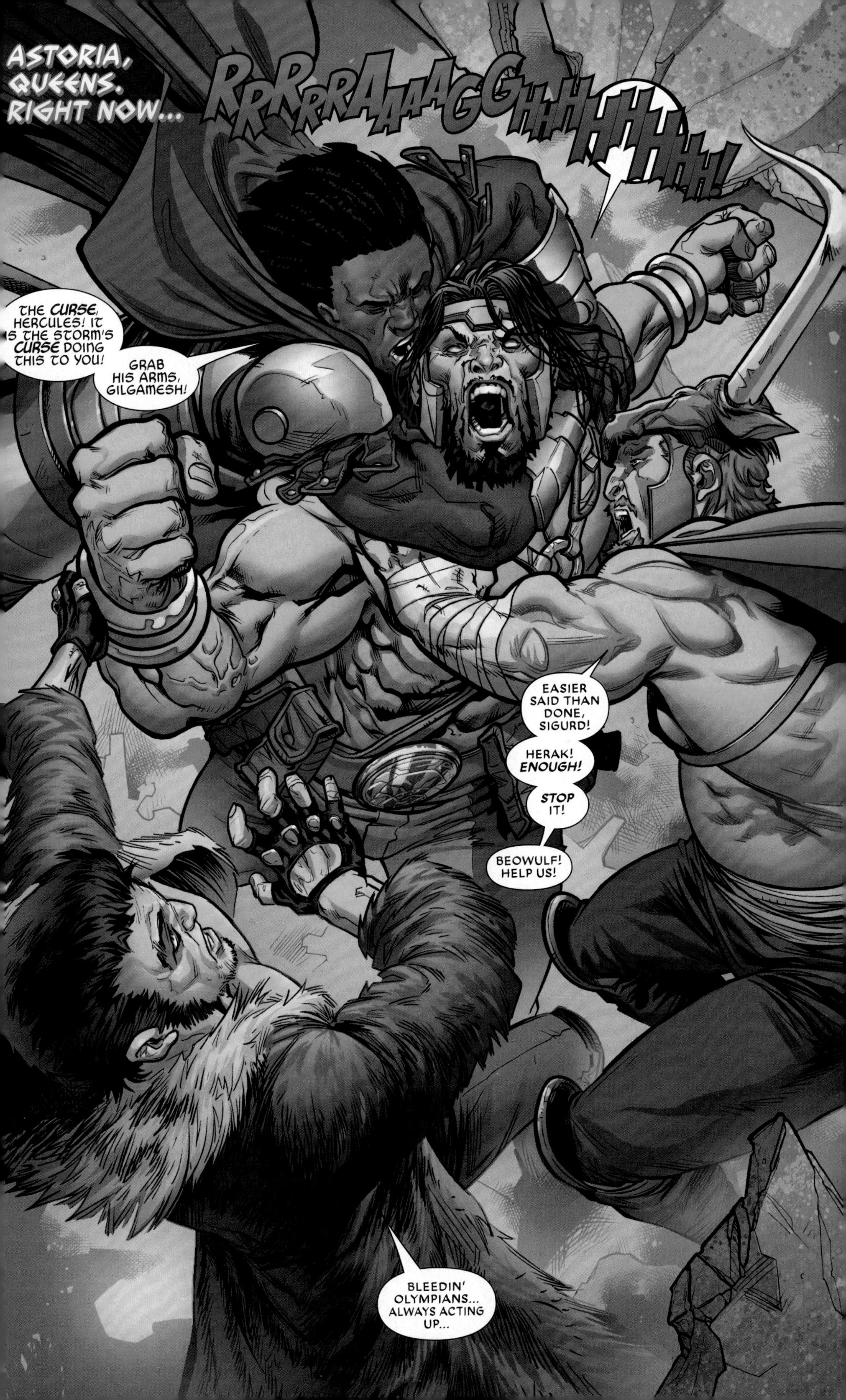
ASTORIA, QUEENS. RIGHT NOW...
RRRRRAAAAGGHHHHHHHH!
THE CURSE, HERCULES! IT IS THE STORM'S CURSE DOING THIS TO YOU!
GRAB HIS ARMS, GILGAMESH!
EASIER SAID THAN DONE, SIGURD!
HERAK! ENOUGH!
STOP IT!
BEOWULF! HELP US!
BLEEDIN' OLYMPIANS... ALWAYS ACTING UP...

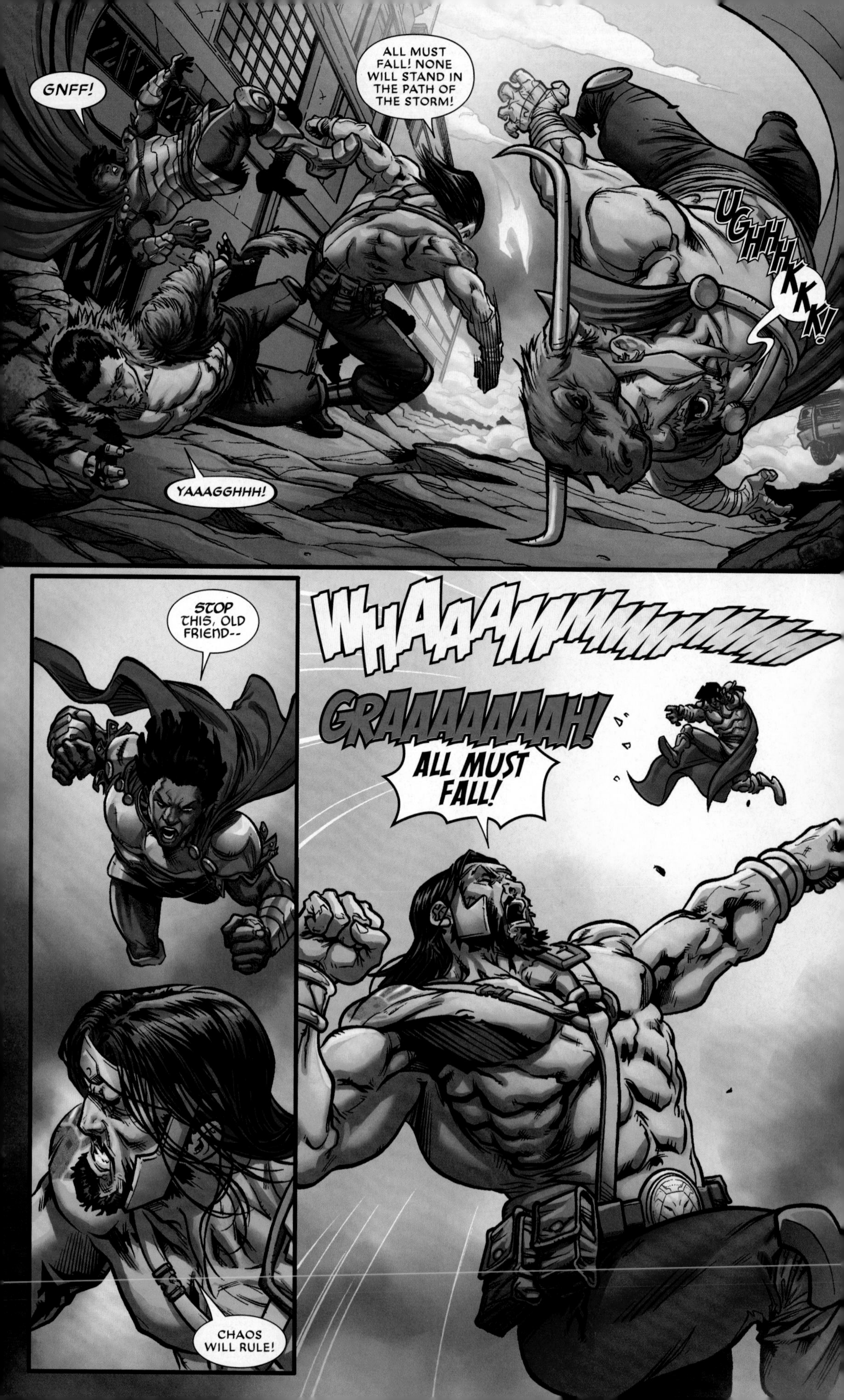
GNFF!
ALL MUST FALL! NONE WILL STAND IN THE PATH OF THE STORM!
UGHHHKKK!
YAAAGGHHH!
STOP THIS, OLD FRIEND--
CHAOS WILL RULE!
WHAAAMMMMMMMM
GRAAAAAAAAH!
ALL MUST FALL!

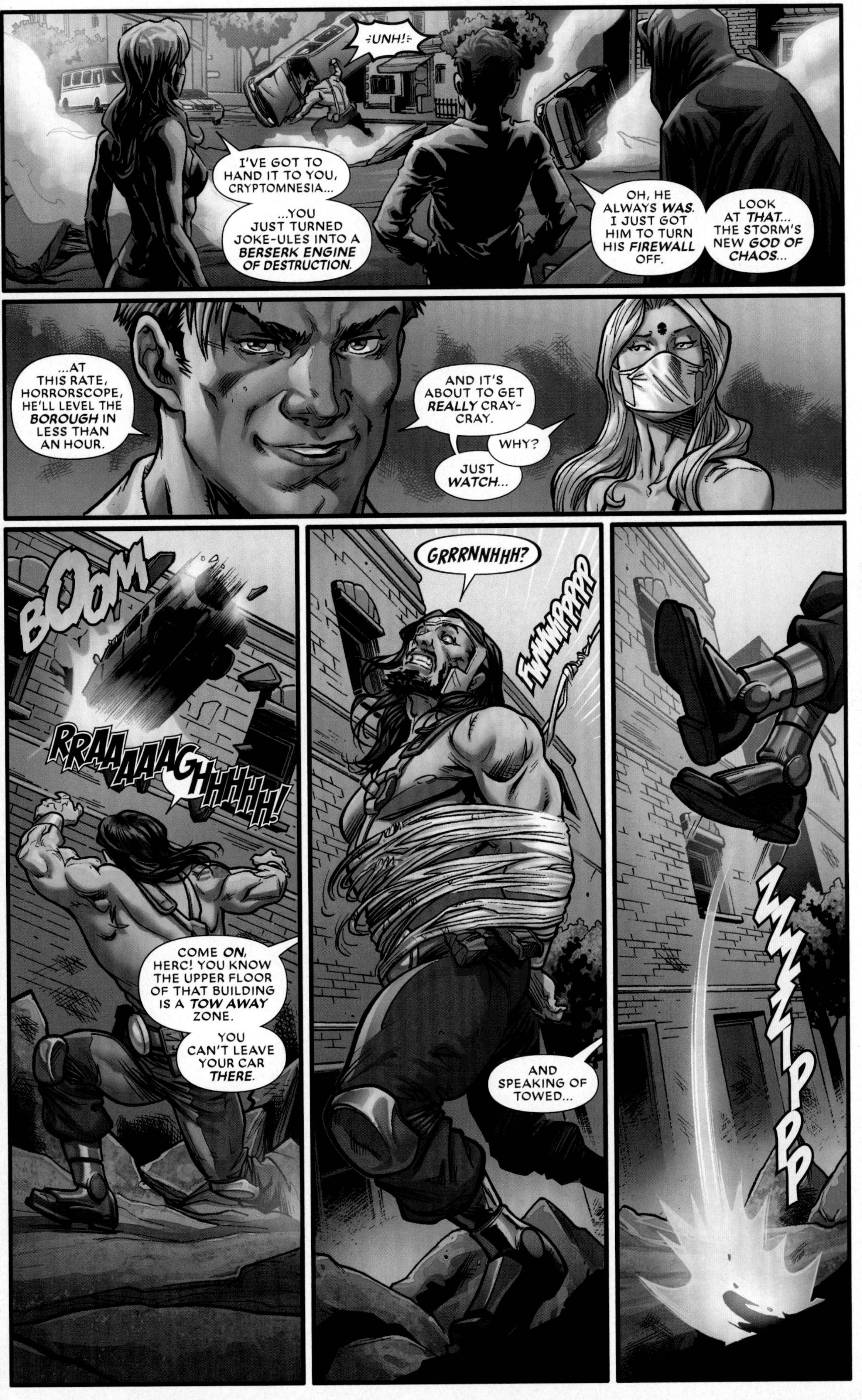
UNH!
I'VE GOT TO HAND IT TO YOU, CRYPTOMNESIA...
...YOU JUST TURNED JOKE-ULES INTO A BERSERK ENGINE OF DESTRUCTION.
OH, HE ALWAYS WAS. I JUST GOT HIM TO TURN HIS FIREWALL OFF.
LOOK AT THAT... THE STORM'S NEW GOD OF CHAOS...
...AT THIS RATE, HORRORSCOPE, HE'LL LEVEL THE BOROUGH IN LESS THAN AN HOUR.
AND IT'S ABOUT TO GET REALLY CRAY-CRAY.
WHY?
JUST WATCH...
BOOM
RRAAAAAAGHHHHH!
COME ON, HERC! YOU KNOW THE UPPER FLOOR OF THAT BUILDING IS A TOW AWAY ZONE.
YOU CAN'T LEAVE YOUR CAR THERE.
GRRRNHHH?
FWWWIPPPP
AND SPEAKING OF TOWED...
ZZZZIPPP

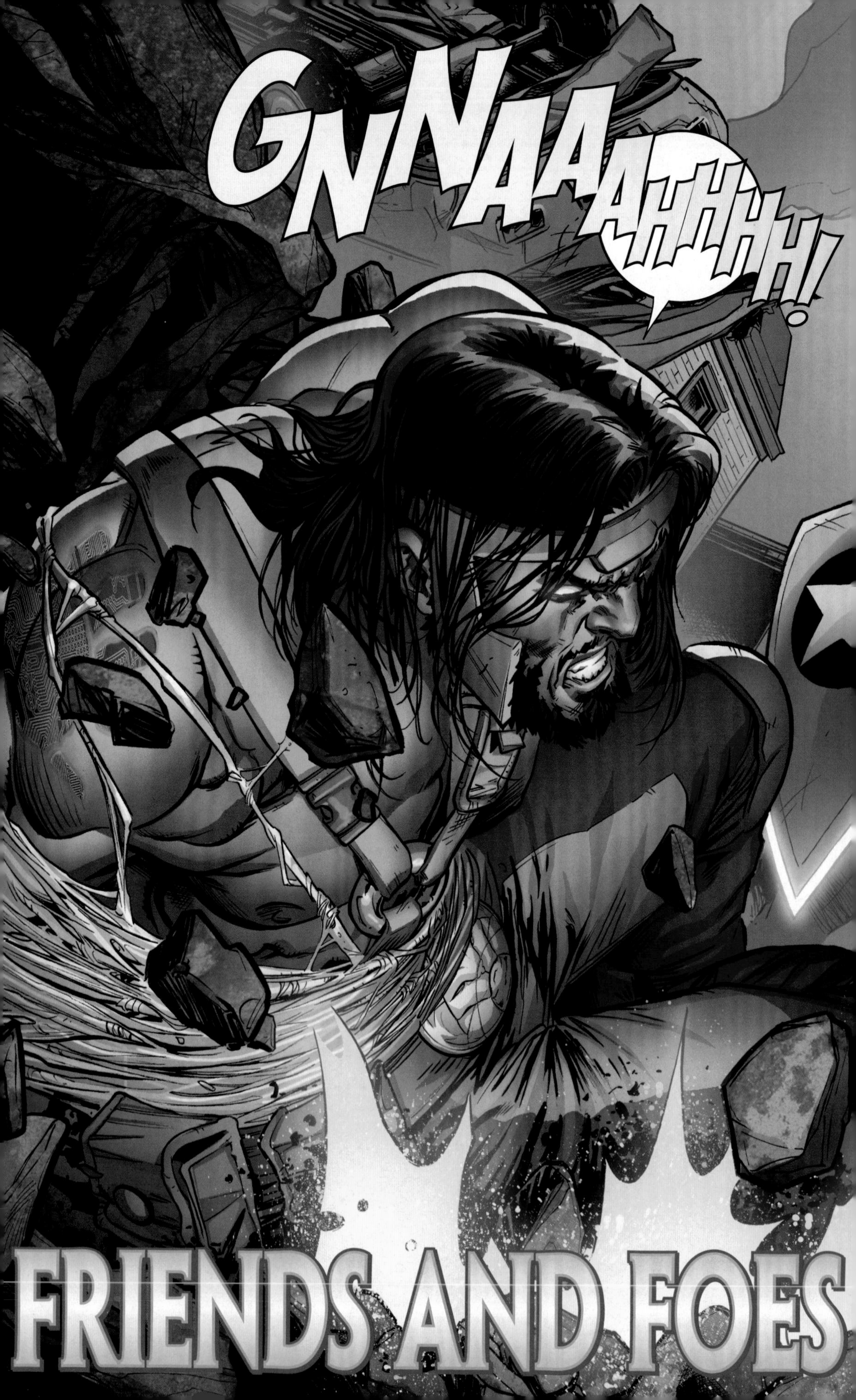
GNAAAHHHH!
FRIENDS AND FOES

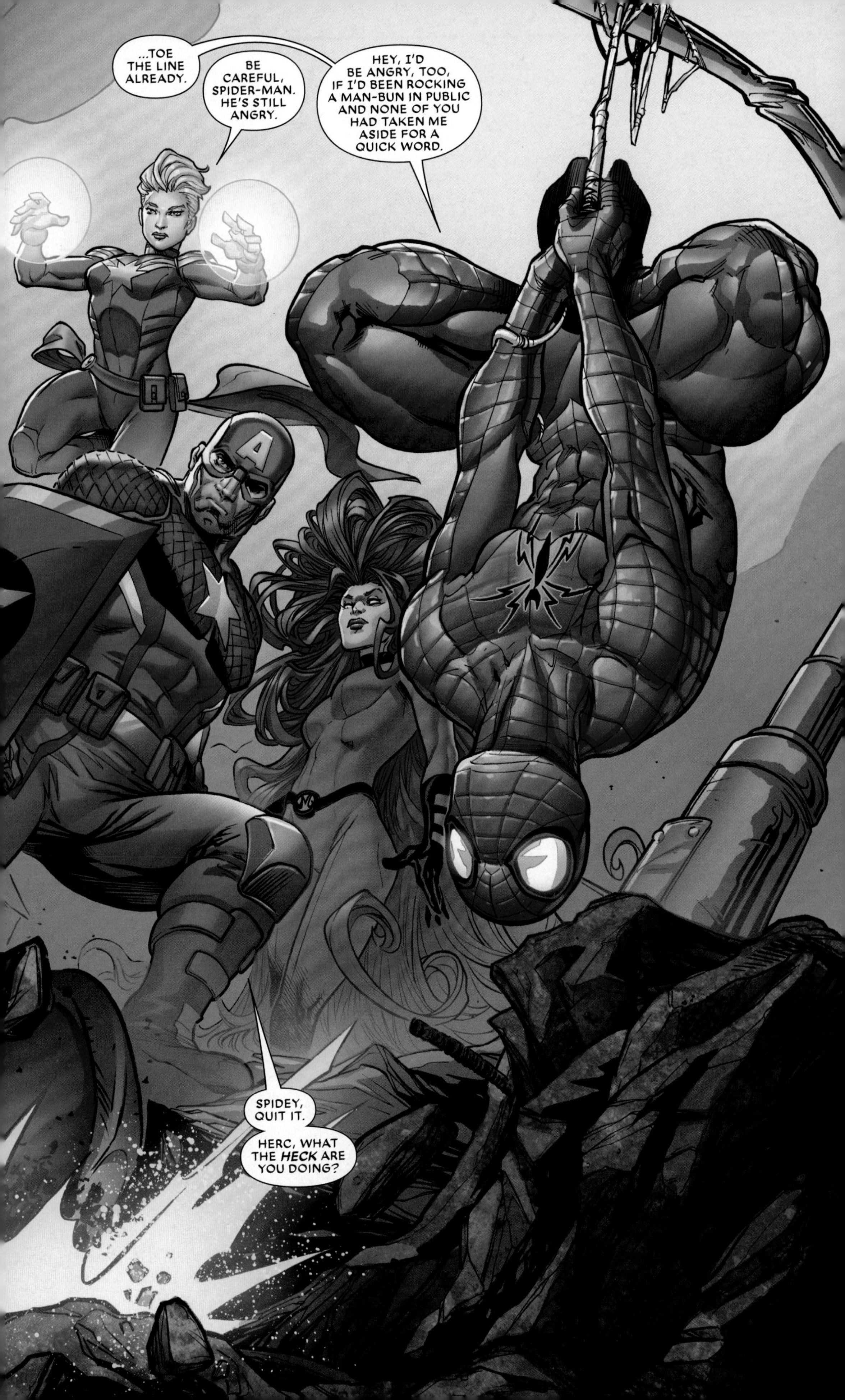
...TOE THE LINE ALREADY.
BE CAREFUL, SPIDER-MAN. HE'S STILL ANGRY.
HEY, I'D BE ANGRY, TOO, IF I'D BEEN ROCKING A MAN-BUN IN PUBLIC AND NONE OF YOU HAD TAKEN ME ASIDE FOR A QUICK WORD.
SPIDEY, QUIT IT.
HERC, WHAT THE HECK ARE YOU DOING?

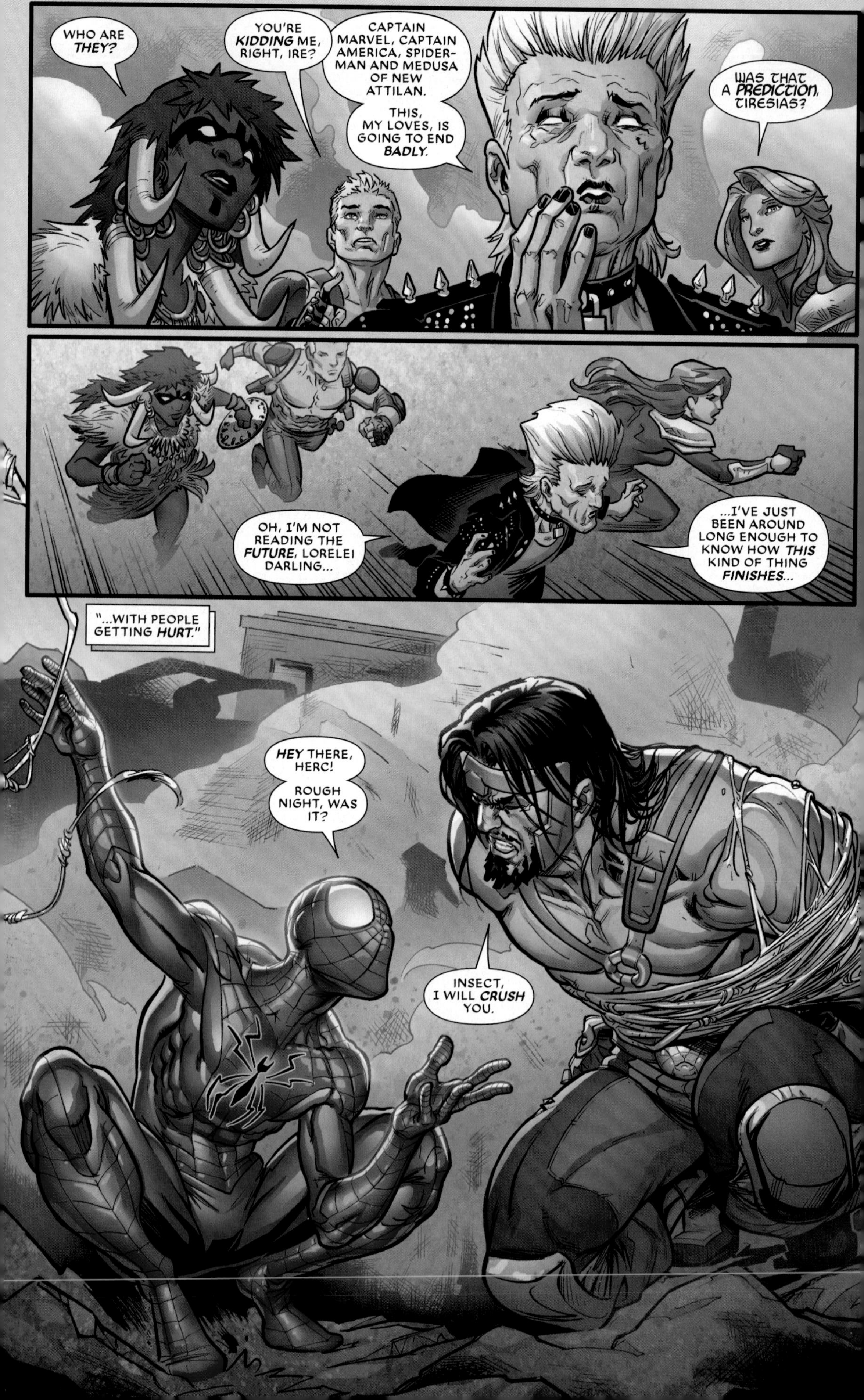
WHO ARE THEY?
YOU'RE KIDDING ME, RIGHT, IRE?
CAPTAIN MARVEL, CAPTAIN AMERICA, SPIDER-MAN AND MEDUSA OF NEW ATTILAN.
THIS, MY LOVES, IS GOING TO END BADLY.
WAS THAT A PREDICTION, TIRESIAS?
OH, I'M NOT READING THE FUTURE, LORELEI DARLING...
...I'VE JUST BEEN AROUND LONG ENOUGH TO KNOW HOW THIS KIND OF THING FINISHES...
"...WITH PEOPLE GETTING HURT."
HEY THERE, HERC!
ROUGH NIGHT, WAS IT?
INSECT, I WILL CRUSH YOU.

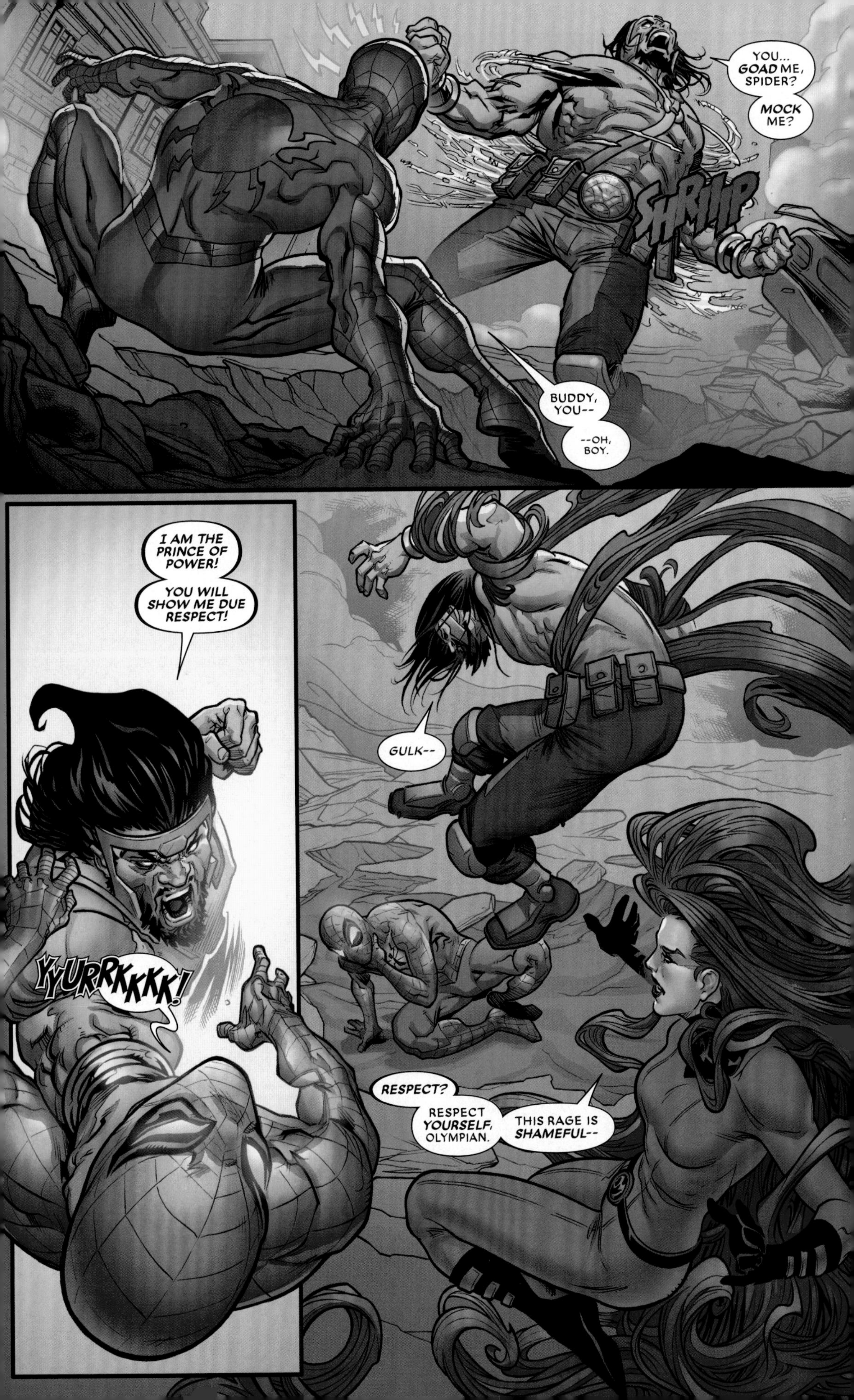
YOU... GOAD ME, SPIDER?
MOCK ME?
BUDDY, YOU--
--OH, BOY.
I AM THE PRINCE OF POWER!
YOU WILL SHOW ME DUE RESPECT!
YYURRKKKK!
GULK--
RESPECT?
RESPECT YOURSELF, OLYMPIAN.
THIS RAGE IS SHAMEFUL--

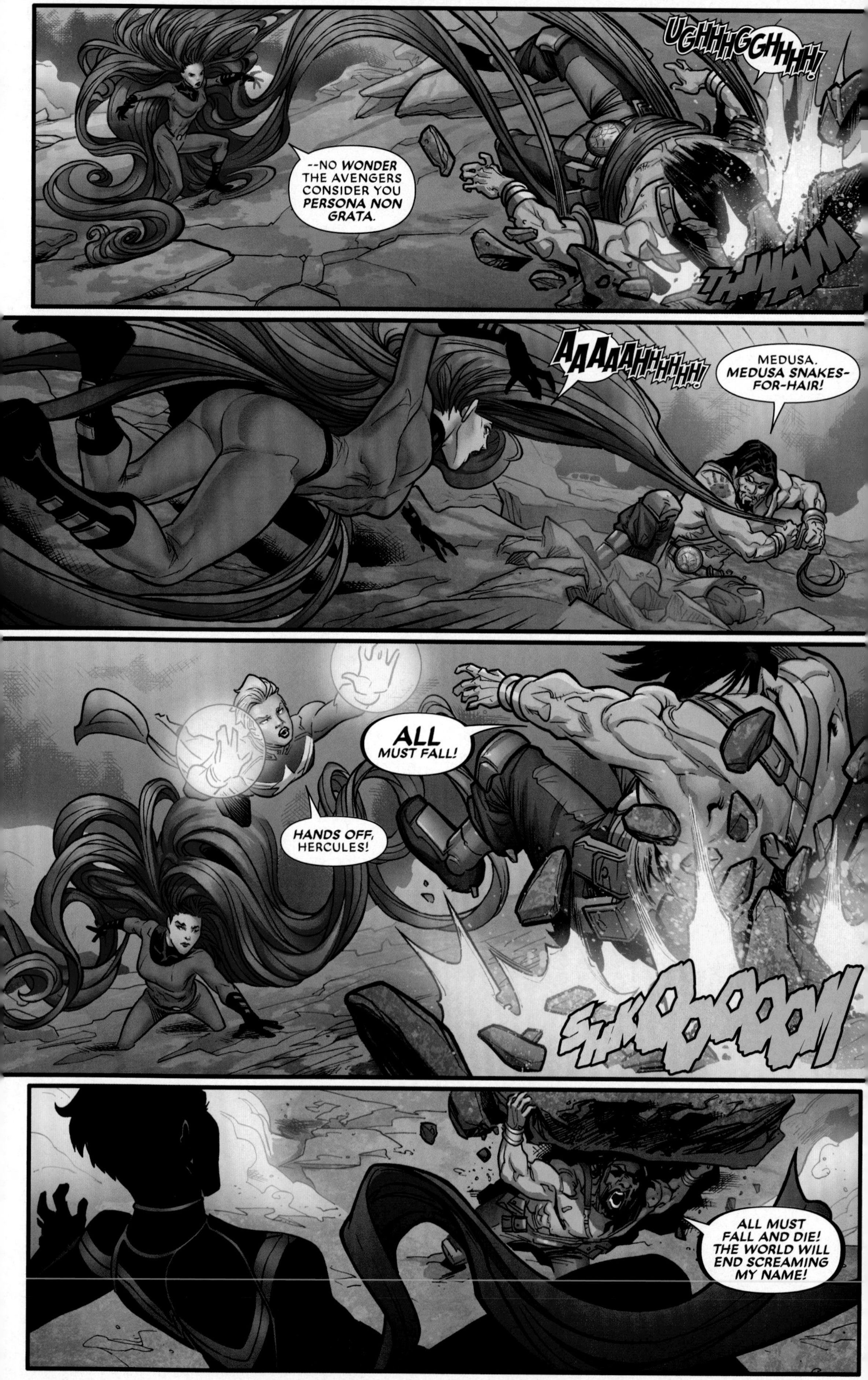
UGHHHGGHHHH!
--NO WONDER THE AVENGERS CONSIDER YOU PERSONA NON GRATA.
THWAM
AAAAAHHHHHH!
MEDUSA. MEDUSA SNAKES-FOR-HAIR!
ALL MUST FALL!
HANDS OFF, HERCULES!
SHKOOOOOM
ALL MUST FALL AND DIE! THE WORLD WILL END SCREAMING MY NAME!

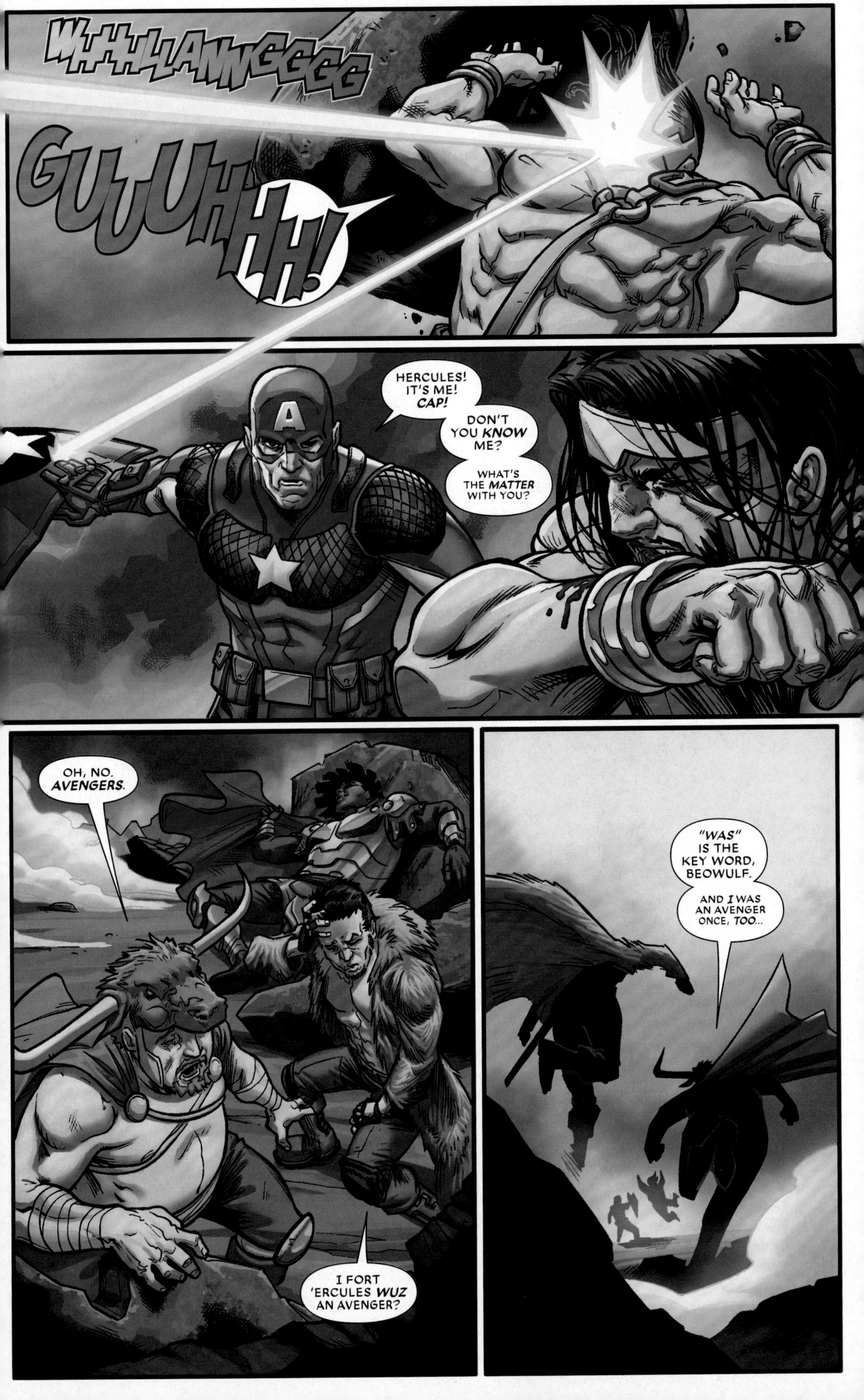
WHHLLANNGGGG
GUUUHHH!
HERCULES! IT'S ME! CAP!
DON'T YOU KNOW ME?
WHAT'S THE MATTER WITH YOU?
OH, NO. AVENGERS.
I FORT 'ERCULES WUZ AN AVENGER?
"WAS" IS THE KEY WORD, BEOWULF.
AND I WAS AN AVENGER ONCE, TOO...

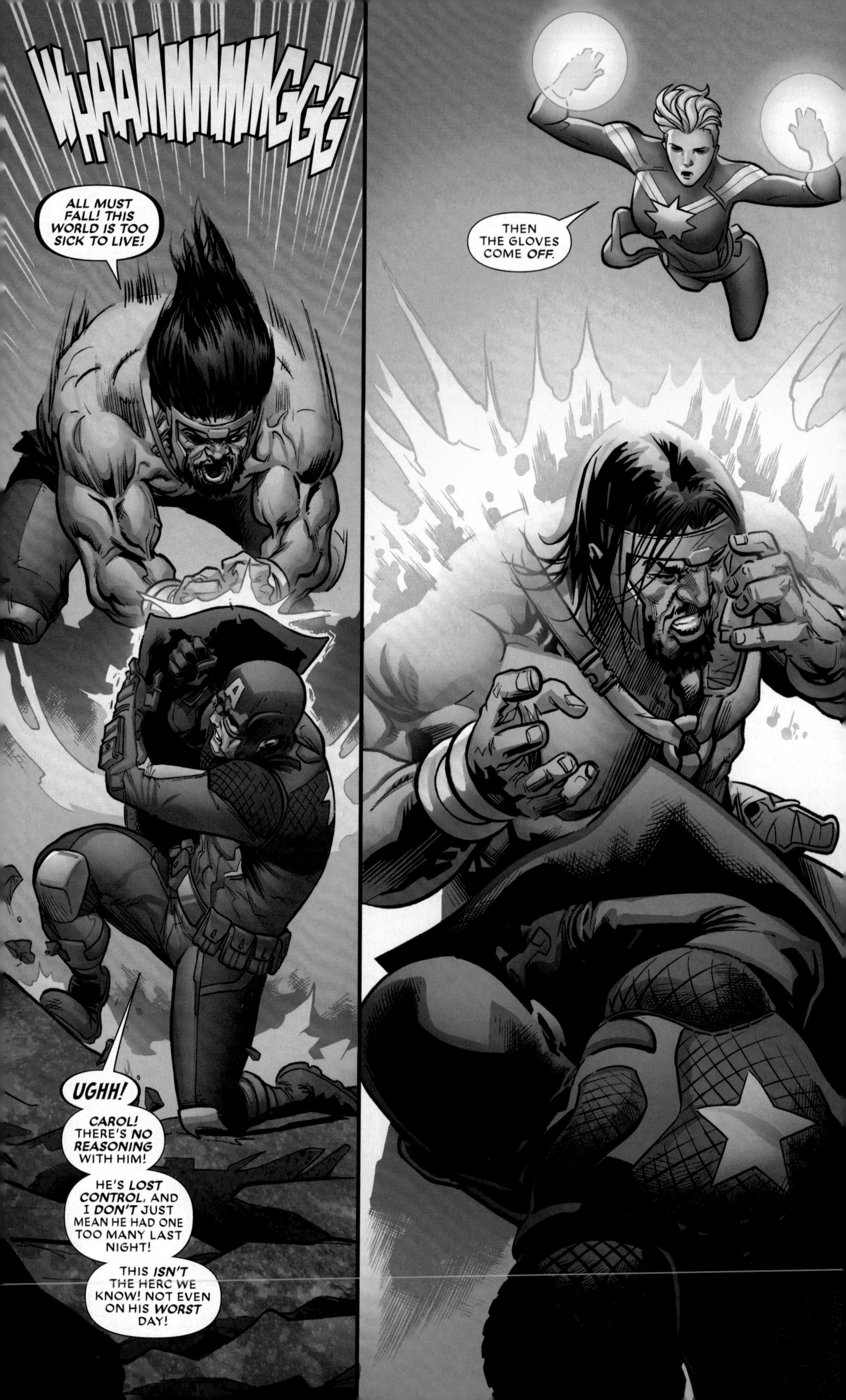
WHAAMMMMMGGG
ALL MUST FALL! THIS WORLD IS TOO SICK TO LIVE!
UGHH!
CAROL! THERE'S NO REASONING WITH HIM!
HE'S LOST CONTROL, AND I DON'T JUST MEAN HE HAD ONE TOO MANY LAST NIGHT!
THIS ISN'T THE HERC WE KNOW! NOT EVEN ON HIS WORST DAY!
THEN THE GLOVES COME OFF.

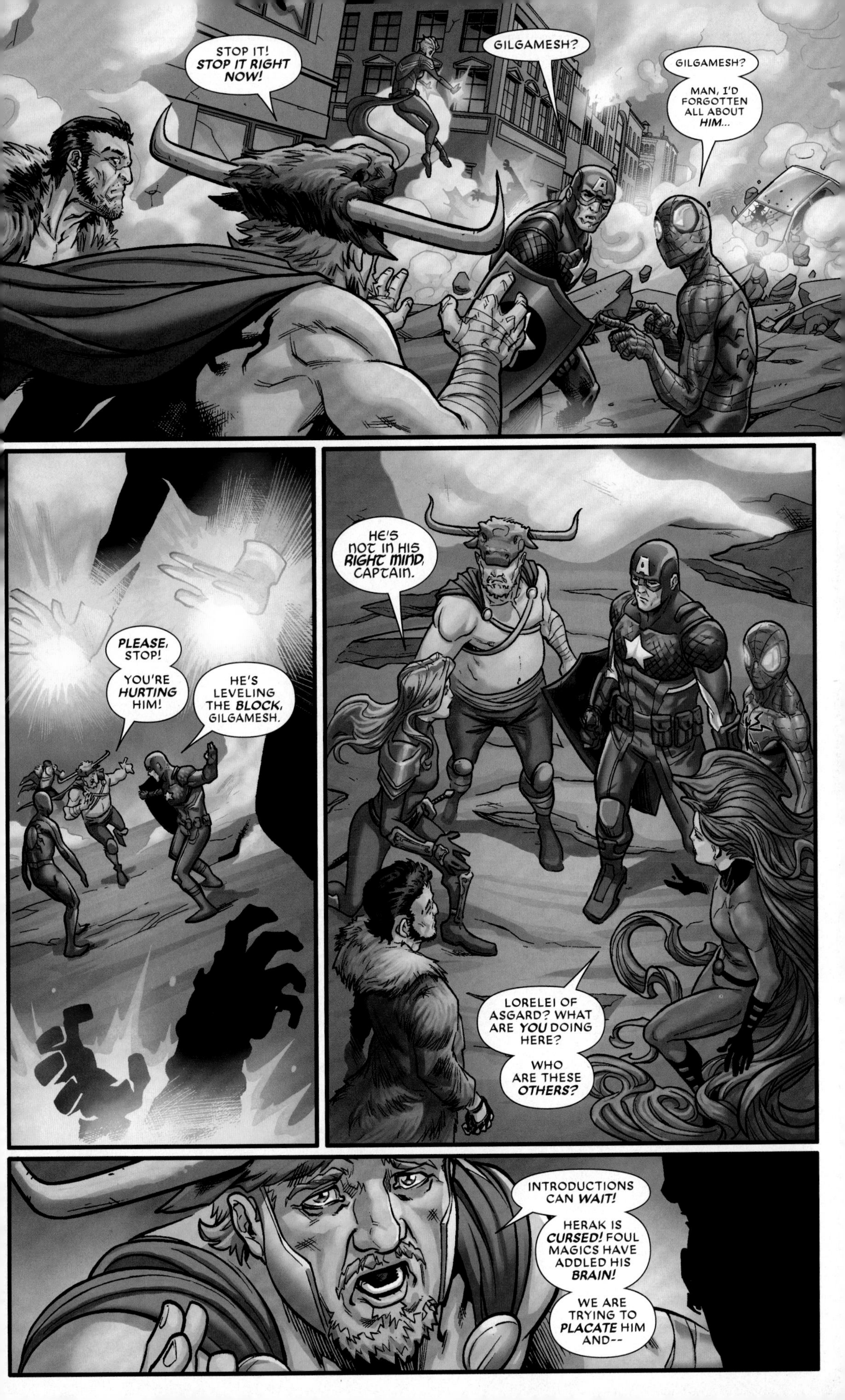
STOP IT! STOP IT RIGHT NOW!
GILGAMESH?
GILGAMESH?
MAN, I'D FORGOTTEN ALL ABOUT HIM...
PLEASE, STOP!
YOU'RE HURTING HIM!
HE'S LEVELING THE BLOCK, GILGAMESH.
HE'S NOT IN HIS RIGHT MIND, CAPTAIN.
LORELEI OF ASGARD? WHAT ARE YOU DOING HERE?
WHO ARE THESE OTHERS?
INTRODUCTIONS CAN WAIT!
HERAK IS CURSED! FOUL MAGICS HAVE ADDLED HIS BRAIN!
WE ARE TRYING TO PLACATE HIM AND--

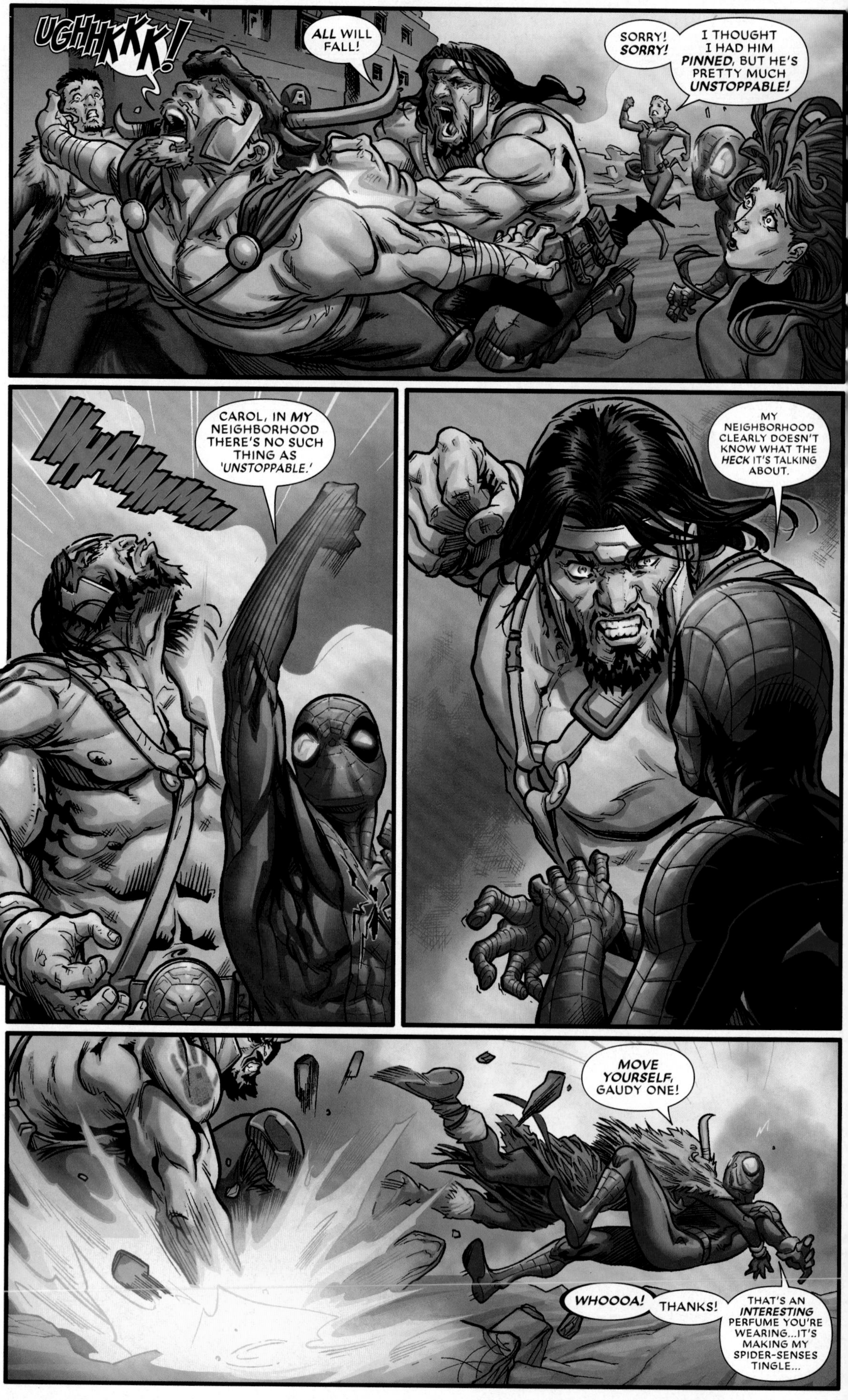
UGHHKKK!
ALL WILL FALL!
SORRY! SORRY!
I THOUGHT I HAD HIM PINNED, BUT HE'S PRETTY MUCH UNSTOPPABLE!
WHAMMMM
CAROL, IN MY NEIGHBORHOOD THERE'S NO SUCH THING AS 'UNSTOPPABLE.'
MY NEIGHBORHOOD CLEARLY DOESN'T KNOW WHAT THE HECK IT'S TALKING ABOUT.
MOVE YOURSELF, GAUDY ONE!
WHOOOA!
THANKS!
THAT'S AN INTERESTING PERFUME YOU'RE WEARING...IT'S MAKING MY SPIDER-SENSES TINGLE...

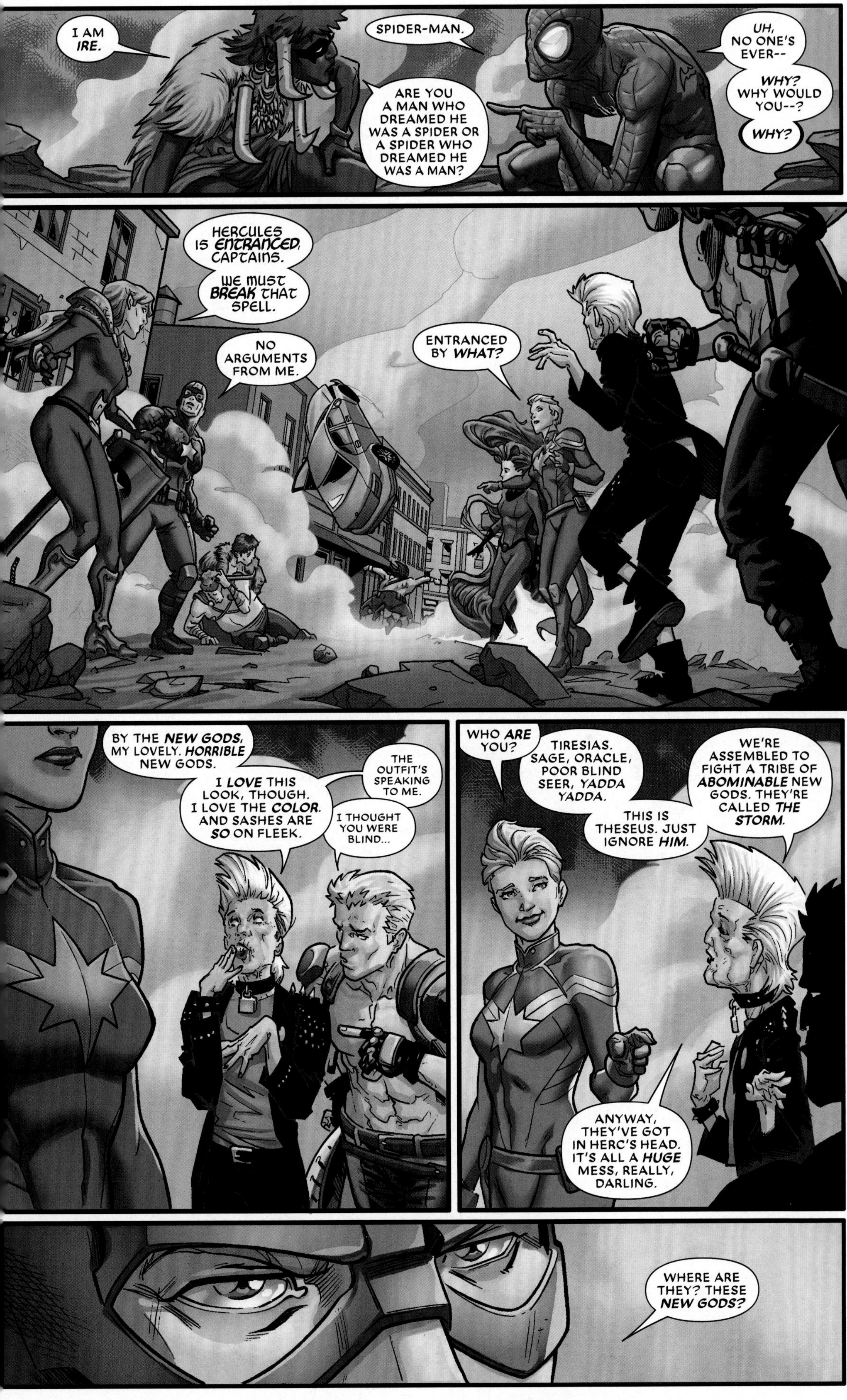

I AM IRE.
SPIDER-MAN.
ARE YOU A MAN WHO DREAMED HE WAS A SPIDER OR A SPIDER WHO DREAMED HE WAS A MAN?
UH, NO ONE'S EVER--
WHY? WHY WOULD YOU--?
WHY?
HERCULES IS ENTRANCED, CAPTAINS.
WE MUST BREAK THAT SPELL.
NO ARGUMENTS FROM ME.
ENTRANCED BY WHAT?
BY THE NEW GODS, MY LOVELY. HORRIBLE NEW GODS.
I LOVE THIS LOOK, THOUGH. I LOVE THE COLOR. AND SASHES ARE SO ON FLEEK.
THE OUTFIT'S SPEAKING TO ME.
I THOUGHT YOU WERE BLIND...
WHO ARE YOU?
TIRESIAS. SAGE, ORACLE, POOR BLIND SEER, YADDA YADDA.
THIS IS THESEUS. JUST IGNORE HIM.
WE'RE ASSEMBLED TO FIGHT A TRIBE OF ABOMINABLE NEW GODS. THEY'RE CALLED THE STORM.
ANYWAY, THEY'VE GOT IN HERC'S HEAD. IT'S ALL A HUGE MESS, REALLY, DARLING.
WHERE ARE THEY? THESE NEW GODS?

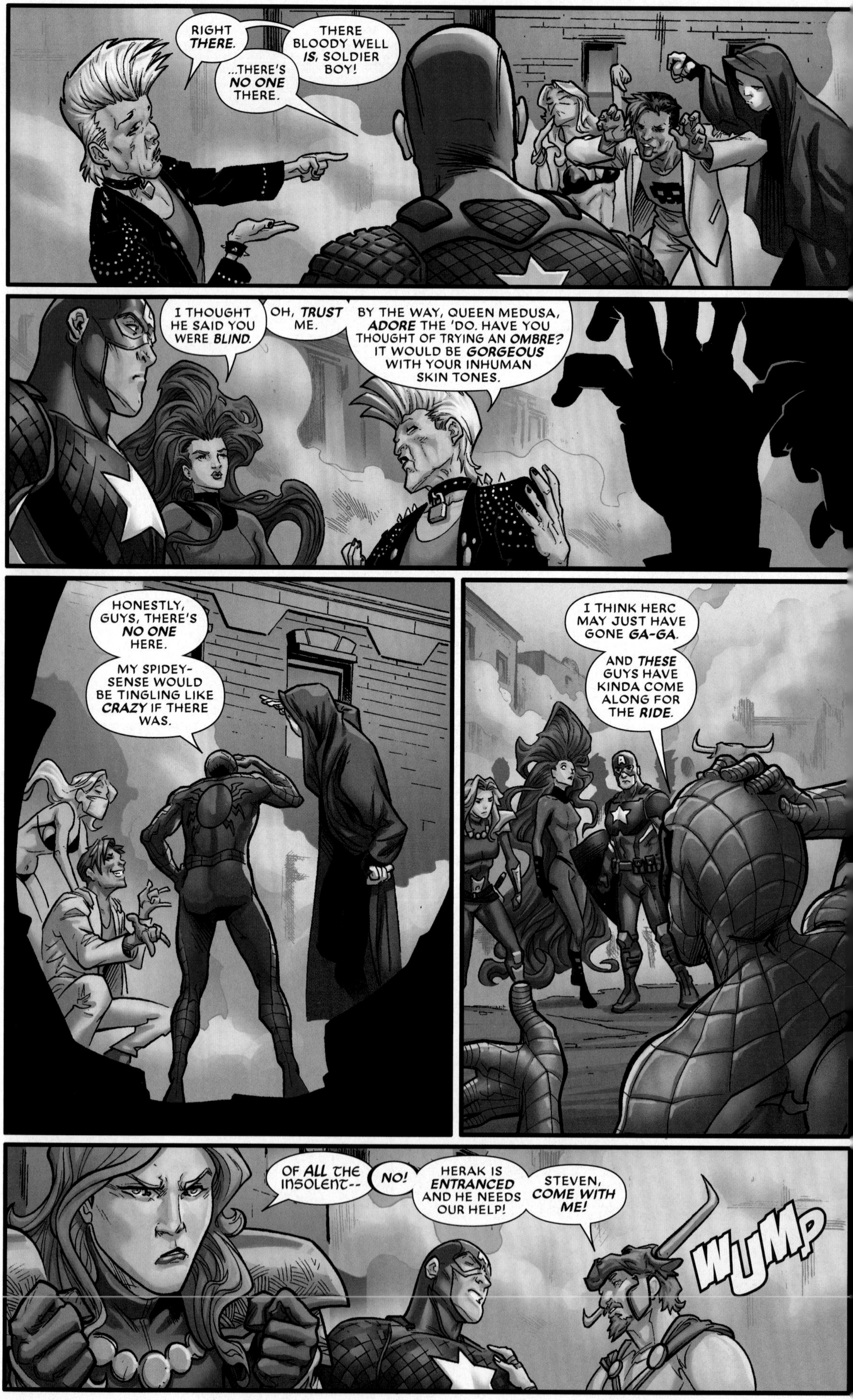
RIGHT *THERE.*
...THERE'S *NO ONE* THERE.
THERE BLOODY WELL *IS,* SOLDIER BOY!
I THOUGHT HE SAID YOU WERE *BLIND.*
OH, *TRUST* ME.
BY THE WAY, QUEEN MEDUSA, *ADORE* THE 'DO. HAVE YOU THOUGHT OF TRYING AN *OMBRE?* IT WOULD BE *GORGEOUS* WITH YOUR INHUMAN SKIN TONES.
HONESTLY, GUYS, THERE'S *NO ONE* HERE.
MY SPIDEY-SENSE WOULD BE TINGLING LIKE *CRAZY* IF THERE WAS.
I THINK HERC MAY JUST HAVE GONE *GA-GA.*
AND *THESE* GUYS HAVE KINDA COME ALONG FOR THE *RIDE.*
OF *ALL* THE INSOLENT--
NO!
HERAK IS *ENTRANCED* AND HE NEEDS OUR HELP!
STEVEN, *COME WITH ME!*
WUMP

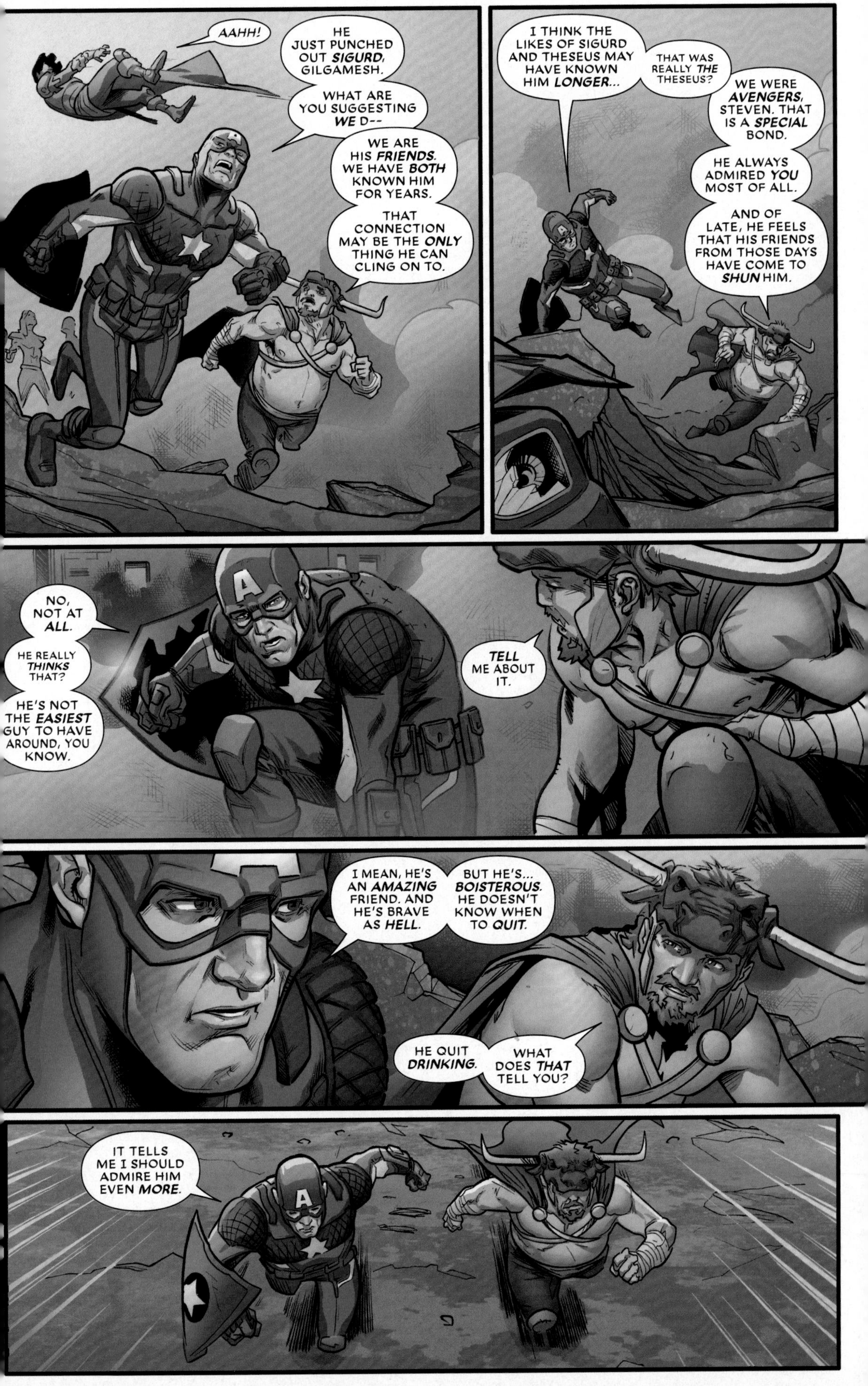
AAHH!
HE JUST PUNCHED OUT SIGURD, GILGAMESH.
WHAT ARE YOU SUGGESTING WE D--
WE ARE HIS FRIENDS. WE HAVE BOTH KNOWN HIM FOR YEARS.
THAT CONNECTION MAY BE THE ONLY THING HE CAN CLING ON TO.
I THINK THE LIKES OF SIGURD AND THESEUS MAY HAVE KNOWN HIM LONGER...
THAT WAS REALLY THE THESEUS?
WE WERE AVENGERS, STEVEN. THAT IS A SPECIAL BOND.
HE ALWAYS ADMIRED YOU MOST OF ALL.
AND OF LATE, HE FEELS THAT HIS FRIENDS FROM THOSE DAYS HAVE COME TO SHUN HIM.
NO, NOT AT ALL.
HE REALLY THINKS THAT?
HE'S NOT THE EASIEST GUY TO HAVE AROUND, YOU KNOW.
TELL ME ABOUT IT.
I MEAN, HE'S AN AMAZING FRIEND. AND HE'S BRAVE AS HELL.
BUT HE'S... BOISTEROUS. HE DOESN'T KNOW WHEN TO QUIT.
HE QUIT DRINKING.
WHAT DOES THAT TELL YOU?
IT TELLS ME I SHOULD ADMIRE HIM EVEN MORE.

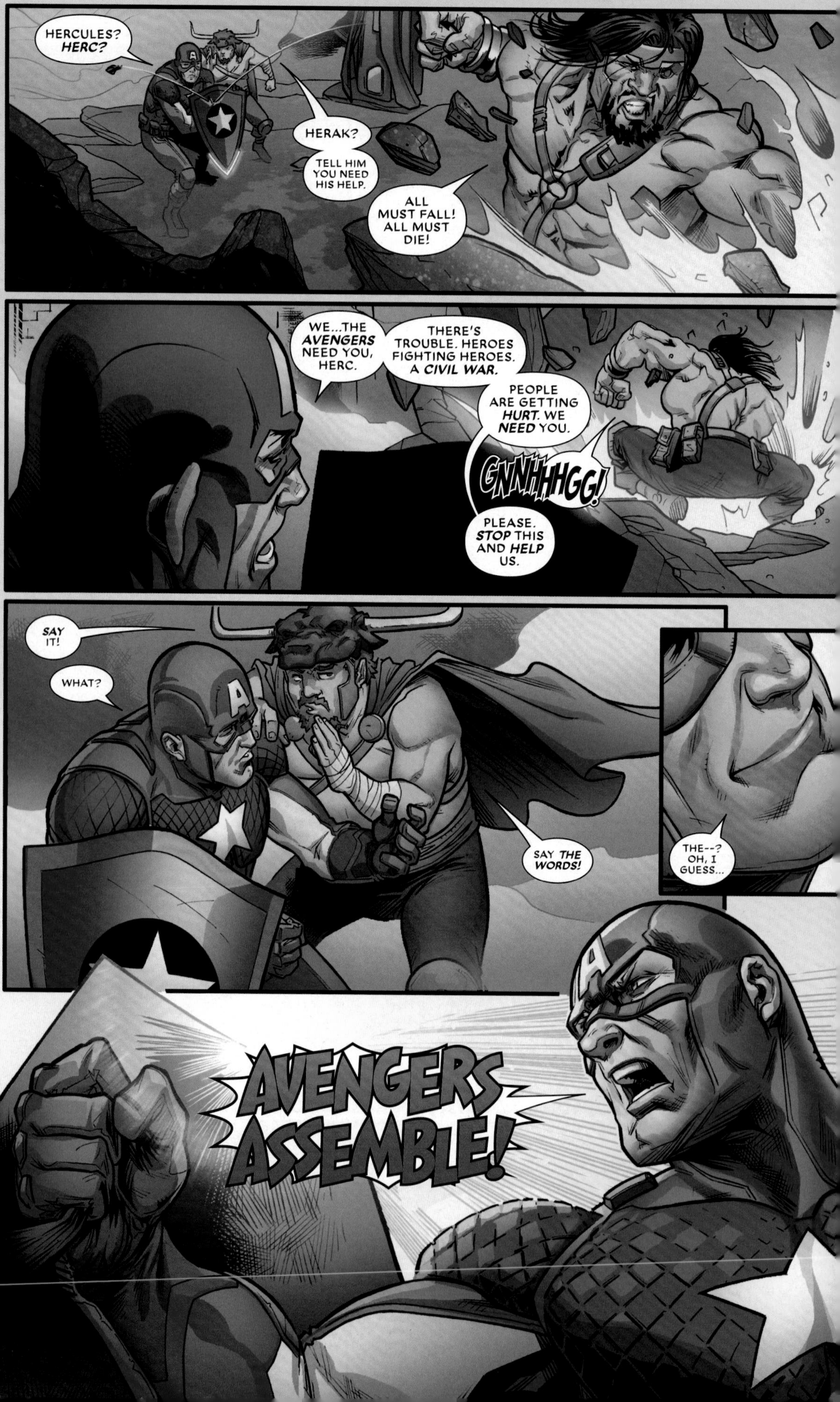
HERCULES? HERC?
HERAK?
TELL HIM YOU NEED HIS HELP.
ALL MUST FALL! ALL MUST DIE!
WE...THE AVENGERS NEED YOU, HERC.
THERE'S TROUBLE. HEROES FIGHTING HEROES. A CIVIL WAR.
PEOPLE ARE GETTING HURT. WE NEED YOU.
GNNHHHGG!
PLEASE. STOP THIS AND HELP US.
SAY IT!
WHAT?
SAY THE WORDS!
THE--? OH, I GUESS...
AVENGERS ASSEMBLE!

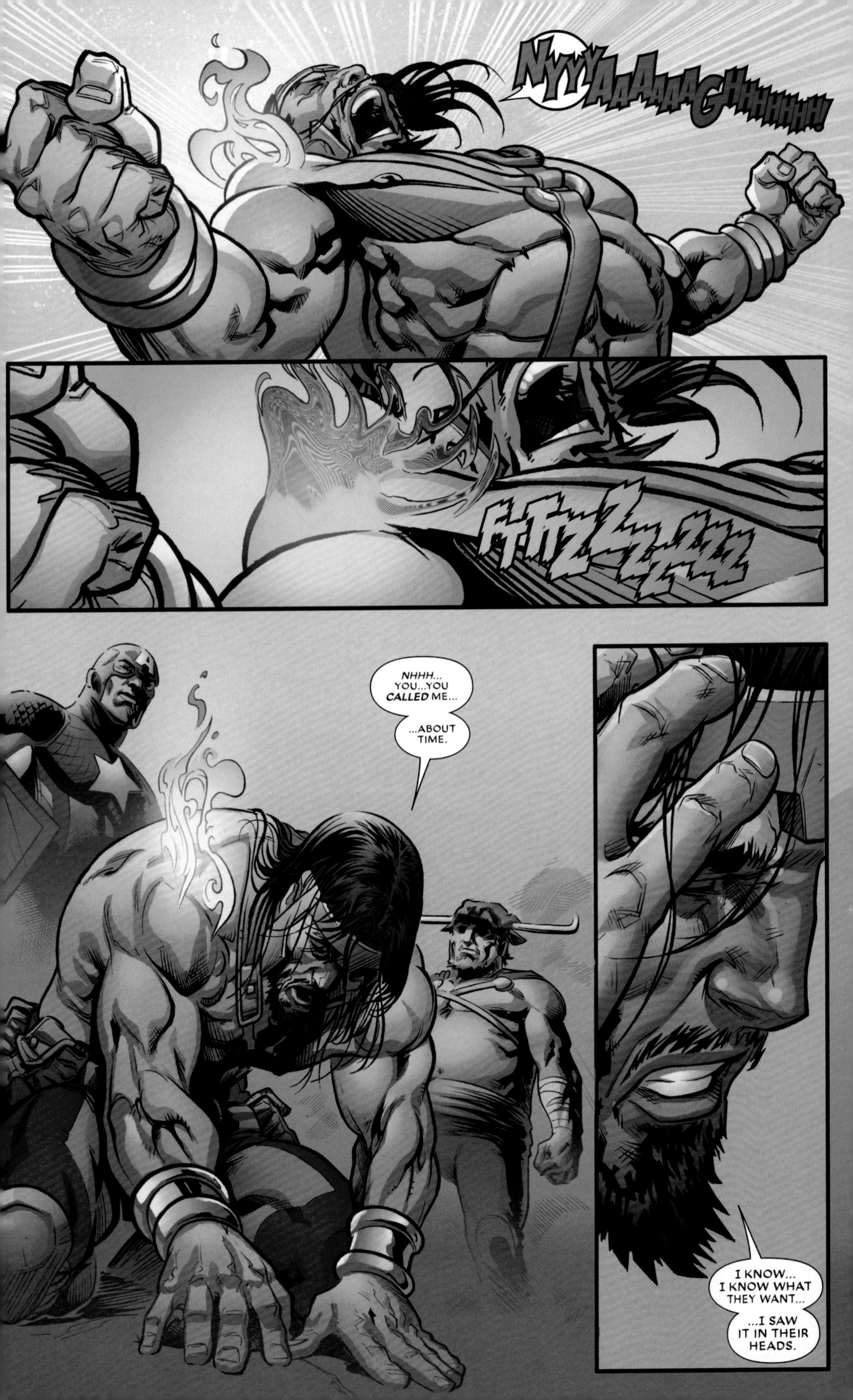

NYYYAAAAAAGHHHHHH!
FFTTZZZZZZZZ
NHHH... YOU...YOU CALLED ME...
...ABOUT TIME.
I KNOW... I KNOW WHAT THEY WANT...
...I SAW IT IN THEIR HEADS.

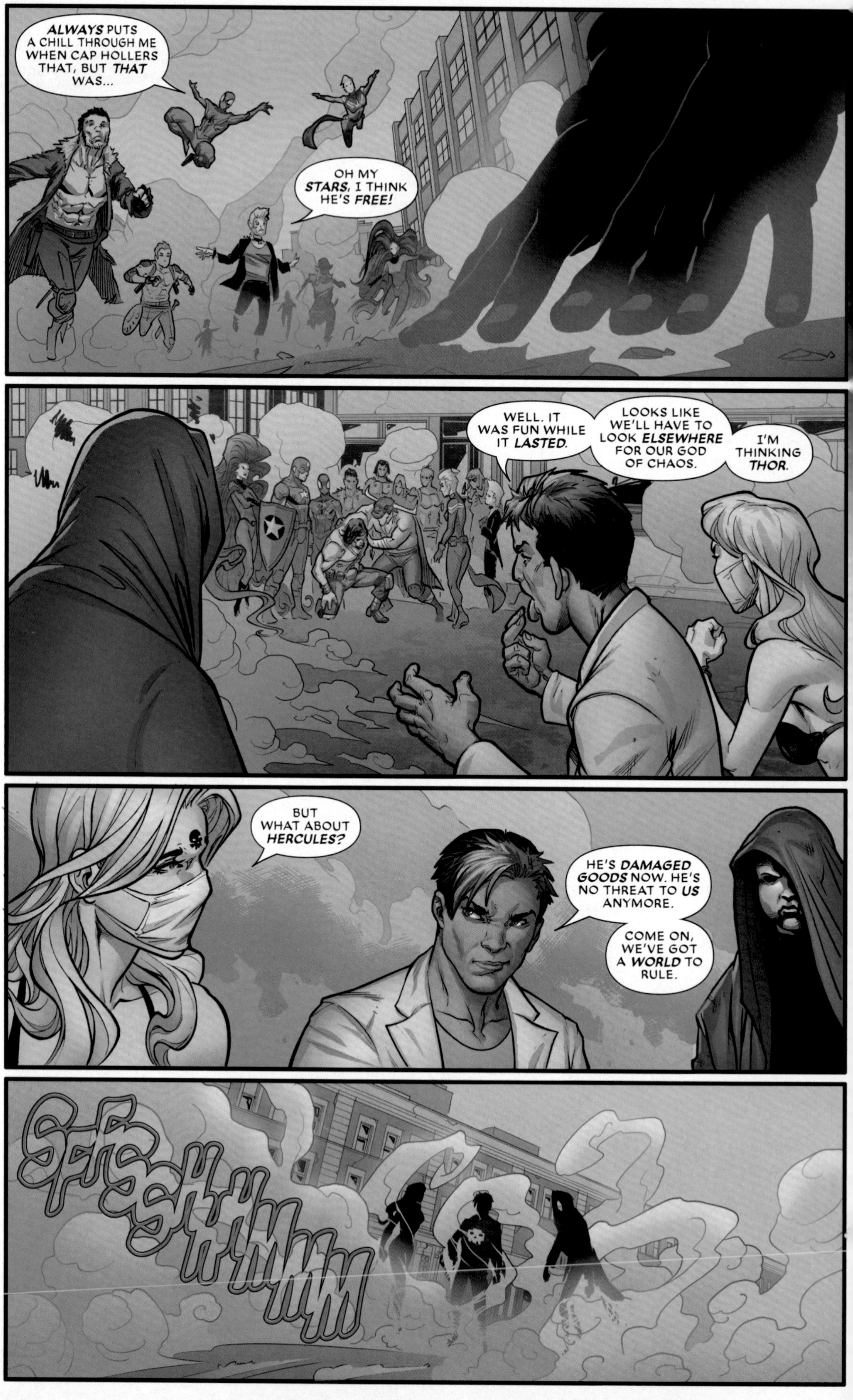
ALWAYS PUTS A CHILL THROUGH ME WHEN CAP HOLLERS THAT, BUT THAT WAS...
OH MY STARS, I THINK HE'S FREE!
WELL. IT WAS FUN WHILE IT LASTED.
LOOKS LIKE WE'LL HAVE TO LOOK ELSEWHERE FOR OUR GOD OF CHAOS.
I'M THINKING THOR.
BUT WHAT ABOUT HERCULES?
HE'S DAMAGED GOODS NOW. HE'S NO THREAT TO US ANYMORE.
COME ON, WE'VE GOT A WORLD TO RULE.

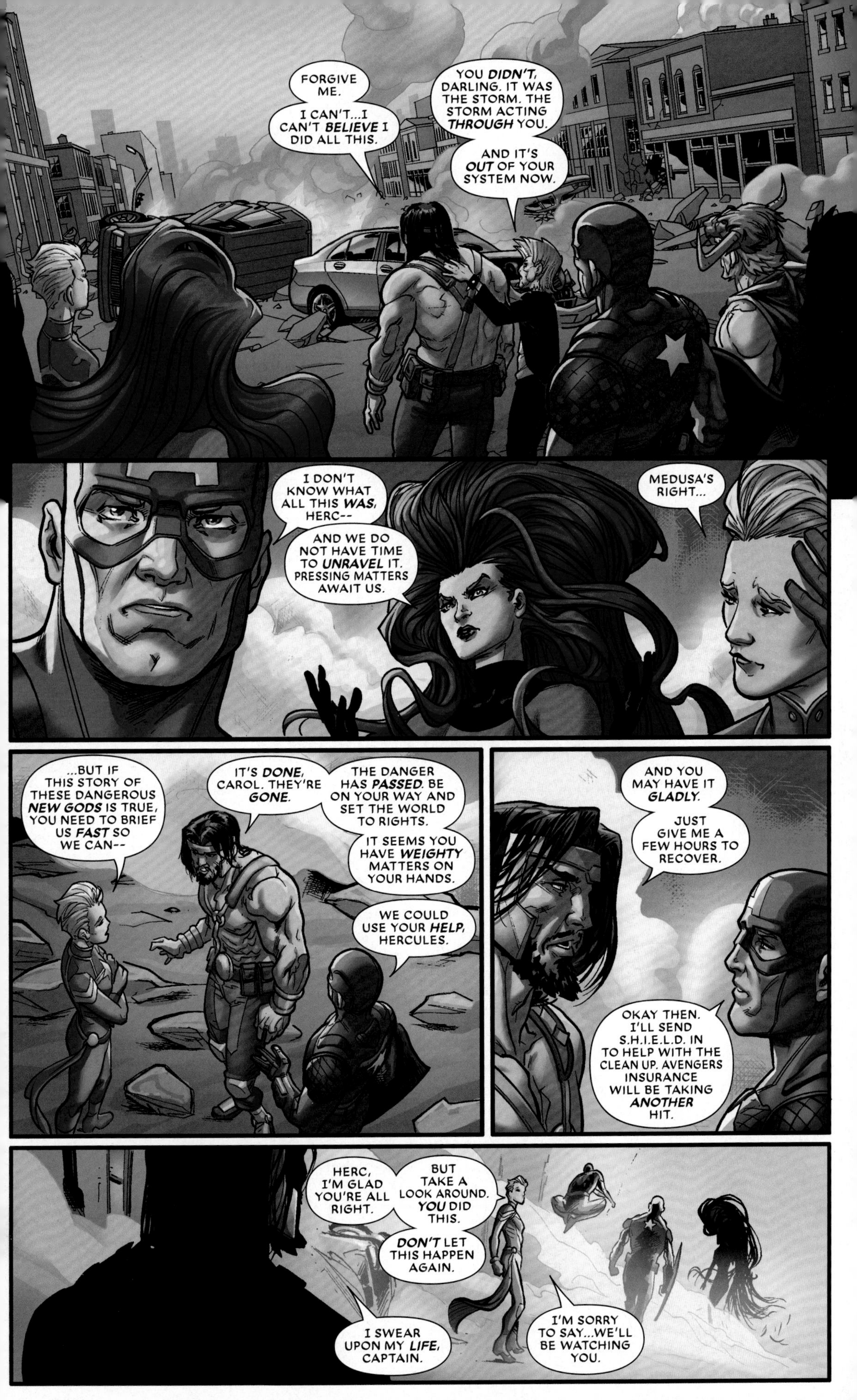
FORGIVE ME.
I CAN'T...I CAN'T BELIEVE I DID ALL THIS.
YOU DIDN'T, DARLING. IT WAS THE STORM. THE STORM ACTING THROUGH YOU.
AND IT'S OUT OF YOUR SYSTEM NOW.
I DON'T KNOW WHAT ALL THIS WAS, HERC--
AND WE DO NOT HAVE TIME TO UNRAVEL IT. PRESSING MATTERS AWAIT US.
MEDUSA'S RIGHT...
...BUT IF THIS STORY OF THESE DANGEROUS NEW GODS IS TRUE, YOU NEED TO BRIEF US FAST SO WE CAN--
IT'S DONE, CAROL. THEY'RE GONE.
THE DANGER HAS PASSED. BE ON YOUR WAY AND SET THE WORLD TO RIGHTS.
IT SEEMS YOU HAVE WEIGHTY MATTERS ON YOUR HANDS.
WE COULD USE YOUR HELP, HERCULES.
AND YOU MAY HAVE IT GLADLY.
JUST GIVE ME A FEW HOURS TO RECOVER.
OKAY THEN. I'LL SEND S.H.I.E.L.D. IN TO HELP WITH THE CLEAN UP. AVENGERS INSURANCE WILL BE TAKING ANOTHER HIT.
HERC, I'M GLAD YOU'RE ALL RIGHT.
BUT TAKE A LOOK AROUND. YOU DID THIS.
DON'T LET THIS HAPPEN AGAIN.
I SWEAR UPON MY LIFE, CAPTAIN.
I'M SORRY TO SAY...WE'LL BE WATCHING YOU.

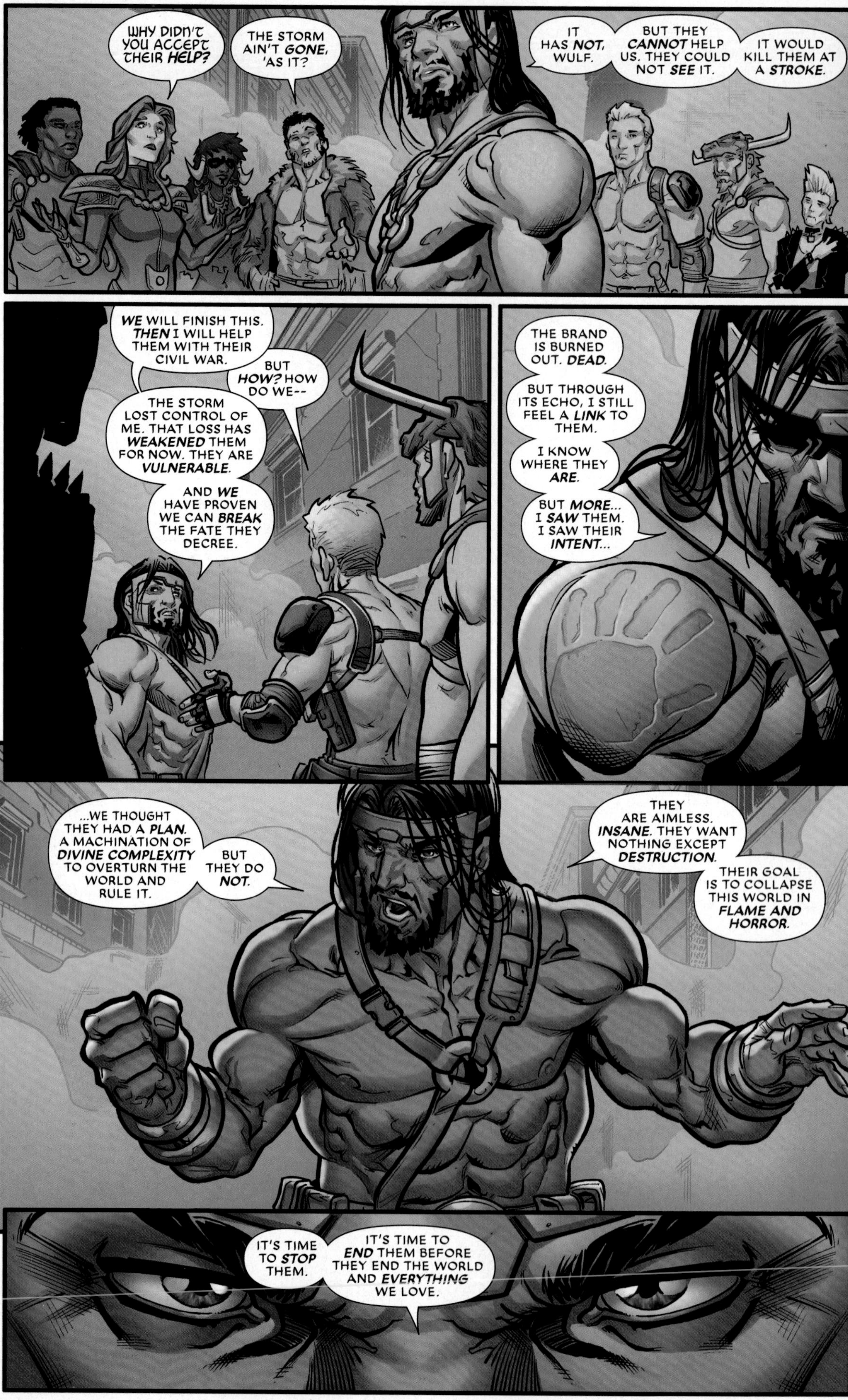
WHY DIDN'T YOU ACCEPT THEIR HELP?
THE STORM AIN'T GONE, 'AS IT?
IT HAS NOT, WULF.
BUT THEY CANNOT HELP US. THEY COULD NOT SEE IT.
IT WOULD KILL THEM AT A STROKE.
WE WILL FINISH THIS. THEN I WILL HELP THEM WITH THEIR CIVIL WAR.
BUT HOW? HOW DO WE--
THE STORM LOST CONTROL OF ME. THAT LOSS HAS WEAKENED THEM FOR NOW. THEY ARE VULNERABLE.
AND WE HAVE PROVEN WE CAN BREAK THE FATE THEY DECREE.
THE BRAND IS BURNED OUT. DEAD.
BUT THROUGH ITS ECHO, I STILL FEEL A LINK TO THEM.
I KNOW WHERE THEY ARE.
BUT MORE... I SAW THEM. I SAW THEIR INTENT...
...WE THOUGHT THEY HAD A PLAN. A MACHINATION OF DIVINE COMPLEXITY TO OVERTURN THE WORLD AND RULE IT.
BUT THEY DO NOT.
THEY ARE AIMLESS. INSANE. THEY WANT NOTHING EXCEPT DESTRUCTION.
THEIR GOAL IS TO COLLAPSE THIS WORLD IN FLAME AND HORROR.
IT'S TIME TO STOP THEM.
IT'S TIME TO END THEM BEFORE THEY END THE WORLD AND EVERYTHING WE LOVE.

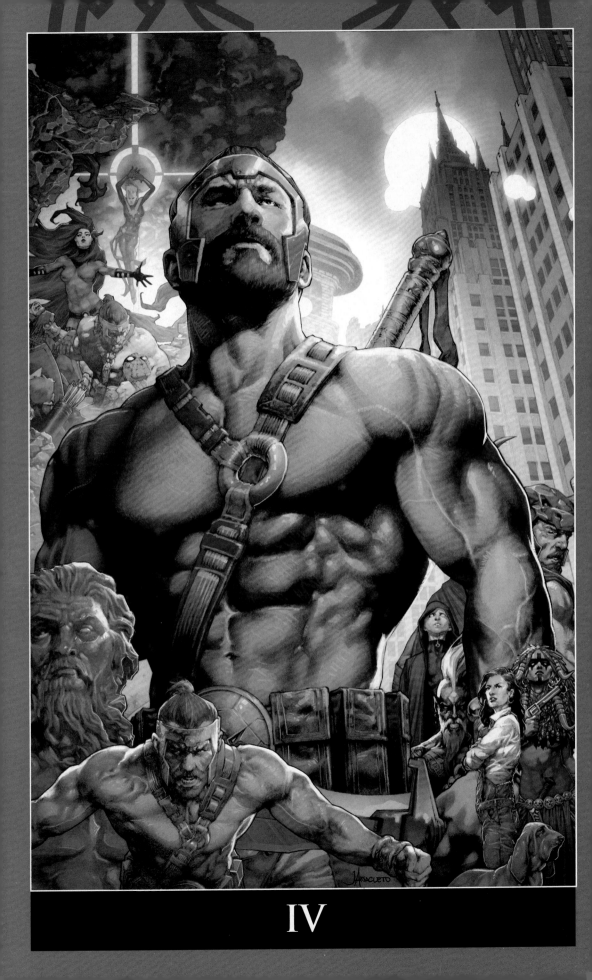

IV

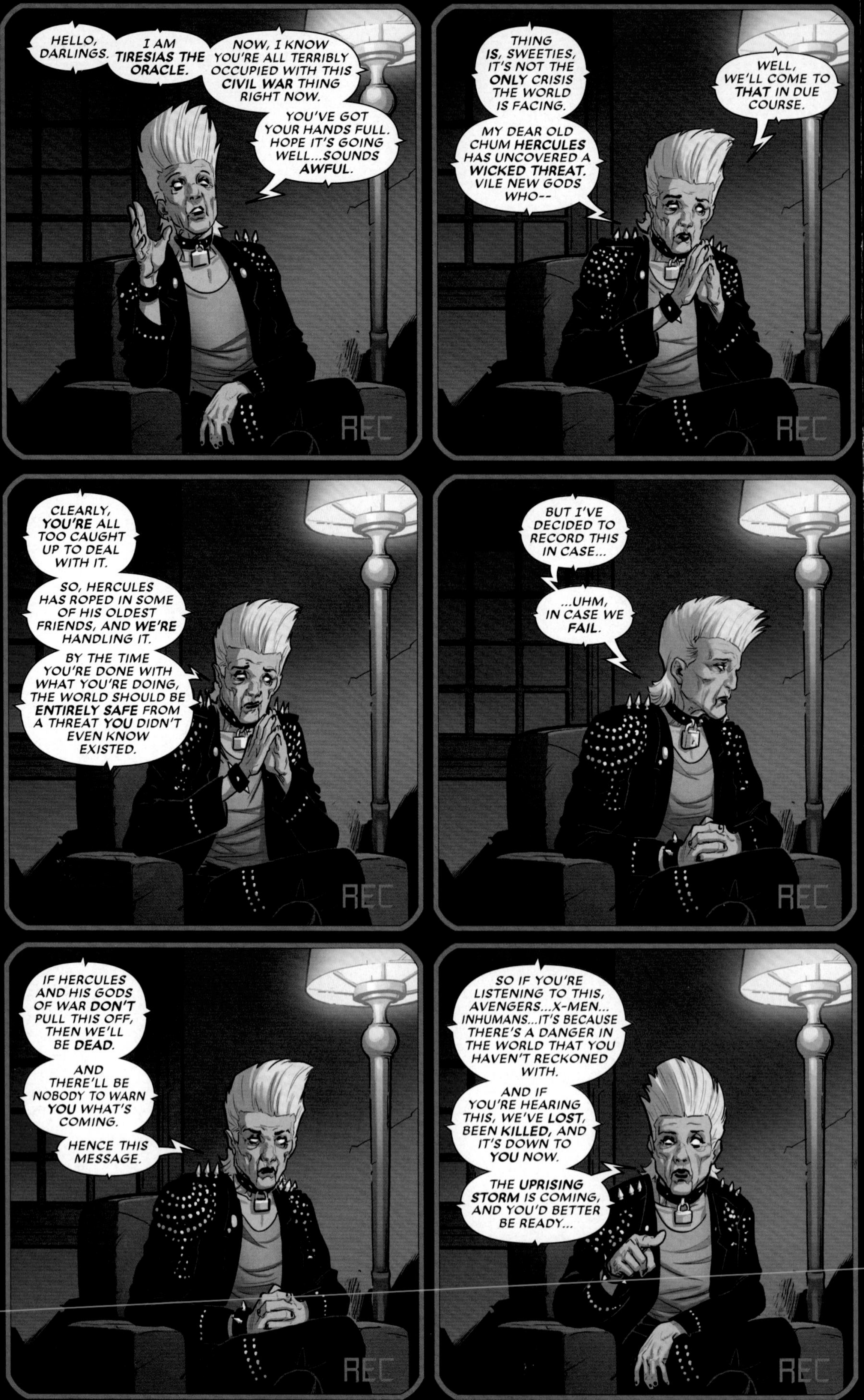
HELLO, DARLINGS.
I AM TIRESIAS THE ORACLE.
NOW, I KNOW YOU'RE ALL TERRIBLY OCCUPIED WITH THIS CIVIL WAR THING RIGHT NOW.
YOU'VE GOT YOUR HANDS FULL. HOPE IT'S GOING WELL...SOUNDS AWFUL.
REC
THING IS, SWEETIES, IT'S NOT THE ONLY CRISIS THE WORLD IS FACING.
MY DEAR OLD CHUM HERCULES HAS UNCOVERED A WICKED THREAT. VILE NEW GODS WHO--
WELL, WE'LL COME TO THAT IN DUE COURSE.
REC
CLEARLY, YOU'RE ALL TOO CAUGHT UP TO DEAL WITH IT.
SO, HERCULES HAS ROPED IN SOME OF HIS OLDEST FRIENDS, AND WE'RE HANDLING IT.
BY THE TIME YOU'RE DONE WITH WHAT YOU'RE DOING, THE WORLD SHOULD BE ENTIRELY SAFE FROM A THREAT YOU DIDN'T EVEN KNOW EXISTED.
REC
BUT I'VE DECIDED TO RECORD THIS IN CASE...
...UHM, IN CASE WE FAIL.
REC
IF HERCULES AND HIS GODS OF WAR DON'T PULL THIS OFF, THEN WE'LL BE DEAD.
AND THERE'LL BE NOBODY TO WARN YOU WHAT'S COMING.
HENCE THIS MESSAGE.
REC
SO IF YOU'RE LISTENING TO THIS, AVENGERS...X-MEN... INHUMANS...IT'S BECAUSE THERE'S A DANGER IN THE WORLD THAT YOU HAVEN'T RECKONED WITH.
AND IF YOU'RE HEARING THIS, WE'VE LOST, BEEN KILLED, AND IT'S DOWN TO YOU NOW.
THE UPRISING STORM IS COMING, AND YOU'D BETTER BE READY...
REC

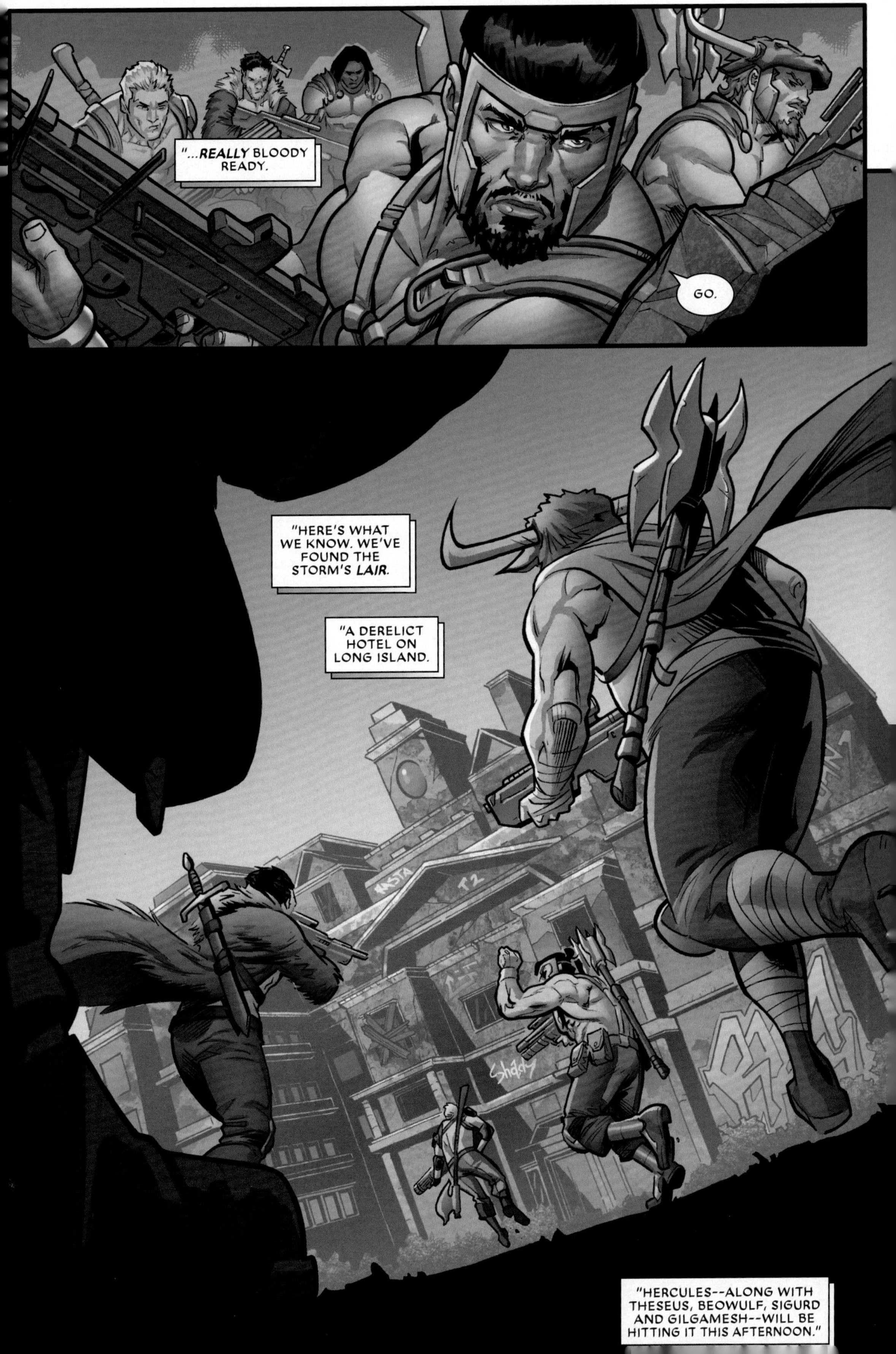
"...REALLY BLOODY READY.
GO.
"HERE'S WHAT WE KNOW. WE'VE FOUND THE STORM'S LAIR.
"A DERELICT HOTEL ON LONG ISLAND.
"HERCULES--ALONG WITH THESEUS, BEOWULF, SIGURD AND GILGAMESH--WILL BE HITTING IT THIS AFTERNOON."

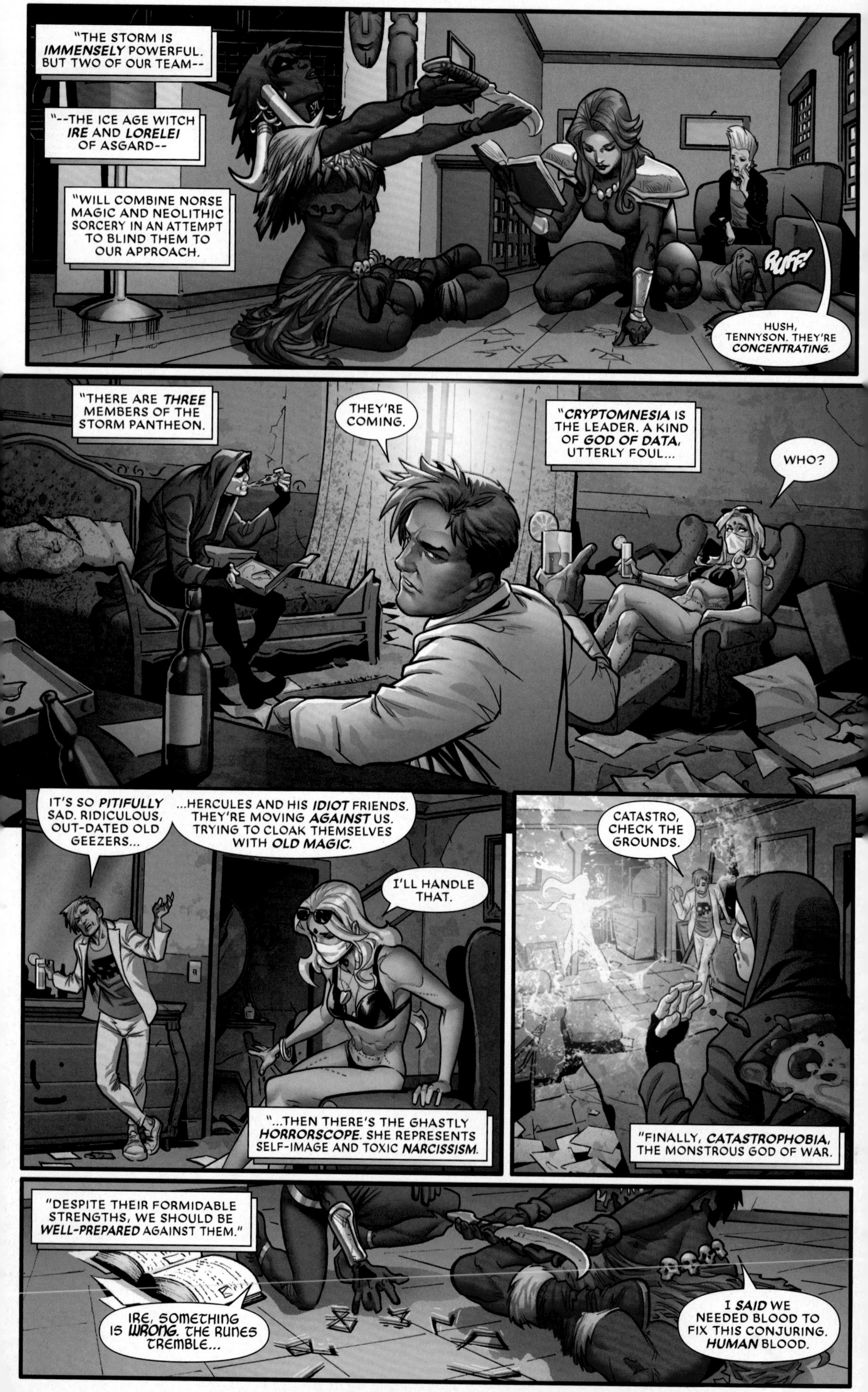
"THE STORM IS IMMENSELY POWERFUL. BUT TWO OF OUR TEAM--
"--THE ICE AGE WITCH IRE AND LORELEI OF ASGARD--
"WILL COMBINE NORSE MAGIC AND NEOLITHIC SORCERY IN AN ATTEMPT TO BLIND THEM TO OUR APPROACH.
RUFF!
HUSH, TENNYSON. THEY'RE CONCENTRATING.
"THERE ARE THREE MEMBERS OF THE STORM PANTHEON.
THEY'RE COMING.
"CRYPTOMNESIA IS THE LEADER. A KIND OF GOD OF DATA, UTTERLY FOUL...
WHO?
IT'S SO PITIFULLY SAD. RIDICULOUS, OUT-DATED OLD GEEZERS...
...HERCULES AND HIS IDIOT FRIENDS. THEY'RE MOVING AGAINST US. TRYING TO CLOAK THEMSELVES WITH OLD MAGIC.
I'LL HANDLE THAT.
"...THEN THERE'S THE GHASTLY HORRORSCOPE. SHE REPRESENTS SELF-IMAGE AND TOXIC NARCISSISM.
CATASTRO, CHECK THE GROUNDS.
"FINALLY, CATASTROPHOBIA, THE MONSTROUS GOD OF WAR.
"DESPITE THEIR FORMIDABLE STRENGTHS, WE SHOULD BE WELL-PREPARED AGAINST THEM."
IRE, SOMETHING IS WRONG. THE RUNES TREMBLE...
I SAID WE NEEDED BLOOD TO FIX THIS CONJURING. HUMAN BLOOD.

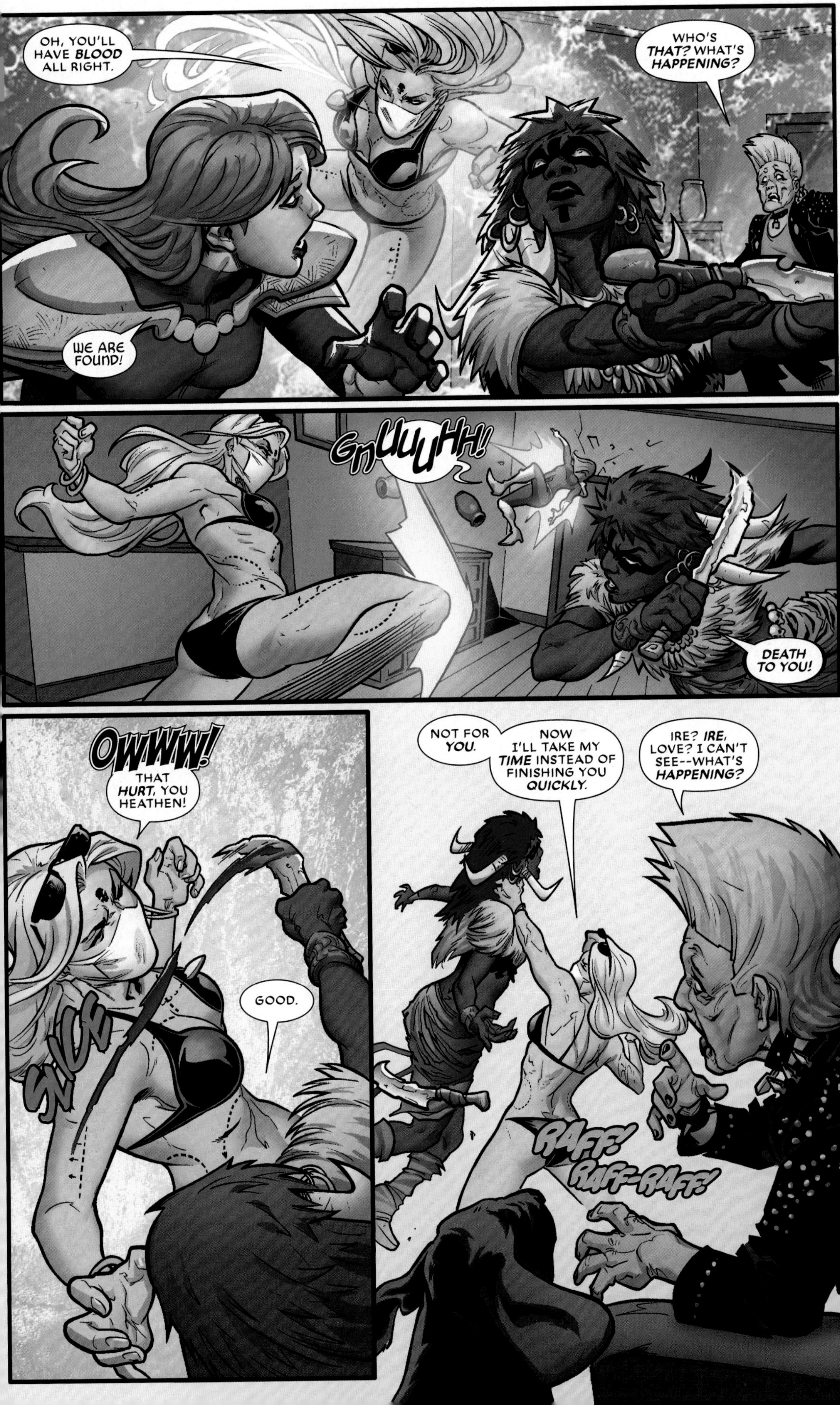

OH, YOU'LL HAVE BLOOD ALL RIGHT.
WE ARE FOUND!
WHO'S THAT? WHAT'S HAPPENING?
GNUUUHH!
DEATH TO YOU!
OWWW!
THAT HURT, YOU HEATHEN!
GOOD.
SLICE
NOT FOR YOU.
NOW I'LL TAKE MY TIME INSTEAD OF FINISHING YOU QUICKLY.
IRE? IRE, LOVE? I CAN'T SEE--WHAT'S HAPPENING?
RAFF! RAFF-RAFF!

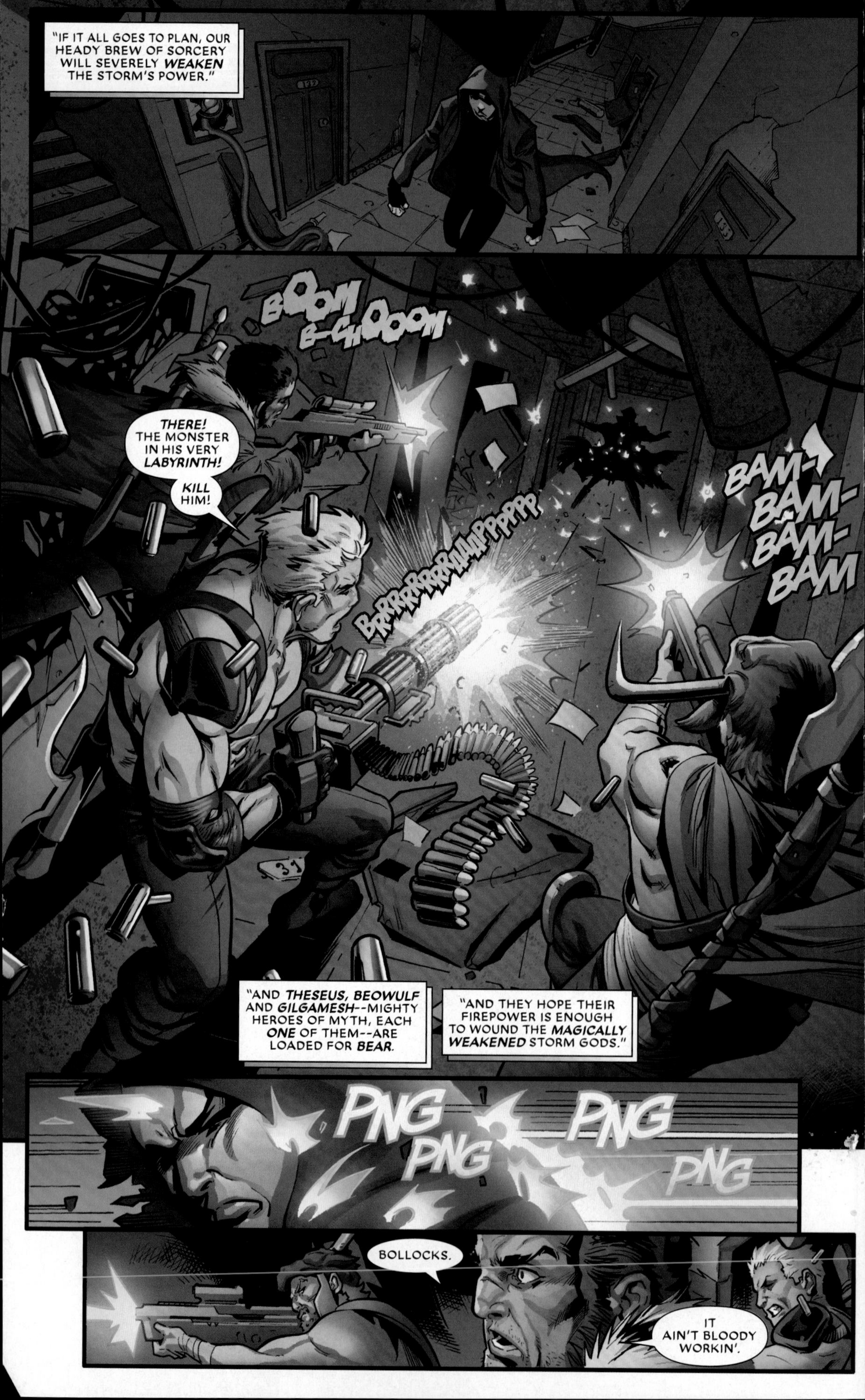
"IF IT ALL GOES TO PLAN, OUR HEADY BREW OF SORCERY WILL SEVERELY WEAKEN THE STORM'S POWER."
BOOM B-CHOOOM
THERE! THE MONSTER IN HIS VERY LABYRINTH!
KILL HIM!
BRRRRRRRAAAPPPPPP
BAM-BAM-BAM-BAM
"AND THESEUS, BEOWULF AND GILGAMESH--MIGHTY HEROES OF MYTH, EACH ONE OF THEM--ARE LOADED FOR BEAR.
"AND THEY HOPE THEIR FIREPOWER IS ENOUGH TO WOUND THE MAGICALLY WEAKENED STORM GODS."
PNG PNG PNG PNG
BOLLOCKS.
IT AIN'T BLOODY WORKIN'.

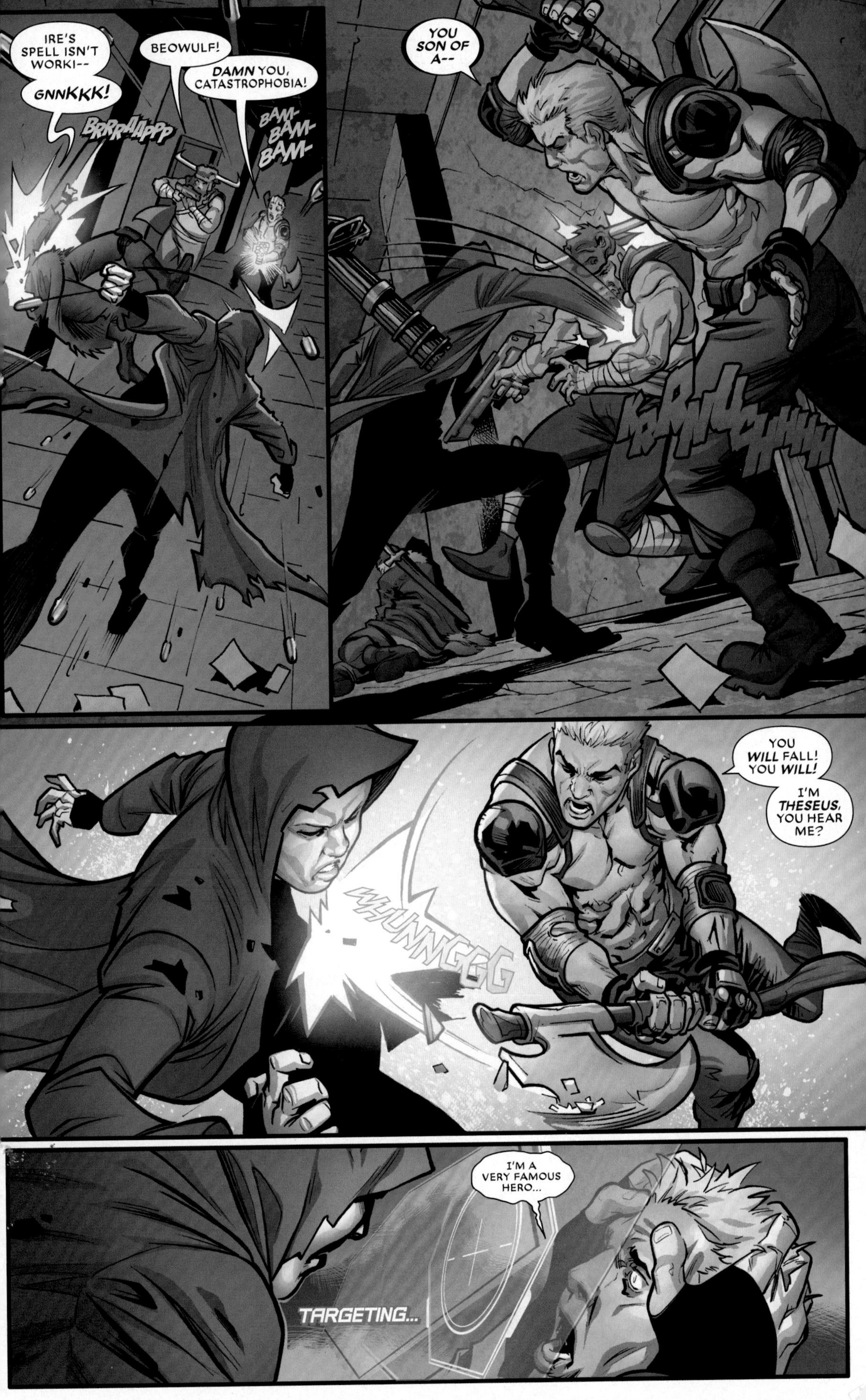
IRE'S SPELL ISN'T WORKI--
GNNKKK!
BEOWULF!
DAMN YOU, CATASTROPHOBIA!
BRRRAAPPP
BAM-BAM-BAM-
YOU SON OF A--
YOU WILL FALL! YOU WILL!
I'M THESEUS, YOU HEAR ME?
I'M A VERY FAMOUS HERO...
TARGETING...

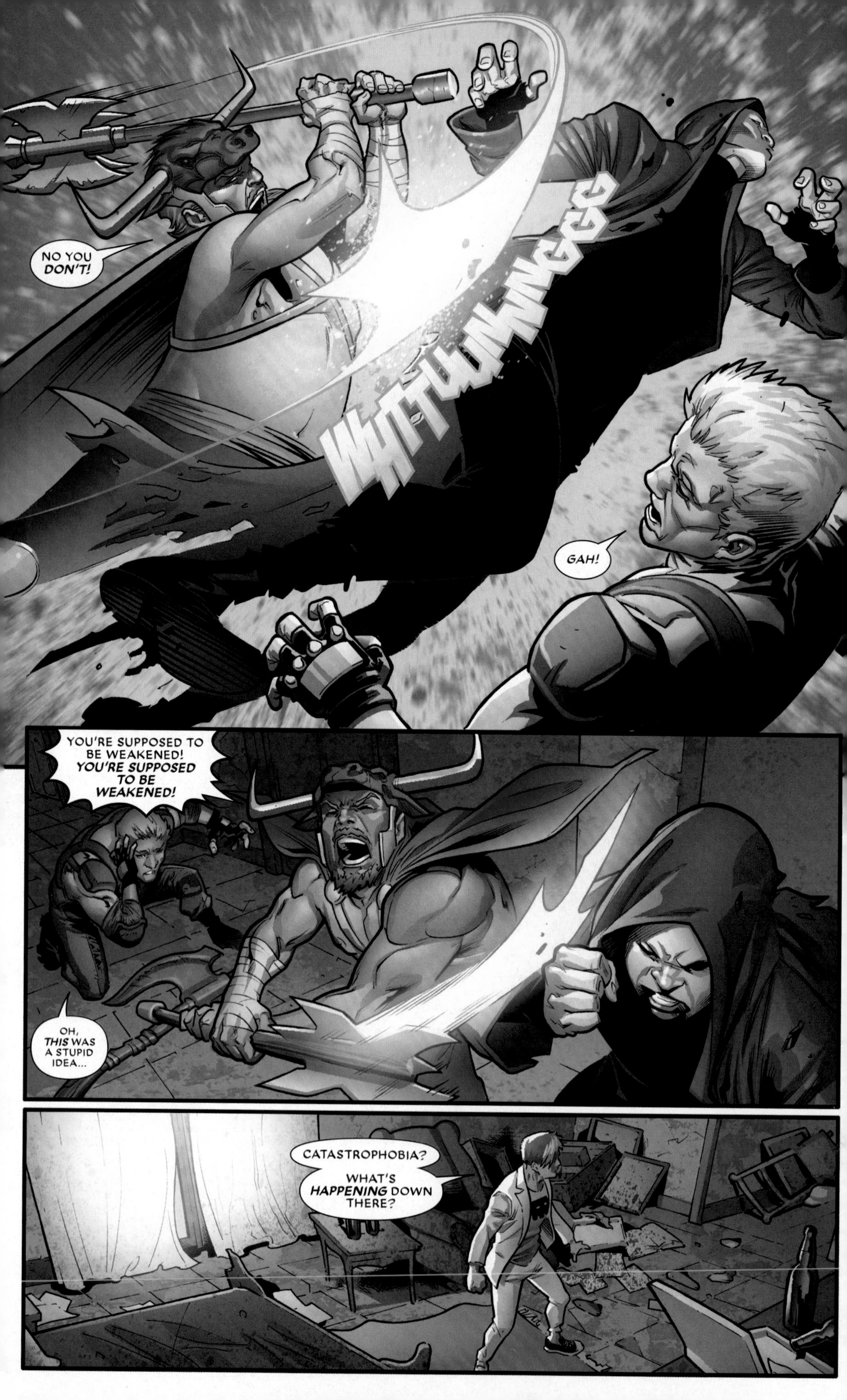
NO YOU DON'T!
WHTTUMWGGG
GAH!
YOU'RE SUPPOSED TO BE WEAKENED! YOU'RE SUPPOSED TO BE WEAKENED!
OH, THIS WAS A STUPID IDEA...
CATASTROPHOBIA?
WHAT'S HAPPENING DOWN THERE?

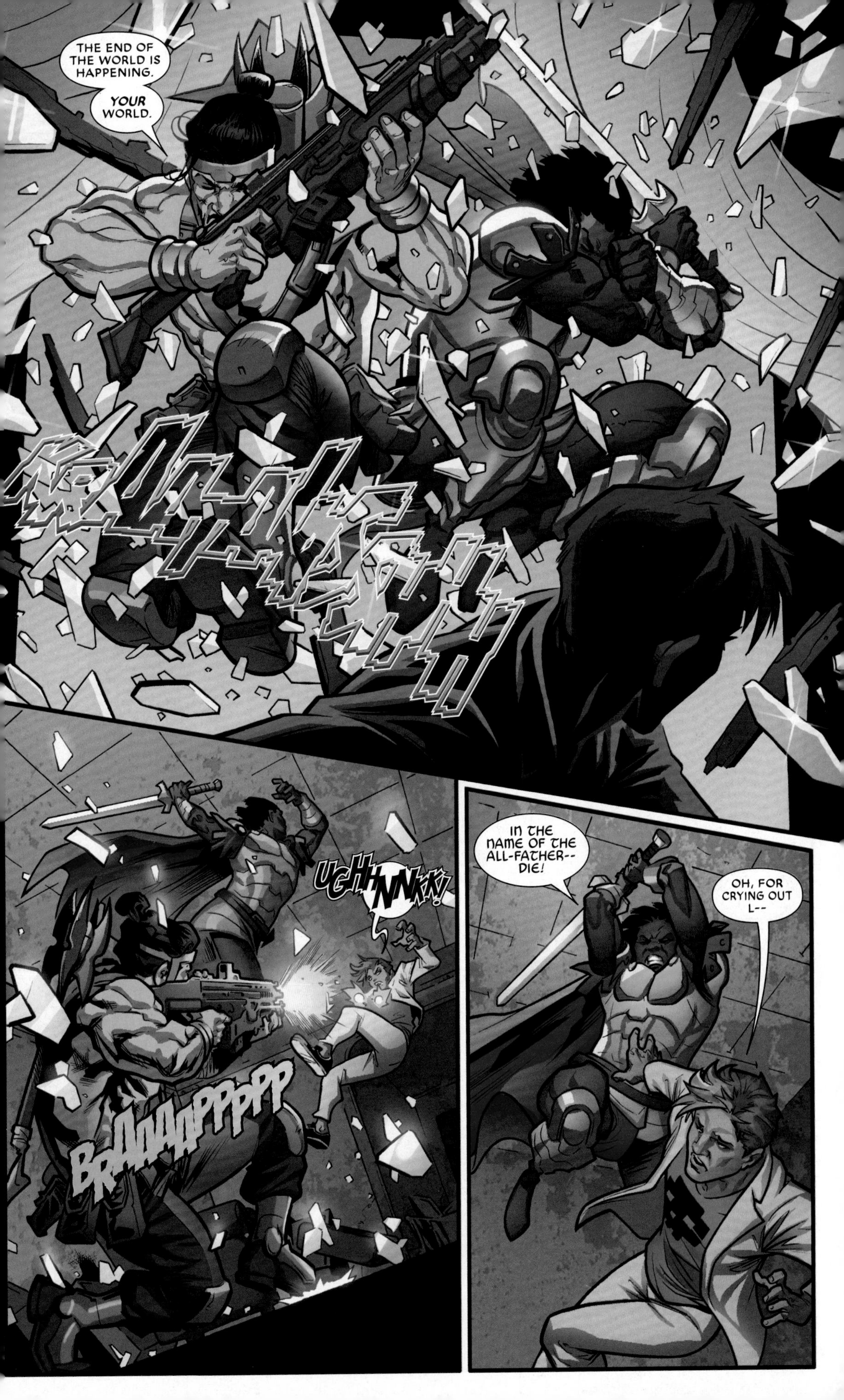

THE END OF THE WORLD IS HAPPENING.
YOUR WORLD.
UGHHNNKK!
BRAAAPPPPPP
IN THE NAME OF THE ALL-FATHER-- DIE!
OH, FOR CRYING OUT L--

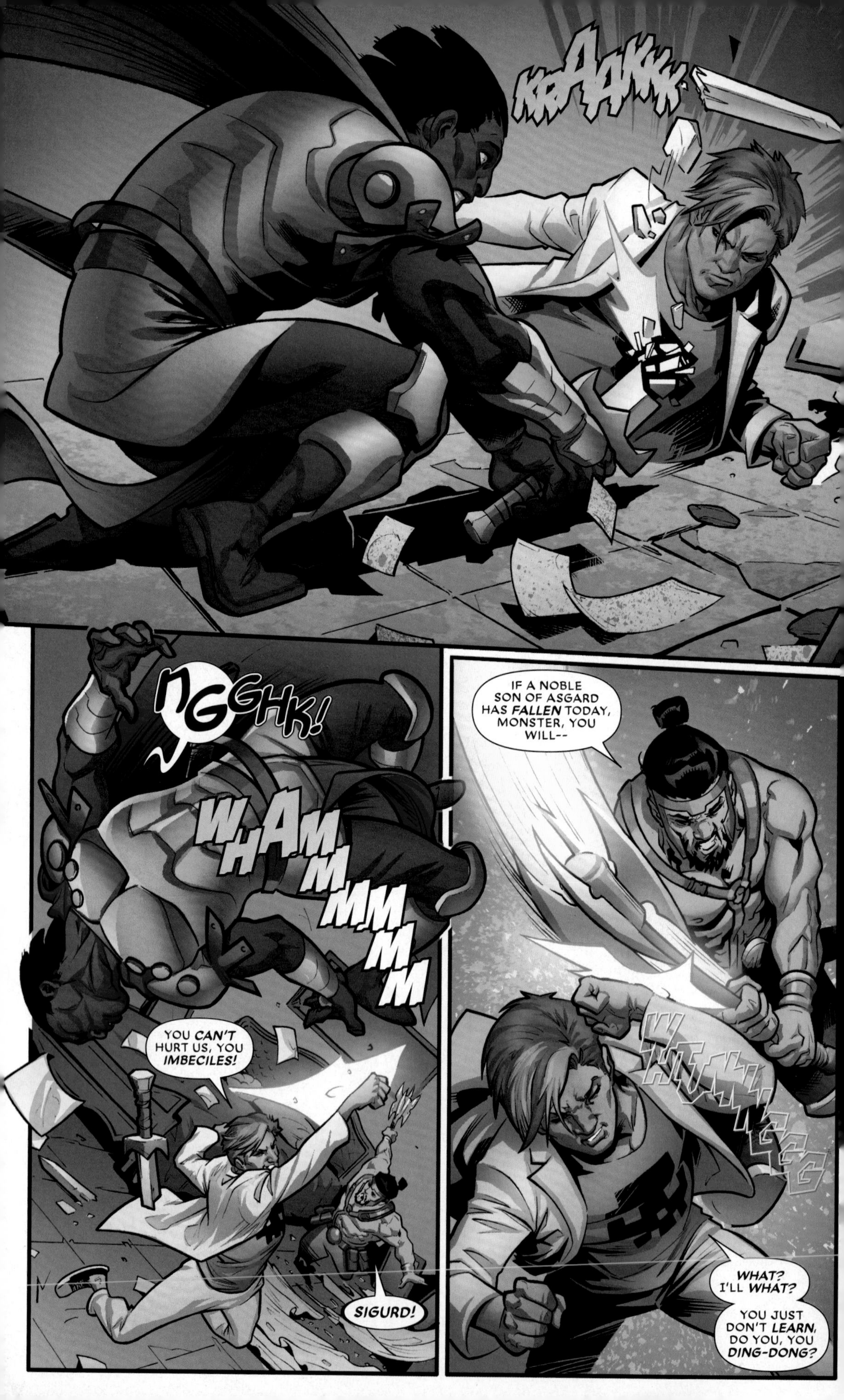
KRAAKKK
NGGHK!
WHAMMMMMM
YOU CAN'T HURT US, YOU IMBECILES!
SIGURD!
IF A NOBLE SON OF ASGARD HAS FALLEN TODAY, MONSTER, YOU WILL--
WHAT? I'LL WHAT?
YOU JUST DON'T LEARN, DO YOU, YOU DING-DONG?

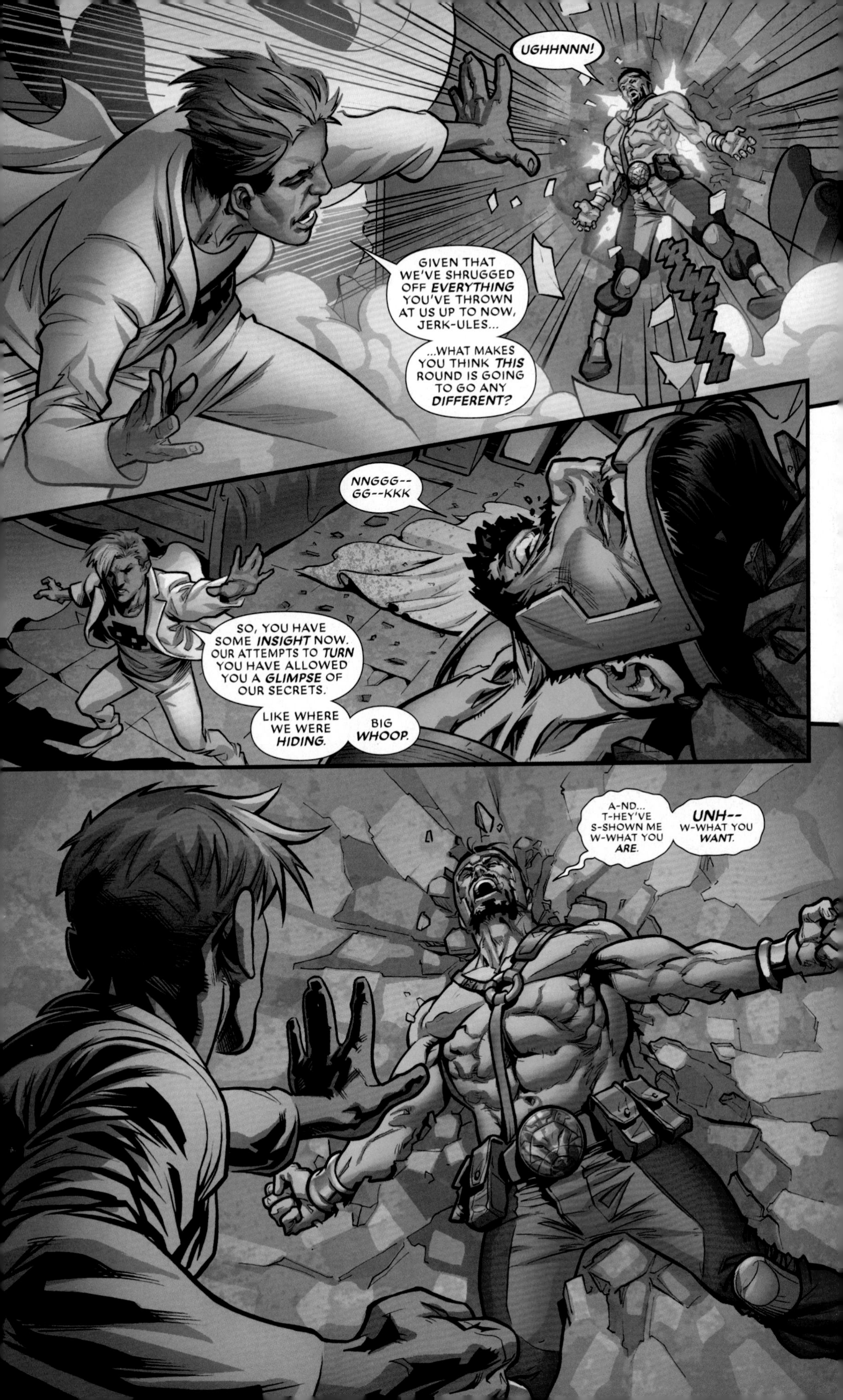
UGHHNNN!
GIVEN THAT WE'VE SHRUGGED OFF EVERYTHING YOU'VE THROWN AT US UP TO NOW, JERK-ULES...
...WHAT MAKES YOU THINK THIS ROUND IS GOING TO GO ANY DIFFERENT?
NNGGG-- GG--KKK
SO, YOU HAVE SOME INSIGHT NOW. OUR ATTEMPTS TO TURN YOU HAVE ALLOWED YOU A GLIMPSE OF OUR SECRETS.
LIKE WHERE WE WERE HIDING.
BIG WHOOP.
A-ND... T-HEY'VE S-SHOWN ME W-WHAT YOU ARE.
UNH-- W-WHAT YOU WANT.

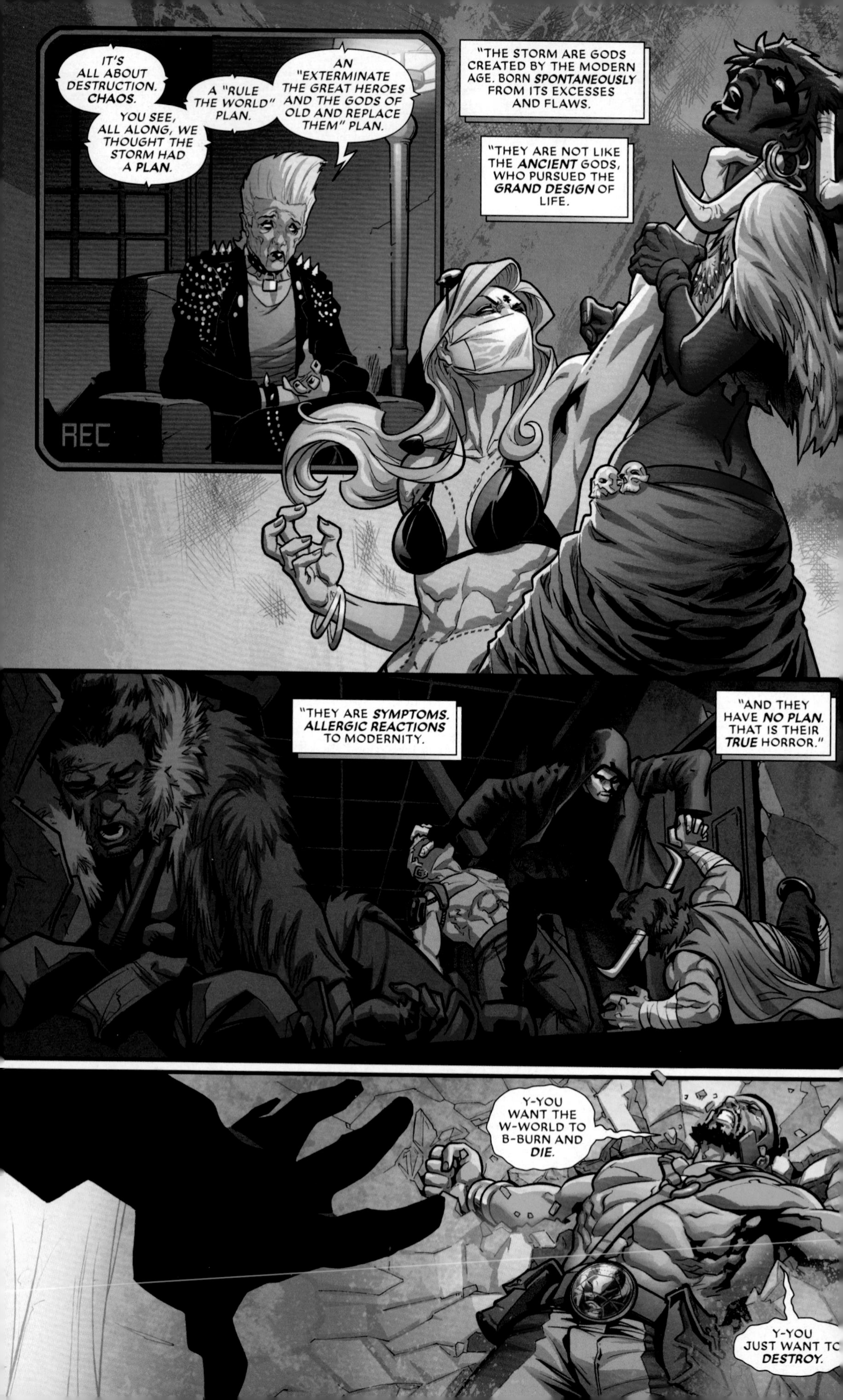

IT'S ALL ABOUT DESTRUCTION. **CHAOS.**
YOU SEE, ALL ALONG, WE THOUGHT THE STORM HAD A **PLAN.**
A "RULE THE WORLD" PLAN.
AN "EXTERMINATE THE GREAT HEROES AND THE GODS OF OLD AND REPLACE THEM" PLAN.
REC
"THE STORM ARE GODS CREATED BY THE MODERN AGE. BORN ***SPONTANEOUSLY*** FROM ITS EXCESSES AND FLAWS.
"THEY ARE NOT LIKE THE ***ANCIENT*** GODS, WHO PURSUED THE ***GRAND DESIGN*** OF LIFE.
"THEY ARE ***SYMPTOMS. ALLERGIC REACTIONS*** TO MODERNITY.
"AND THEY HAVE ***NO PLAN.*** THAT IS THEIR ***TRUE*** HORROR."
Y-YOU WANT THE W-WORLD TO B-BURN AND ***DIE.***
Y-YOU JUST WANT TO ***DESTROY.***

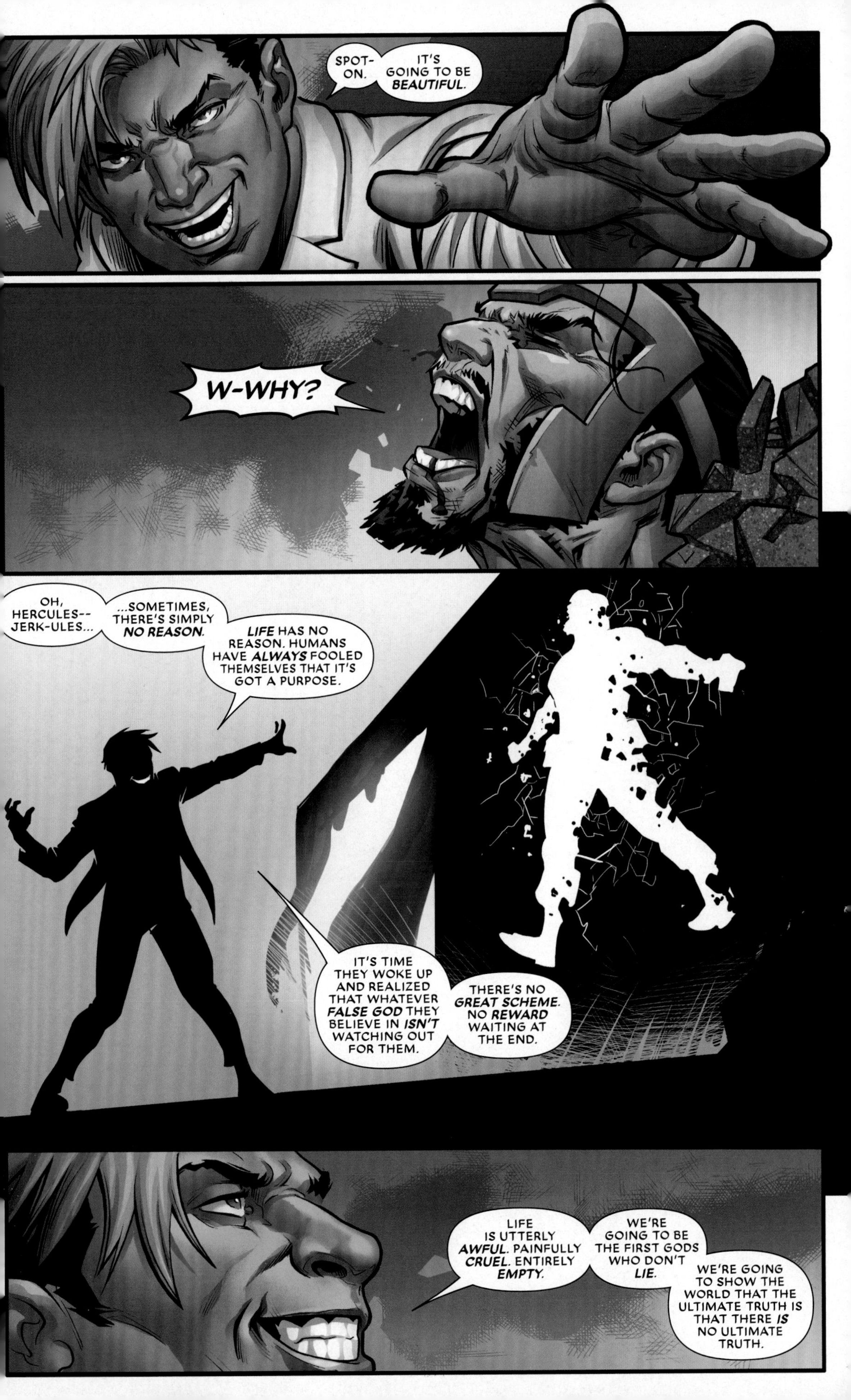
SPOT-ON.
IT'S GOING TO BE BEAUTIFUL.
W-WHY?
OH, HERCULES--JERK-ULES...
...SOMETIMES, THERE'S SIMPLY NO REASON.
LIFE HAS NO REASON. HUMANS HAVE ALWAYS FOOLED THEMSELVES THAT IT'S GOT A PURPOSE.
IT'S TIME THEY WOKE UP AND REALIZED THAT WHATEVER FALSE GOD THEY BELIEVE IN ISN'T WATCHING OUT FOR THEM.
THERE'S NO GREAT SCHEME. NO REWARD WAITING AT THE END.
LIFE IS UTTERLY AWFUL. PAINFULLY CRUEL. ENTIRELY EMPTY.
WE'RE GOING TO BE THE FIRST GODS WHO DON'T LIE.
WE'RE GOING TO SHOW THE WORLD THAT THE ULTIMATE TRUTH IS THAT THERE IS NO ULTIMATE TRUTH.

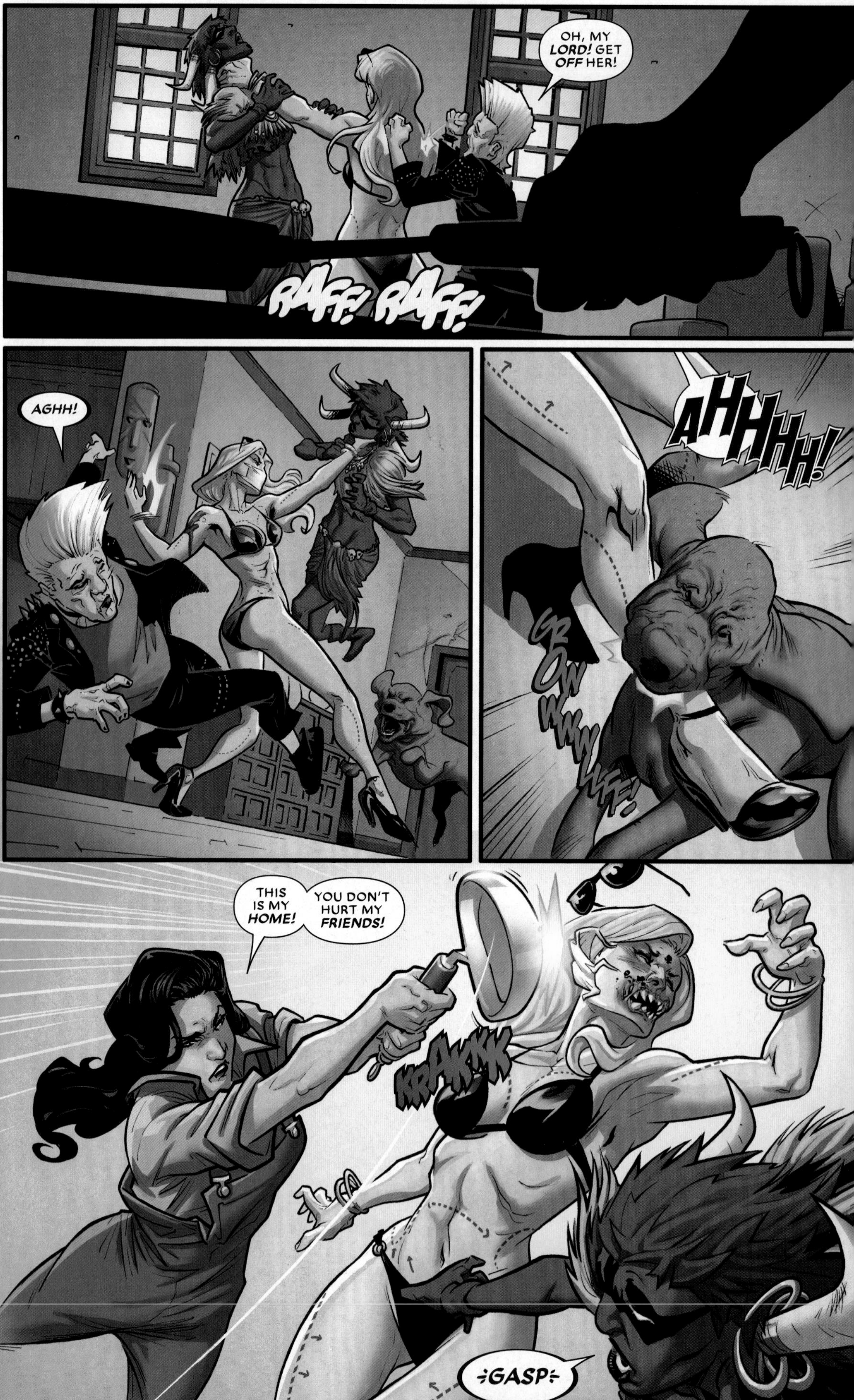

OH, MY LORD! GET OFF HER!
RAFF! RAFF!
AGHH!
AHHHHH!
GROWWWWLFF!
THIS IS MY HOME!
YOU DON'T HURT MY FRIENDS!
KRAKKK
GASP

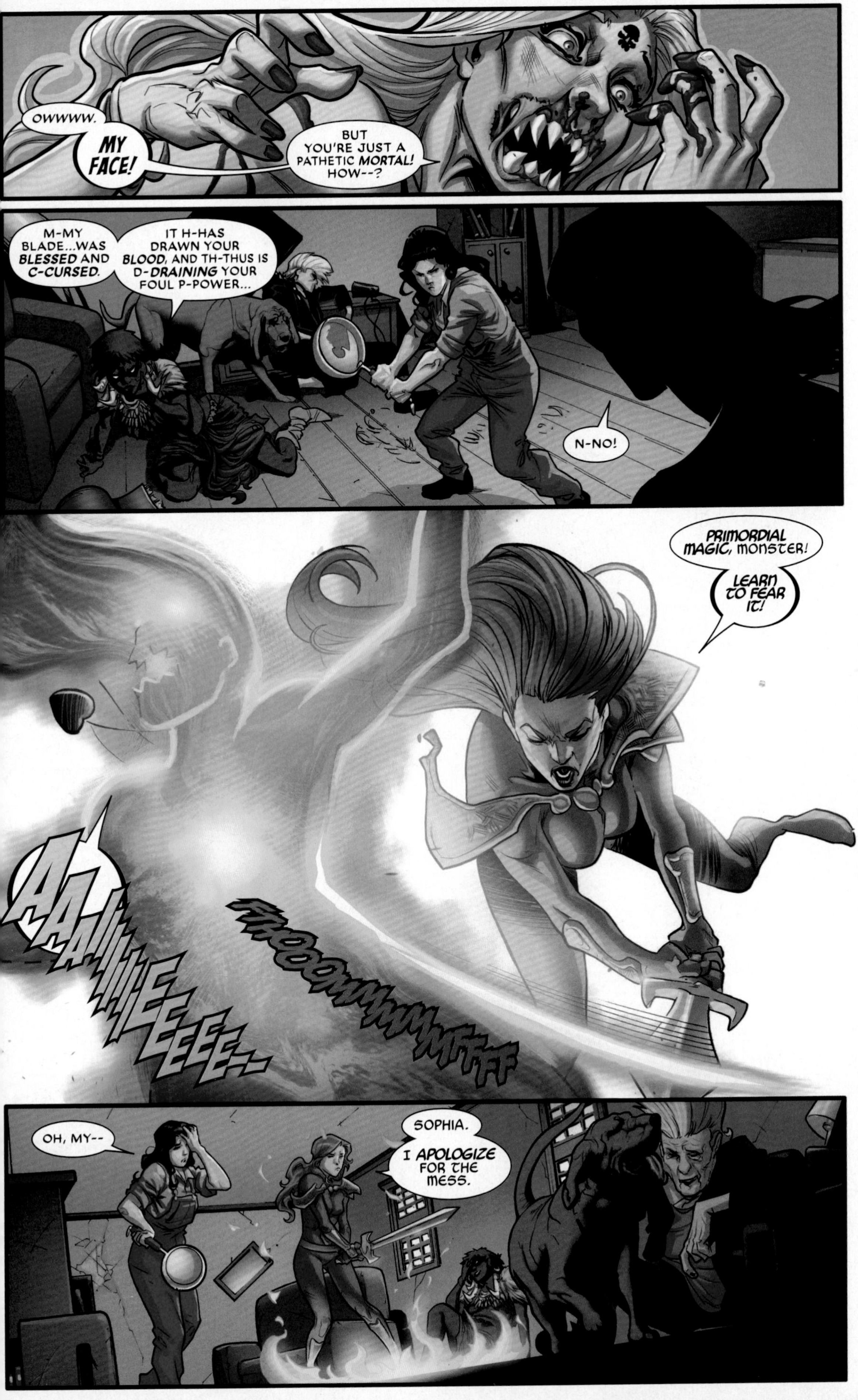
OWWWW.
MY FACE!
BUT YOU'RE JUST A PATHETIC MORTAL! HOW--?
M-MY BLADE...WAS BLESSED AND C-CURSED.
IT H-HAS DRAWN YOUR BLOOD, AND TH-THUS IS D-DRAINING YOUR FOUL P-POWER...
N-NO!
PRIMORDIAL MAGIC, MONSTER!
LEARN TO FEAR IT!
AAAIIIIEEEEE--
FTHOOOMMMMMFFF
OH, MY--
SOPHIA.
I APOLOGIZE FOR THE MESS.

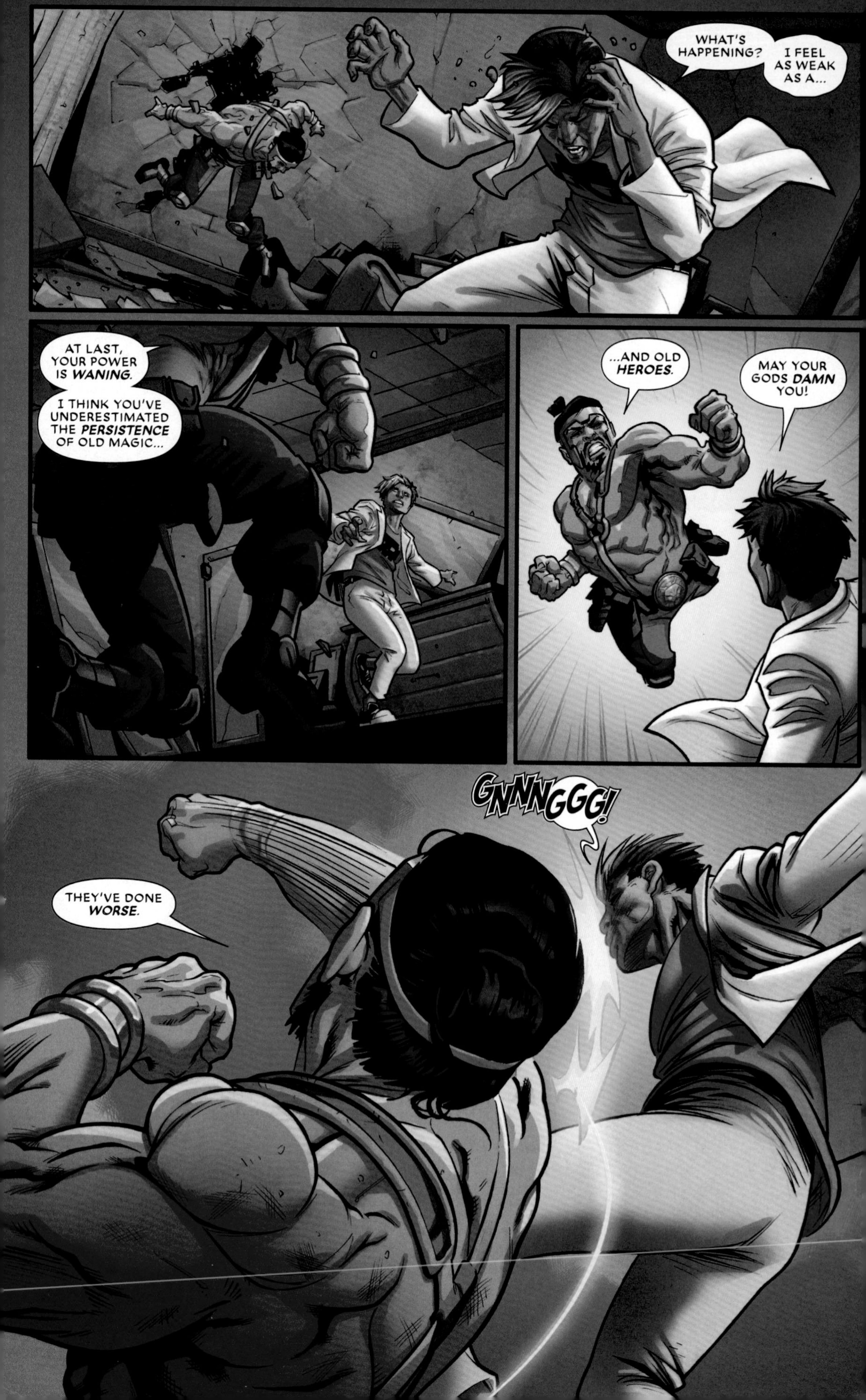
WHAT'S HAPPENING?
I FEEL AS WEAK AS A...
AT LAST, YOUR POWER IS *WANING*.
I THINK YOU'VE UNDERESTIMATED THE *PERSISTENCE* OF OLD MAGIC...
...AND OLD *HEROES*.
MAY YOUR GODS *DAMN* YOU!
GNNNGGG!
THEY'VE DONE *WORSE*.

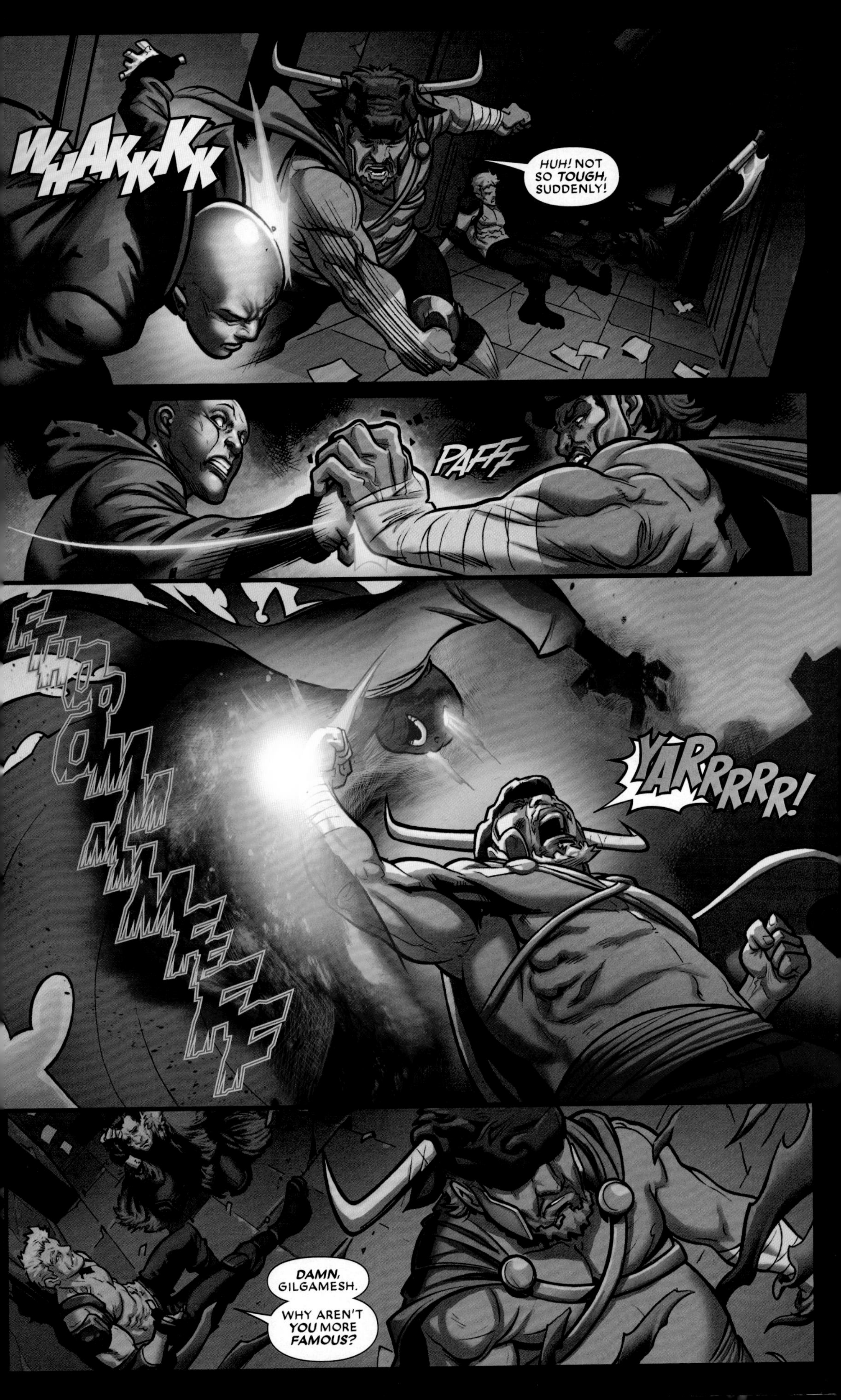
WHAKKKK
HUH! NOT SO TOUGH, SUDDENLY!
PAFFF
YARRRRR!
DAMN, GILGAMESH.
WHY AREN'T YOU MORE FAMOUS?

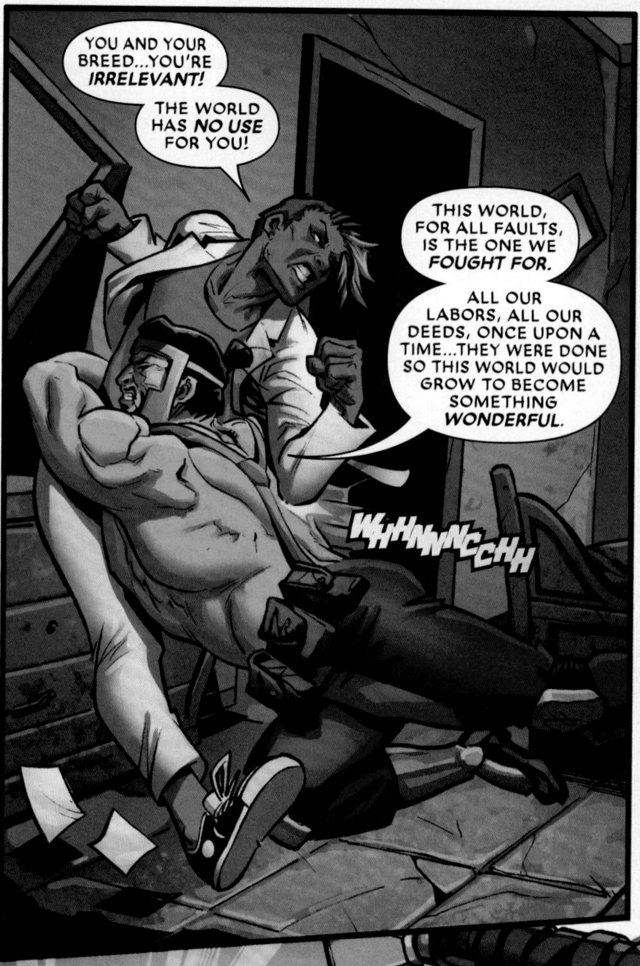
YOU AND YOUR BREED...YOU'RE IRRELEVANT!
THE WORLD HAS NO USE FOR YOU!
THIS WORLD, FOR ALL FAULTS, IS THE ONE WE FOUGHT FOR.
ALL OUR LABORS, ALL OUR DEEDS, ONCE UPON A TIME...THEY WERE DONE SO THIS WORLD WOULD GROW TO BECOME SOMETHING WONDERFUL.
WHHHNNNCCHH

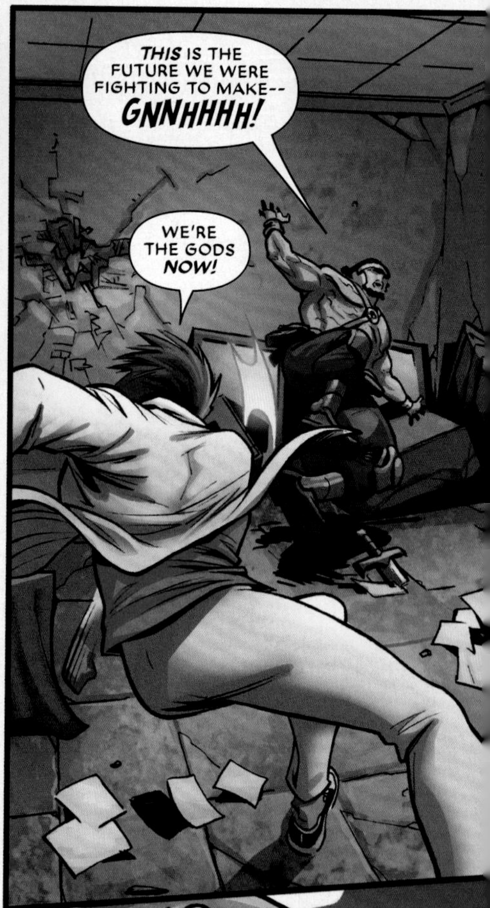
THIS IS THE FUTURE WE WERE FIGHTING TO MAKE-- GNNHHHH!
WE'RE THE GODS NOW!

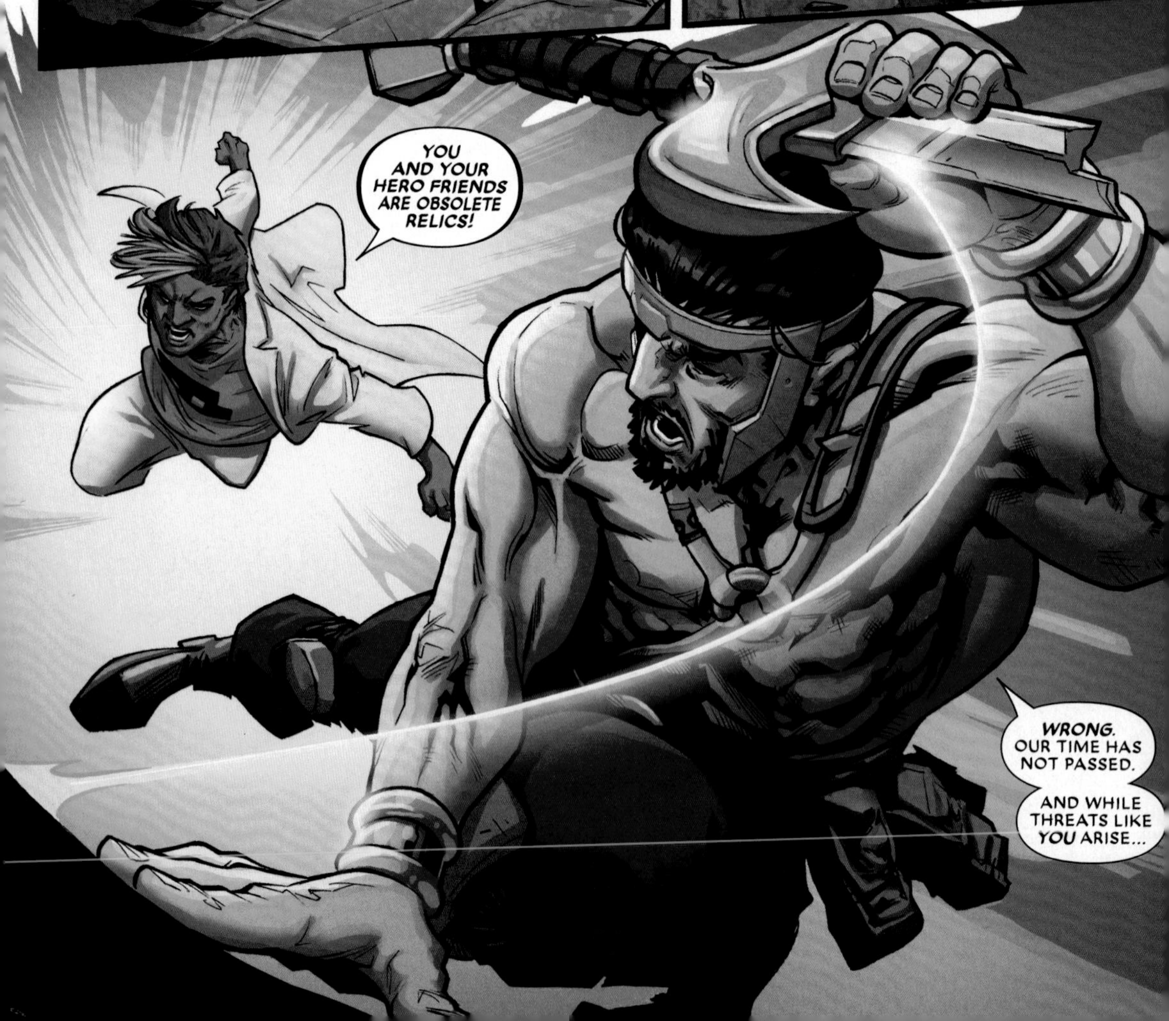
YOU AND YOUR HERO FRIENDS ARE OBSOLETE RELICS!
WRONG. OUR TIME HAS NOT PASSED.
AND WHILE THREATS LIKE YOU ARISE...

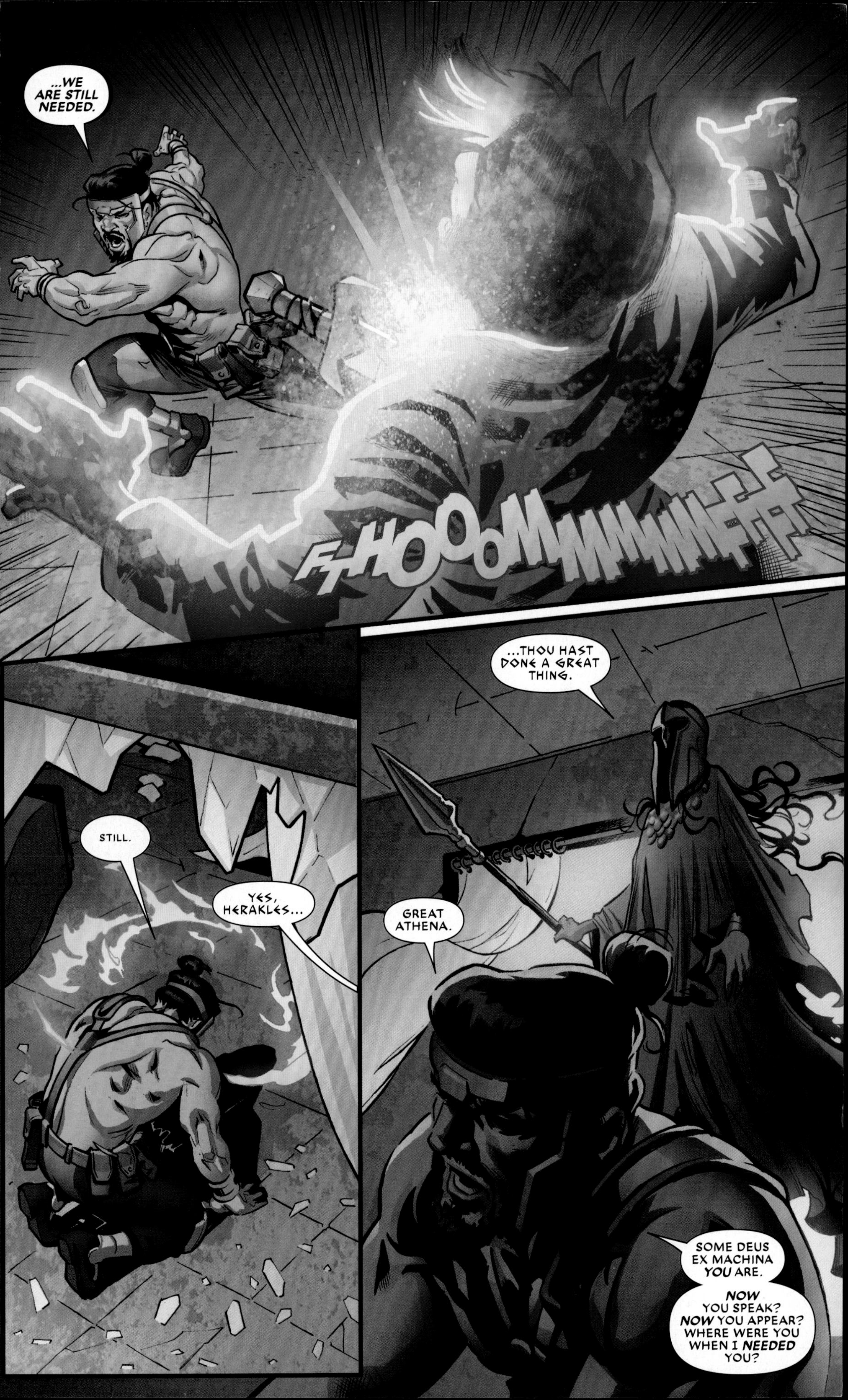
...WE ARE STILL NEEDED.
FT-HOOOMMMMMMFF
...THOU HAST DONE A GREAT THING.
STILL.
YES, HERAKLES...
GREAT ATHENA.
SOME DEUS EX MACHINA *YOU* ARE.
NOW YOU SPEAK? *NOW* YOU APPEAR? WHERE WERE YOU WHEN I *NEEDED* YOU?

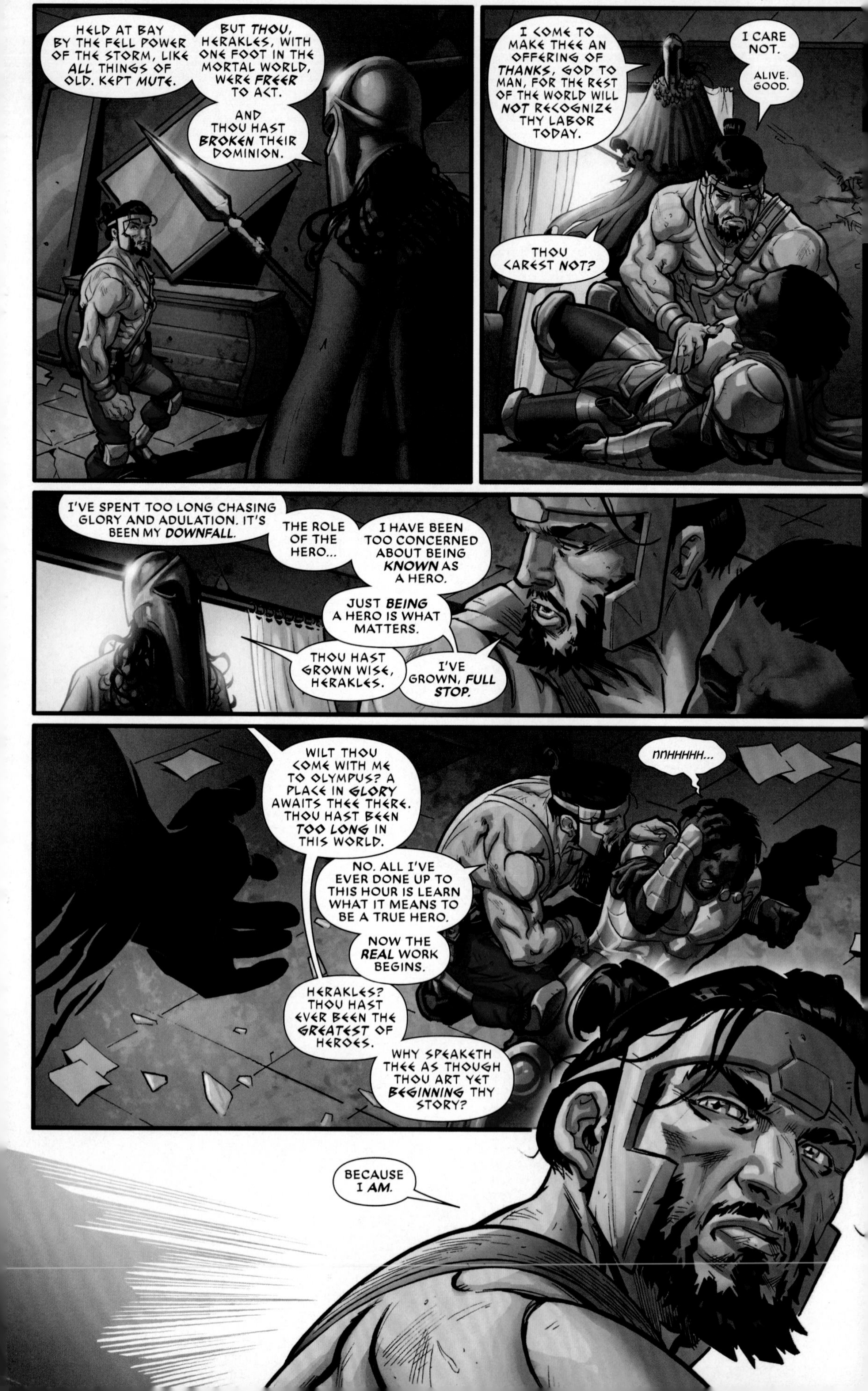
HELD AT BAY BY THE FELL POWER OF THE STORM, LIKE ALL THINGS OF OLD. KEPT MUTE.
BUT THOU, HERAKLES, WITH ONE FOOT IN THE MORTAL WORLD, WERE FREER TO ACT.
AND THOU HAST BROKEN THEIR DOMINION.
I COME TO MAKE THEE AN OFFERING OF THANKS, GOD TO MAN, FOR THE REST OF THE WORLD WILL NOT RECOGNIZE THY LABOR TODAY.
I CARE NOT.
ALIVE. GOOD.
THOU CAREST NOT?
I'VE SPENT TOO LONG CHASING GLORY AND ADULATION. IT'S BEEN MY DOWNFALL.
THE ROLE OF THE HERO...
I HAVE BEEN TOO CONCERNED ABOUT BEING KNOWN AS A HERO.
JUST BEING A HERO IS WHAT MATTERS.
THOU HAST GROWN WISE, HERAKLES.
I'VE GROWN, FULL STOP.
WILT THOU COME WITH ME TO OLYMPUS? A PLACE IN GLORY AWAITS THEE THERE. THOU HAST BEEN TOO LONG IN THIS WORLD.
NNHHHHH...
NO. ALL I'VE EVER DONE UP TO THIS HOUR IS LEARN WHAT IT MEANS TO BE A TRUE HERO.
NOW THE REAL WORK BEGINS.
HERAKLES? THOU HAST EVER BEEN THE GREATEST OF HEROES.
WHY SPEAKETH THEE AS THOUGH THOU ART YET BEGINNING THY STORY?
BECAUSE I AM.

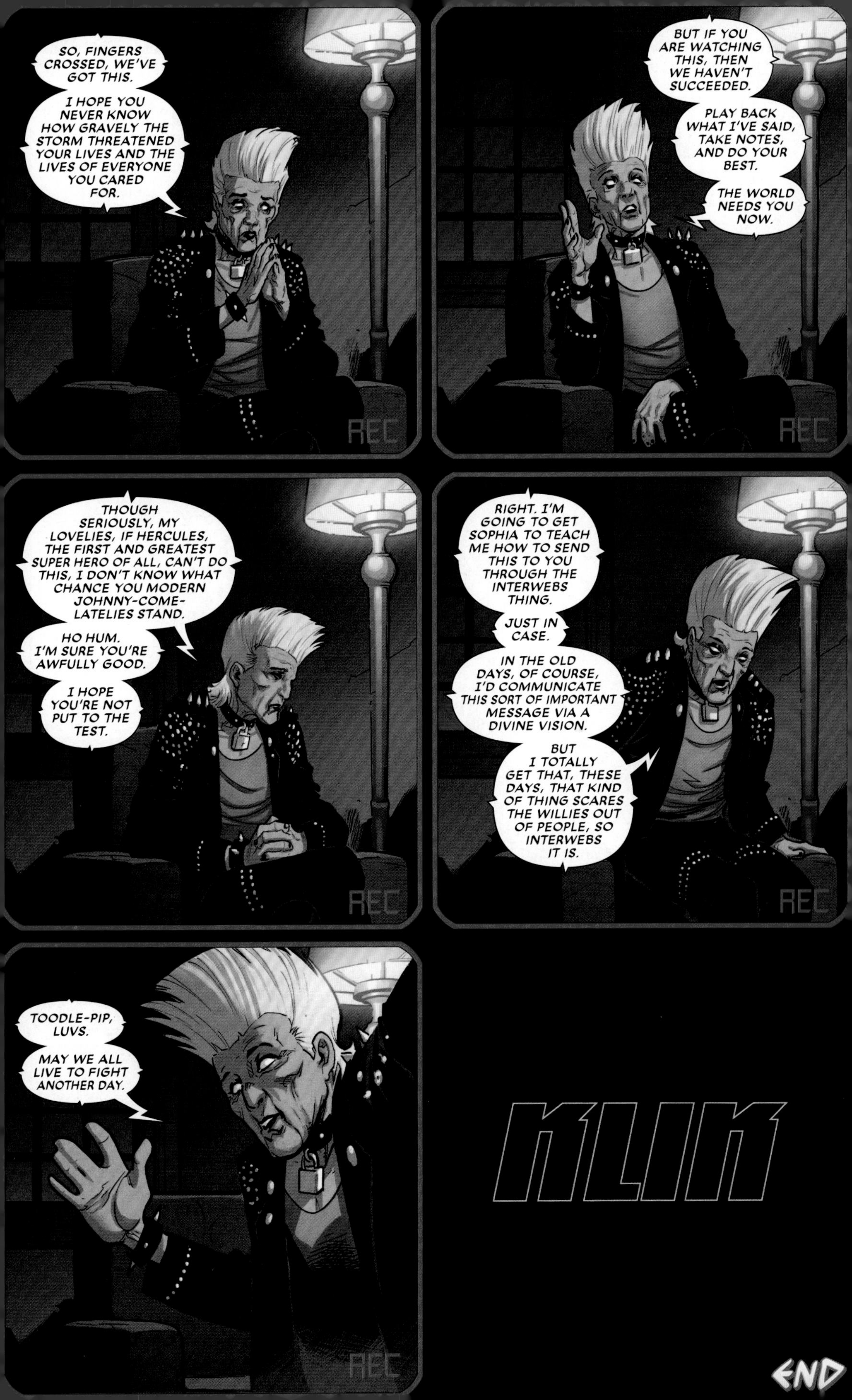
SO, FINGERS CROSSED, WE'VE GOT THIS.
I HOPE YOU NEVER KNOW HOW GRAVELY THE STORM THREATENED YOUR LIVES AND THE LIVES OF EVERYONE YOU CARED FOR.
REC
BUT IF YOU ARE WATCHING THIS, THEN WE HAVEN'T SUCCEEDED.
PLAY BACK WHAT I'VE SAID, TAKE NOTES, AND DO YOUR BEST.
THE WORLD NEEDS YOU NOW.
REC
THOUGH SERIOUSLY, MY LOVELIES, IF HERCULES, THE FIRST AND GREATEST SUPER HERO OF ALL, CAN'T DO THIS, I DON'T KNOW WHAT CHANCE YOU MODERN JOHNNY-COME-LATELIES STAND.
HO HUM. I'M SURE YOU'RE AWFULLY GOOD.
I HOPE YOU'RE NOT PUT TO THE TEST.
REC
RIGHT. I'M GOING TO GET SOPHIA TO TEACH ME HOW TO SEND THIS TO YOU THROUGH THE INTERWEBS THING.
JUST IN CASE.
IN THE OLD DAYS, OF COURSE, I'D COMMUNICATE THIS SORT OF IMPORTANT MESSAGE VIA A DIVINE VISION.
BUT I TOTALLY GET THAT, THESE DAYS, THAT KIND OF THING SCARES THE WILLIES OUT OF PEOPLE, SO INTERWEBS IT IS.
REC
TOODLE-PIP, LUVS.
MAY WE ALL LIVE TO FIGHT ANOTHER DAY.
REC
KLIK
END

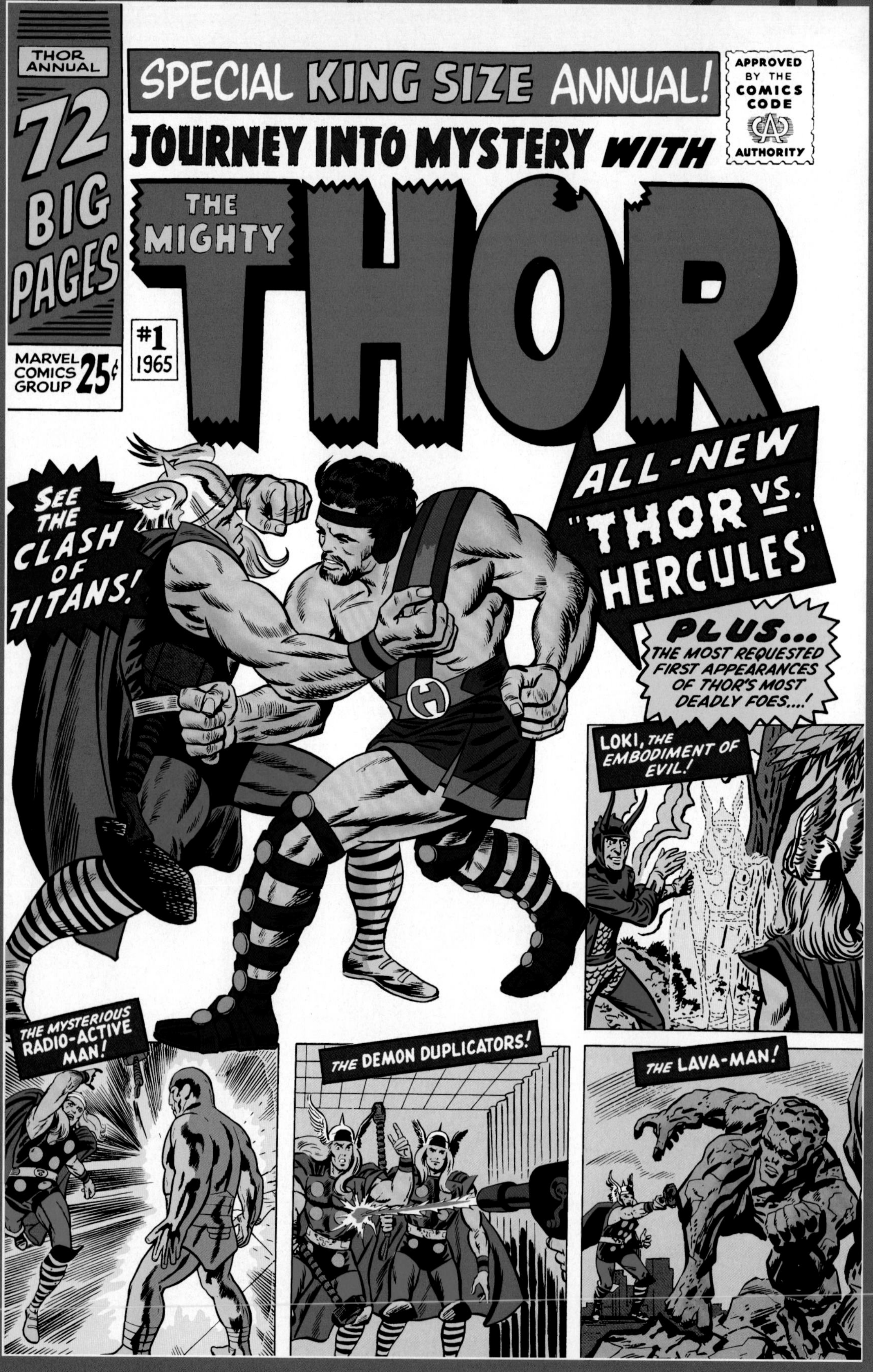
THOR ANNUAL
72 BIG PAGES
MARVEL COMICS GROUP 25¢
SPECIAL KING SIZE ANNUAL!
APPROVED BY THE COMICS CODE AUTHORITY
JOURNEY INTO MYSTERY WITH
THE MIGHTY THOR
#1 1965
SEE THE CLASH OF TITANS!
ALL-NEW "THOR VS. HERCULES"
PLUS... THE MOST REQUESTED FIRST APPEARANCES OF THOR'S MOST DEADLY FOES....!
LOKI, THE EMBODIMENT OF EVIL!
THE MYSTERIOUS RADIO-ACTIVE MAN!
THE DEMON DUPLICATORS!
THE LAVA-MAN!

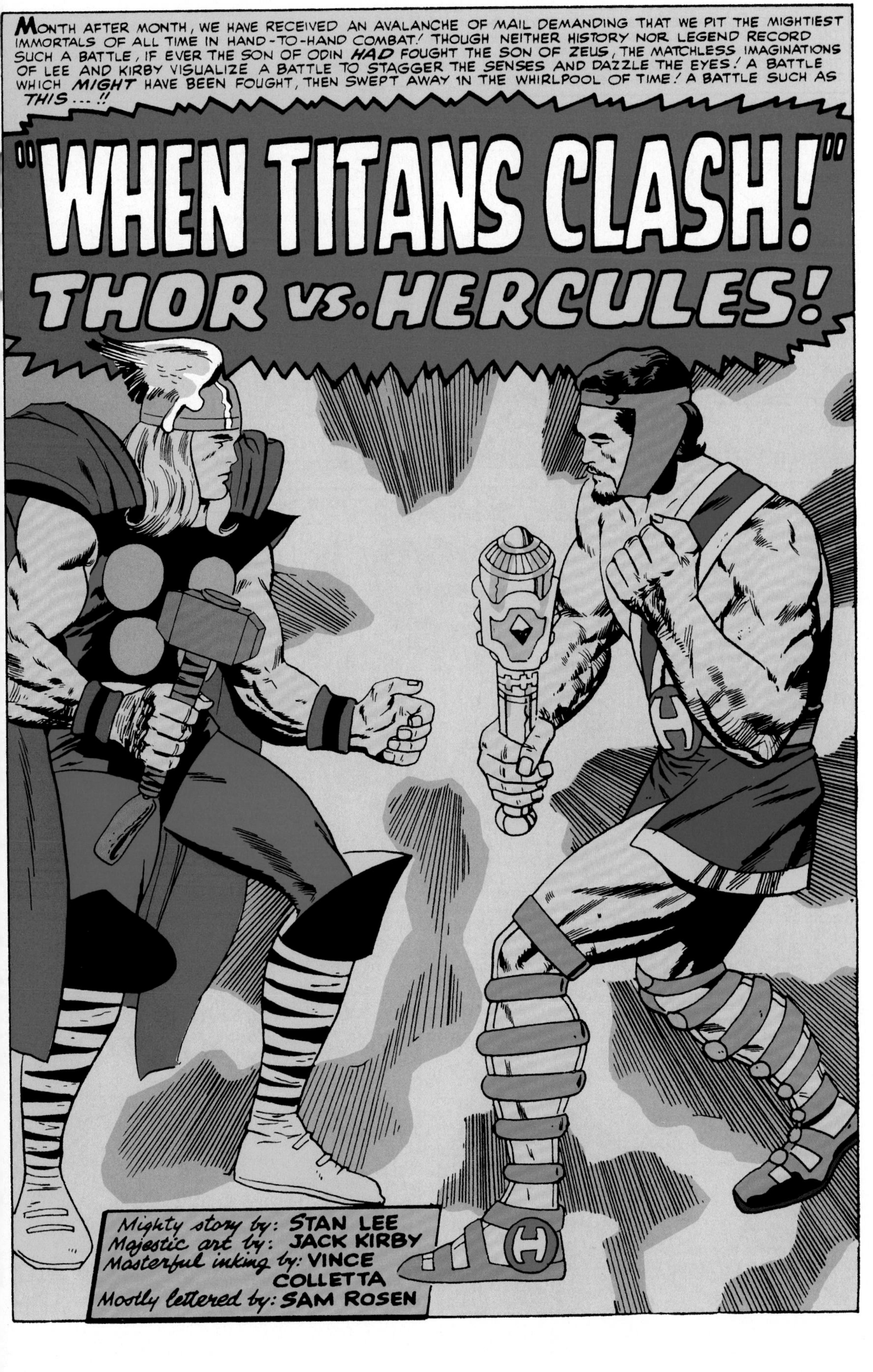
MONTH AFTER MONTH, WE HAVE RECEIVED AN AVALANCHE OF MAIL DEMANDING THAT WE PIT THE MIGHTIEST IMMORTALS OF ALL TIME IN HAND-TO-HAND COMBAT! THOUGH NEITHER HISTORY NOR LEGEND RECORD SUCH A BATTLE, IF EVER THE SON OF ODIN HAD FOUGHT THE SON OF ZEUS, THE MATCHLESS IMAGINATIONS OF LEE AND KIRBY VISUALIZE A BATTLE TO STAGGER THE SENSES AND DAZZLE THE EYES! A BATTLE WHICH MIGHT HAVE BEEN FOUGHT, THEN SWEPT AWAY IN THE WHIRLPOOL OF TIME! A BATTLE SUCH AS THIS...!!
"WHEN TITANS CLASH!"
THOR vs. HERCULES!
Mighty story by: STAN LEE
Majestic art by: JACK KIRBY
Masterful inking by: VINCE COLLETTA
Mostly lettered by: SAM ROSEN

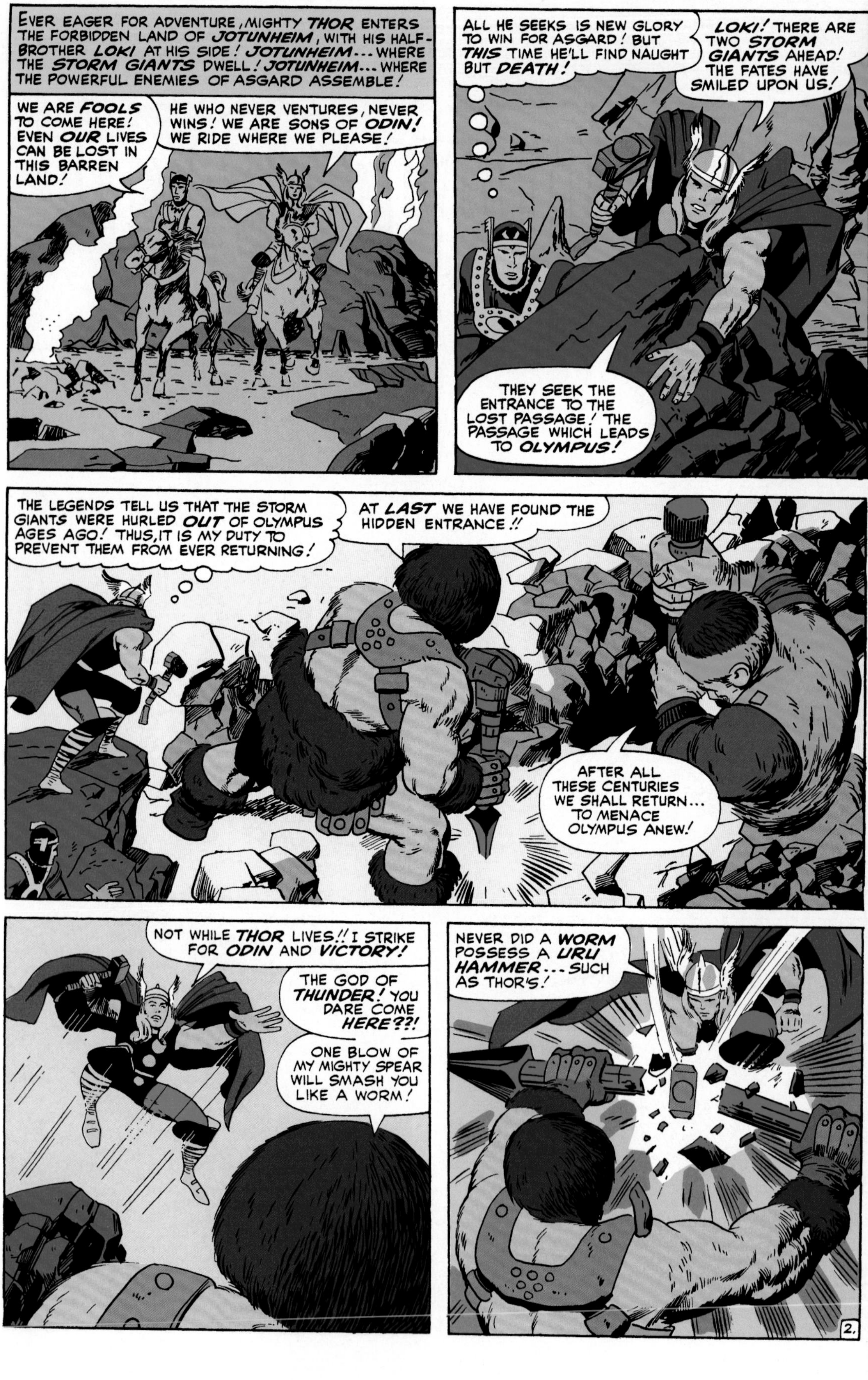

EVER EAGER FOR ADVENTURE, MIGHTY THOR ENTERS THE FORBIDDEN LAND OF JOTUNHEIM, WITH HIS HALF-BROTHER LOKI AT HIS SIDE! JOTUNHEIM... WHERE THE STORM GIANTS DWELL! JOTUNHEIM... WHERE THE POWERFUL ENEMIES OF ASGARD ASSEMBLE!
WE ARE FOOLS TO COME HERE! EVEN OUR LIVES CAN BE LOST IN THIS BARREN LAND!
HE WHO NEVER VENTURES, NEVER WINS! WE ARE SONS OF ODIN! WE RIDE WHERE WE PLEASE!
ALL HE SEEKS IS NEW GLORY TO WIN FOR ASGARD! BUT THIS TIME HE'LL FIND NAUGHT BUT DEATH!
LOKI! THERE ARE TWO STORM GIANTS AHEAD! THE FATES HAVE SMILED UPON US!
THEY SEEK THE ENTRANCE TO THE LOST PASSAGE! THE PASSAGE WHICH LEADS TO OLYMPUS!
THE LEGENDS TELL US THAT THE STORM GIANTS WERE HURLED OUT OF OLYMPUS AGES AGO! THUS, IT IS MY DUTY TO PREVENT THEM FROM EVER RETURNING!
AT LAST WE HAVE FOUND THE HIDDEN ENTRANCE!!
AFTER ALL THESE CENTURIES WE SHALL RETURN... TO MENACE OLYMPUS ANEW!
NOT WHILE THOR LIVES!! I STRIKE FOR ODIN AND VICTORY!
THE GOD OF THUNDER! YOU DARE COME HERE??!
ONE BLOW OF MY MIGHTY SPEAR WILL SMASH YOU LIKE A WORM!
NEVER DID A WORM POSSESS A URU HAMMER... SUCH AS THOR'S!
2.

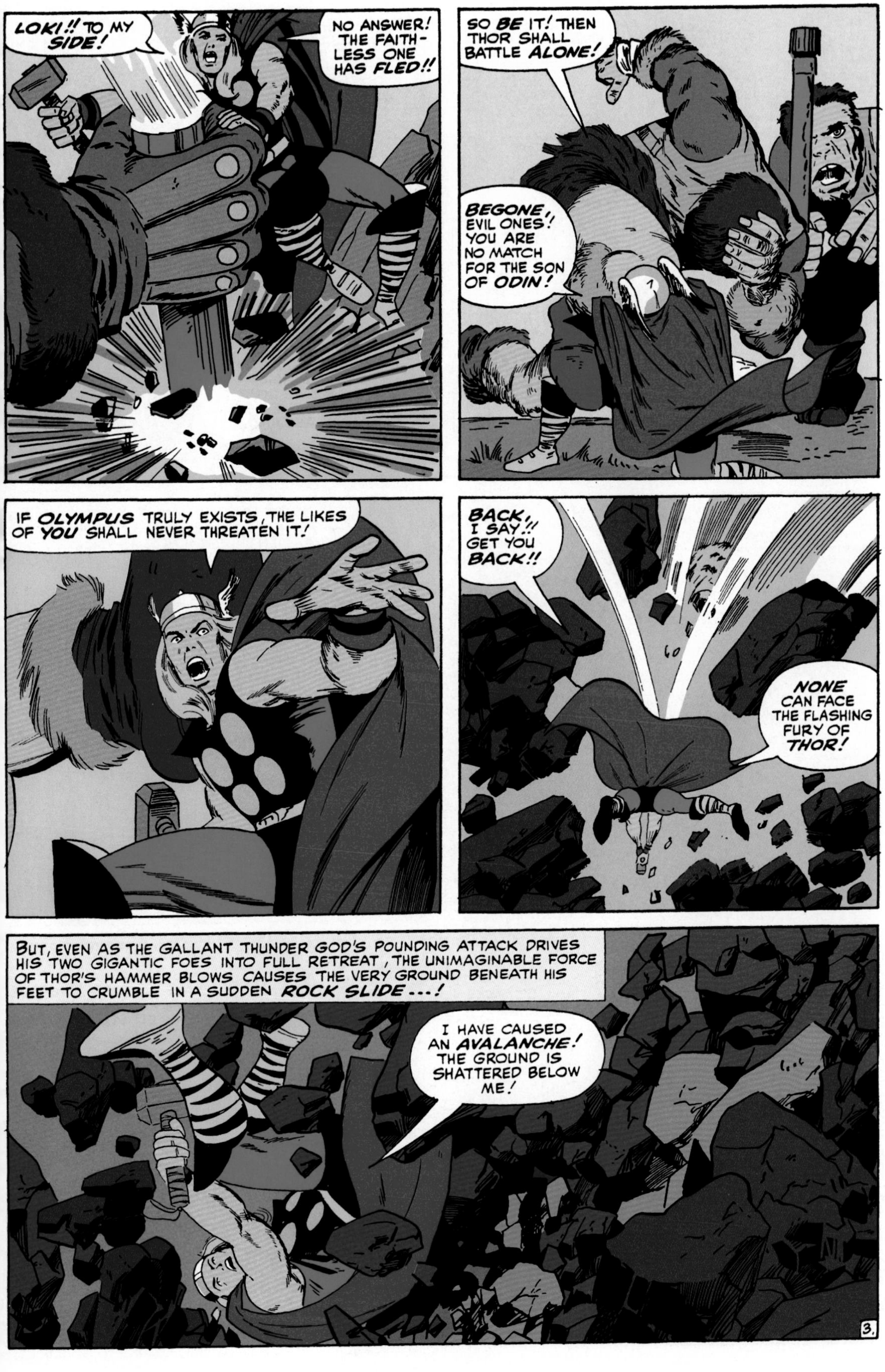
LOKI!! TO MY SIDE!
NO ANSWER! THE FAITH-LESS ONE HAS FLED!!
SO BE IT! THEN THOR SHALL BATTLE ALONE!
BEGONE, EVIL ONES! YOU ARE NO MATCH FOR THE SON OF ODIN!
IF OLYMPUS TRULY EXISTS, THE LIKES OF YOU SHALL NEVER THREATEN IT!
BACK, I SAY!! GET YOU BACK!!
NONE CAN FACE THE FLASHING FURY OF THOR!
BUT, EVEN AS THE GALLANT THUNDER GOD'S POUNDING ATTACK DRIVES HIS TWO GIGANTIC FOES INTO FULL RETREAT, THE UNIMAGINABLE FORCE OF THOR'S HAMMER BLOWS CAUSES THE VERY GROUND BENEATH HIS FEET TO CRUMBLE IN A SUDDEN ROCK SLIDE...!
I HAVE CAUSED AN AVALANCHE! THE GROUND IS SHATTERED BELOW ME!
3.

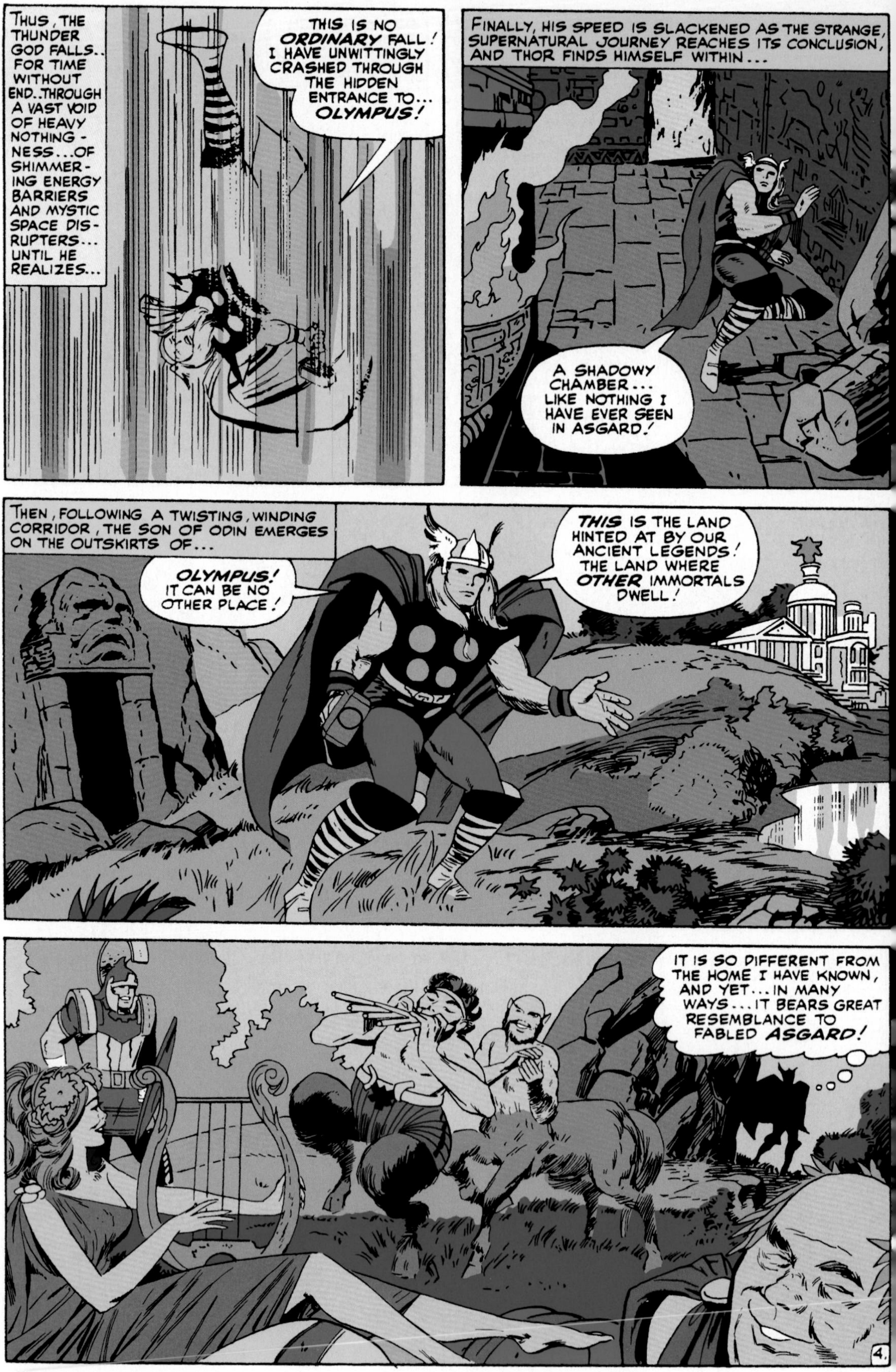
THUS, THE THUNDER GOD FALLS.. FOR TIME WITHOUT END..THROUGH A VAST VOID OF HEAVY NOTHING-NESS...OF SHIMMER-ING ENERGY BARRIERS AND MYSTIC SPACE DIS-RUPTERS... UNTIL HE REALIZES...
THIS IS NO ORDINARY FALL! I HAVE UNWITTINGLY CRASHED THROUGH THE HIDDEN ENTRANCE TO... OLYMPUS!
FINALLY, HIS SPEED IS SLACKENED AS THE STRANGE, SUPERNATURAL JOURNEY REACHES ITS CONCLUSION, AND THOR FINDS HIMSELF WITHIN...
A SHADOWY CHAMBER... LIKE NOTHING I HAVE EVER SEEN IN ASGARD!
THEN, FOLLOWING A TWISTING, WINDING CORRIDOR, THE SON OF ODIN EMERGES ON THE OUTSKIRTS OF...
OLYMPUS! IT CAN BE NO OTHER PLACE!
THIS IS THE LAND HINTED AT BY OUR ANCIENT LEGENDS! THE LAND WHERE OTHER IMMORTALS DWELL!
IT IS SO DIFFERENT FROM THE HOME I HAVE KNOWN, AND YET... IN MANY WAYS... IT BEARS GREAT RESEMBLANCE TO FABLED ASGARD!
4.

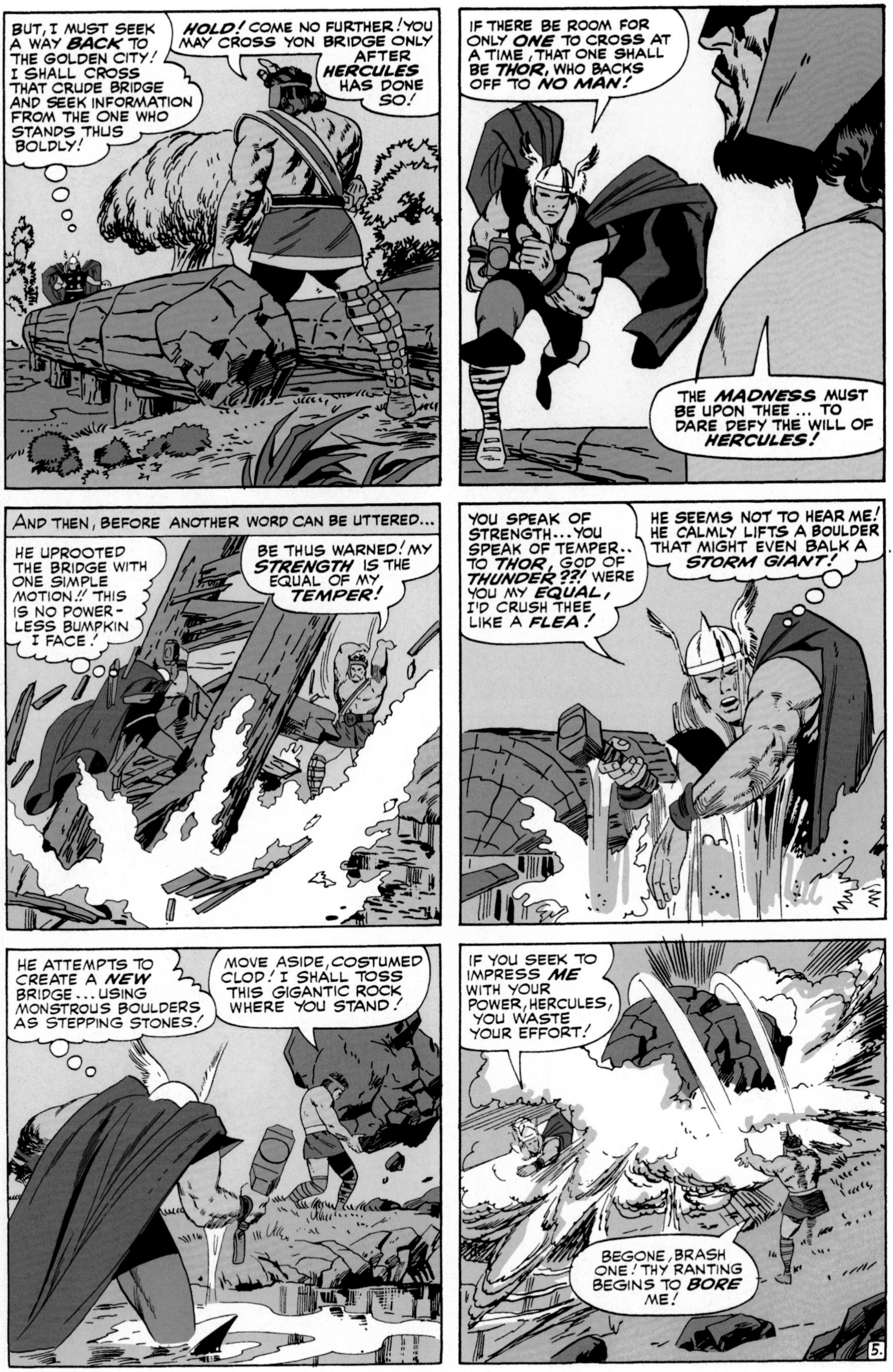

BUT, I MUST SEEK A WAY BACK TO THE GOLDEN CITY! I SHALL CROSS THAT CRUDE BRIDGE AND SEEK INFORMATION FROM THE ONE WHO STANDS THUS BOLDLY!
HOLD! COME NO FURTHER! YOU MAY CROSS YON BRIDGE ONLY AFTER HERCULES HAS DONE SO!
IF THERE BE ROOM FOR ONLY ONE TO CROSS AT A TIME, THAT ONE SHALL BE THOR, WHO BACKS OFF TO NO MAN!
THE MADNESS MUST BE UPON THEE ... TO DARE DEFY THE WILL OF HERCULES!
AND THEN, BEFORE ANOTHER WORD CAN BE UTTERED...
HE UPROOTED THE BRIDGE WITH ONE SIMPLE MOTION!! THIS IS NO POWER-LESS BUMPKIN I FACE!
BE THUS WARNED! MY STRENGTH IS THE EQUAL OF MY TEMPER!
YOU SPEAK OF STRENGTH... YOU SPEAK OF TEMPER.. TO THOR, GOD OF THUNDER??! WERE YOU MY EQUAL, I'D CRUSH THEE LIKE A FLEA!
HE SEEMS NOT TO HEAR ME! HE CALMLY LIFTS A BOULDER THAT MIGHT EVEN BALK A STORM GIANT!
HE ATTEMPTS TO CREATE A NEW BRIDGE... USING MONSTROUS BOULDERS AS STEPPING STONES!
MOVE ASIDE, COSTUMED CLOD! I SHALL TOSS THIS GIGANTIC ROCK WHERE YOU STAND!
IF YOU SEEK TO IMPRESS ME WITH YOUR POWER, HERCULES, YOU WASTE YOUR EFFORT!
BEGONE, BRASH ONE! THY RANTING BEGINS TO BORE ME!
5.

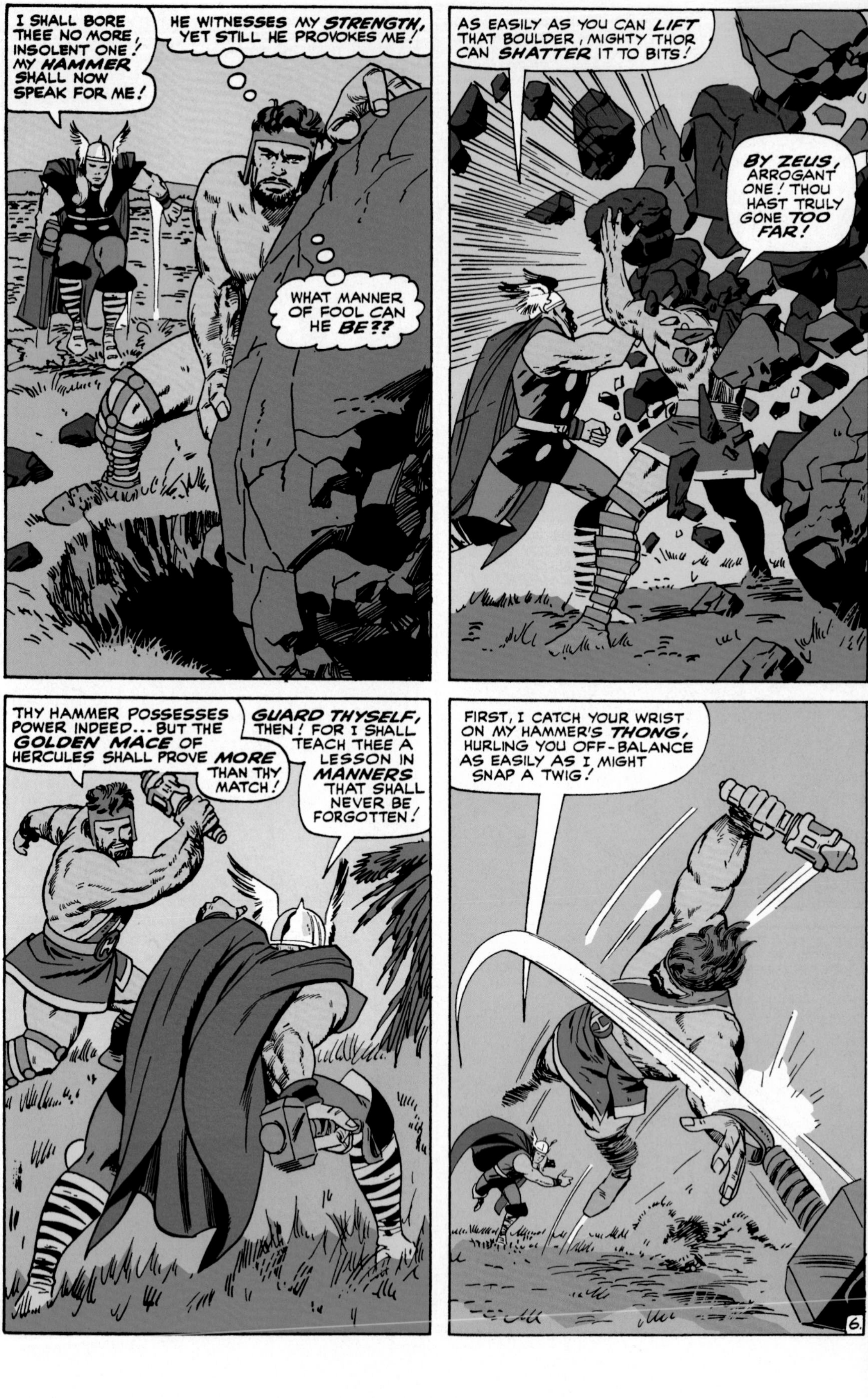
I SHALL BORE THEE NO MORE, INSOLENT ONE! MY HAMMER SHALL NOW SPEAK FOR ME!
HE WITNESSES MY STRENGTH, YET STILL HE PROVOKES ME!
WHAT MANNER OF FOOL CAN HE BE??
AS EASILY AS YOU CAN LIFT THAT BOULDER, MIGHTY THOR CAN SHATTER IT TO BITS!
BY ZEUS, ARROGANT ONE! THOU HAST TRULY GONE TOO FAR!
THY HAMMER POSSESSES POWER INDEED... BUT THE GOLDEN MACE OF HERCULES SHALL PROVE MORE THAN THY MATCH!
GUARD THYSELF, THEN! FOR I SHALL TEACH THEE A LESSON IN MANNERS THAT SHALL NEVER BE FORGOTTEN!
FIRST, I CATCH YOUR WRIST ON MY HAMMER'S THONG, HURLING YOU OFF-BALANCE AS EASILY AS I MIGHT SNAP A TWIG!
6.

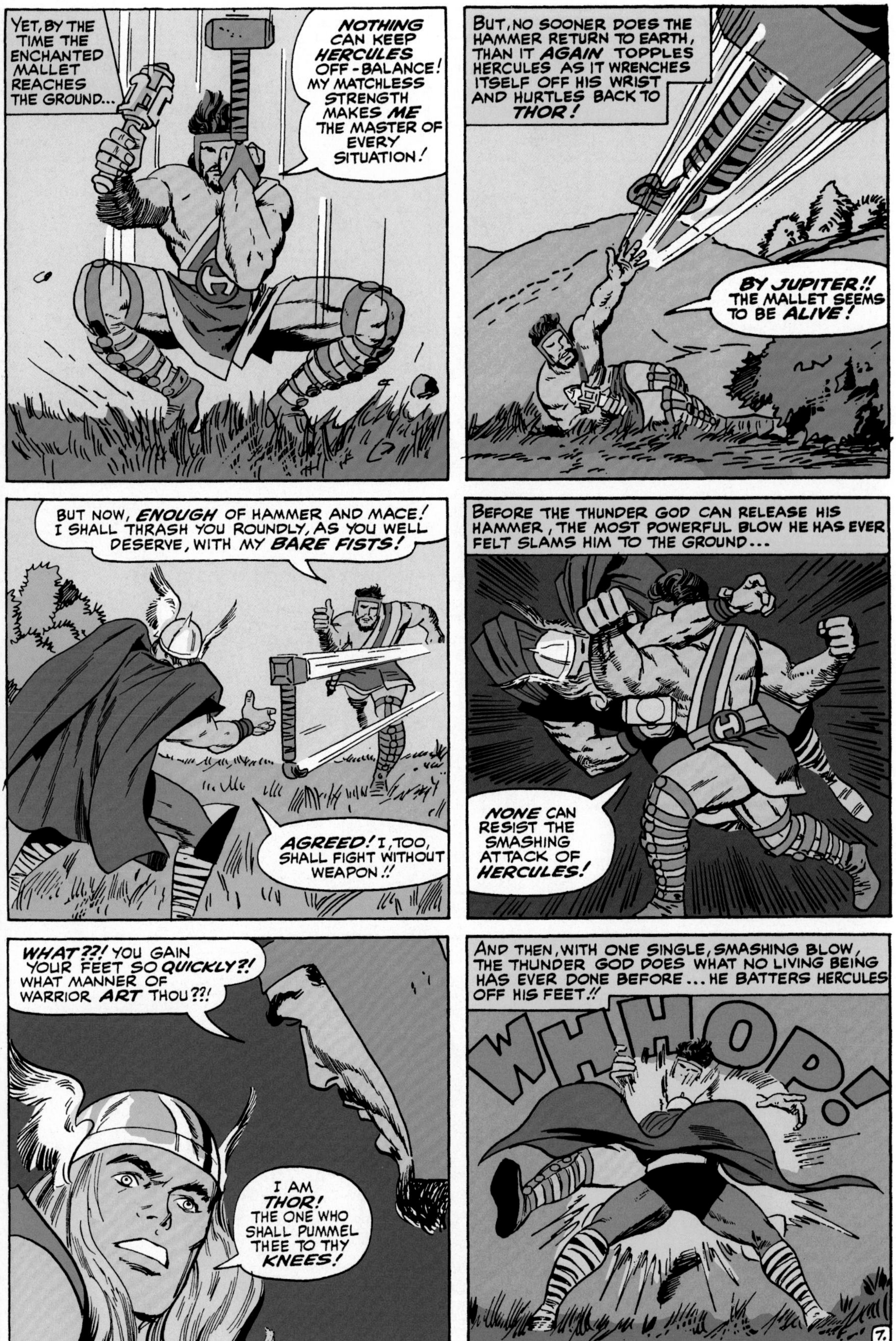
YET, BY THE TIME THE ENCHANTED MALLET REACHES THE GROUND...
NOTHING CAN KEEP HERCULES OFF-BALANCE! MY MATCHLESS STRENGTH MAKES ME THE MASTER OF EVERY SITUATION!
BUT, NO SOONER DOES THE HAMMER RETURN TO EARTH, THAN IT AGAIN TOPPLES HERCULES AS IT WRENCHES ITSELF OFF HIS WRIST AND HURTLES BACK TO THOR!
BY JUPITER!! THE MALLET SEEMS TO BE ALIVE!
BUT NOW, ENOUGH OF HAMMER AND MACE! I SHALL THRASH YOU ROUNDLY, AS YOU WELL DESERVE, WITH MY BARE FISTS!
AGREED! I, TOO, SHALL FIGHT WITHOUT WEAPON!!
BEFORE THE THUNDER GOD CAN RELEASE HIS HAMMER, THE MOST POWERFUL BLOW HE HAS EVER FELT SLAMS HIM TO THE GROUND...
NONE CAN RESIST THE SMASHING ATTACK OF HERCULES!
WHAT??! YOU GAIN YOUR FEET SO QUICKLY?! WHAT MANNER OF WARRIOR ART THOU??!
I AM THOR! THE ONE WHO SHALL PUMMEL THEE TO THY KNEES!
AND THEN, WITH ONE SINGLE, SMASHING BLOW, THE THUNDER GOD DOES WHAT NO LIVING BEING HAS EVER DONE BEFORE... HE BATTERS HERCULES OFF HIS FEET!!
WHHOP!
7.

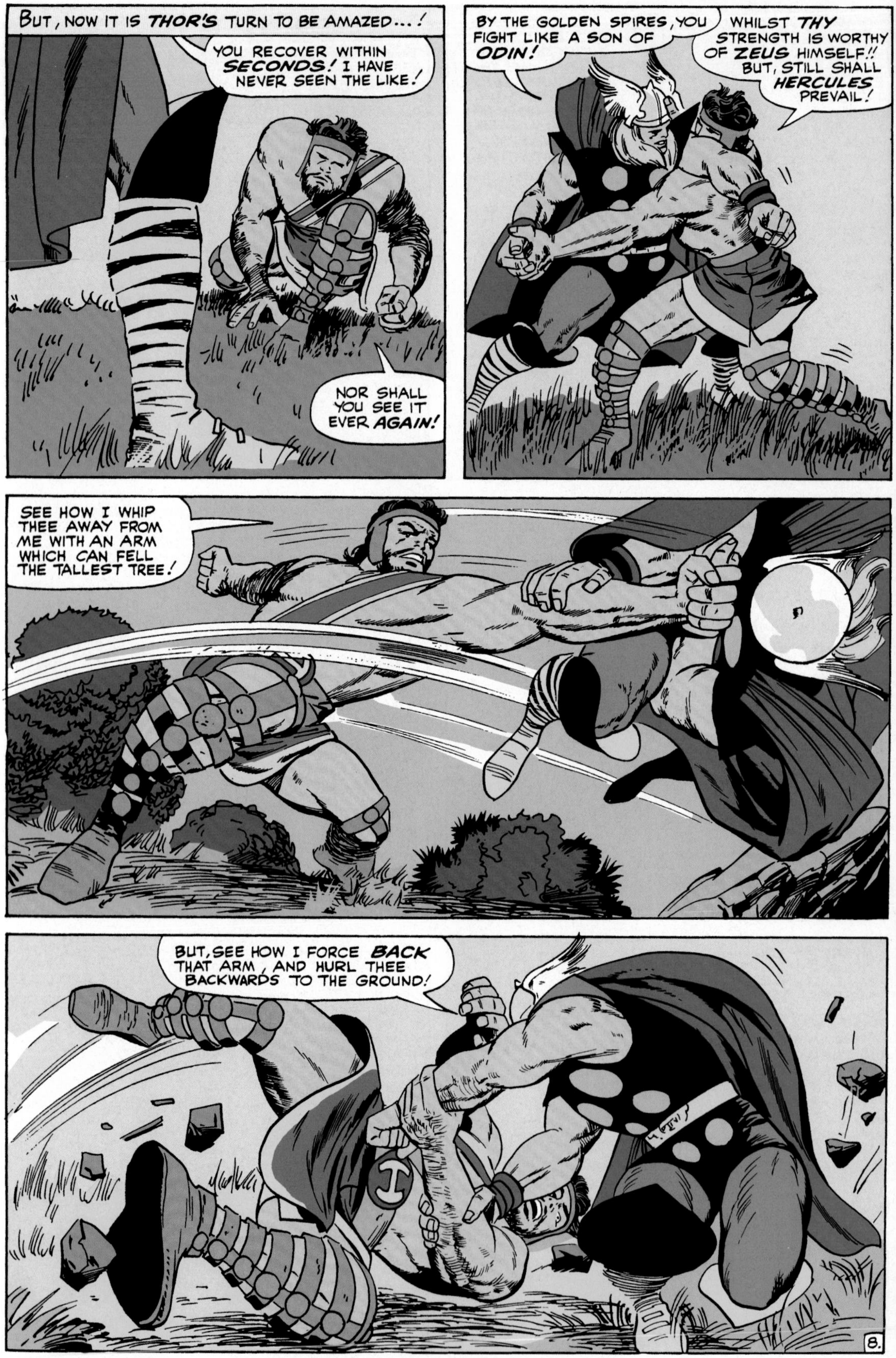
BUT, NOW IT IS THOR'S TURN TO BE AMAZED...!
YOU RECOVER WITHIN SECONDS! I HAVE NEVER SEEN THE LIKE!
NOR SHALL YOU SEE IT EVER AGAIN!
BY THE GOLDEN SPIRES, YOU FIGHT LIKE A SON OF ODIN!
WHILST THY STRENGTH IS WORTHY OF ZEUS HIMSELF!! BUT, STILL SHALL HERCULES PREVAIL!
SEE HOW I WHIP THEE AWAY FROM ME WITH AN ARM WHICH CAN FELL THE TALLEST TREE!
BUT, SEE HOW I FORCE BACK THAT ARM, AND HURL THEE BACKWARDS TO THE GROUND!
8.

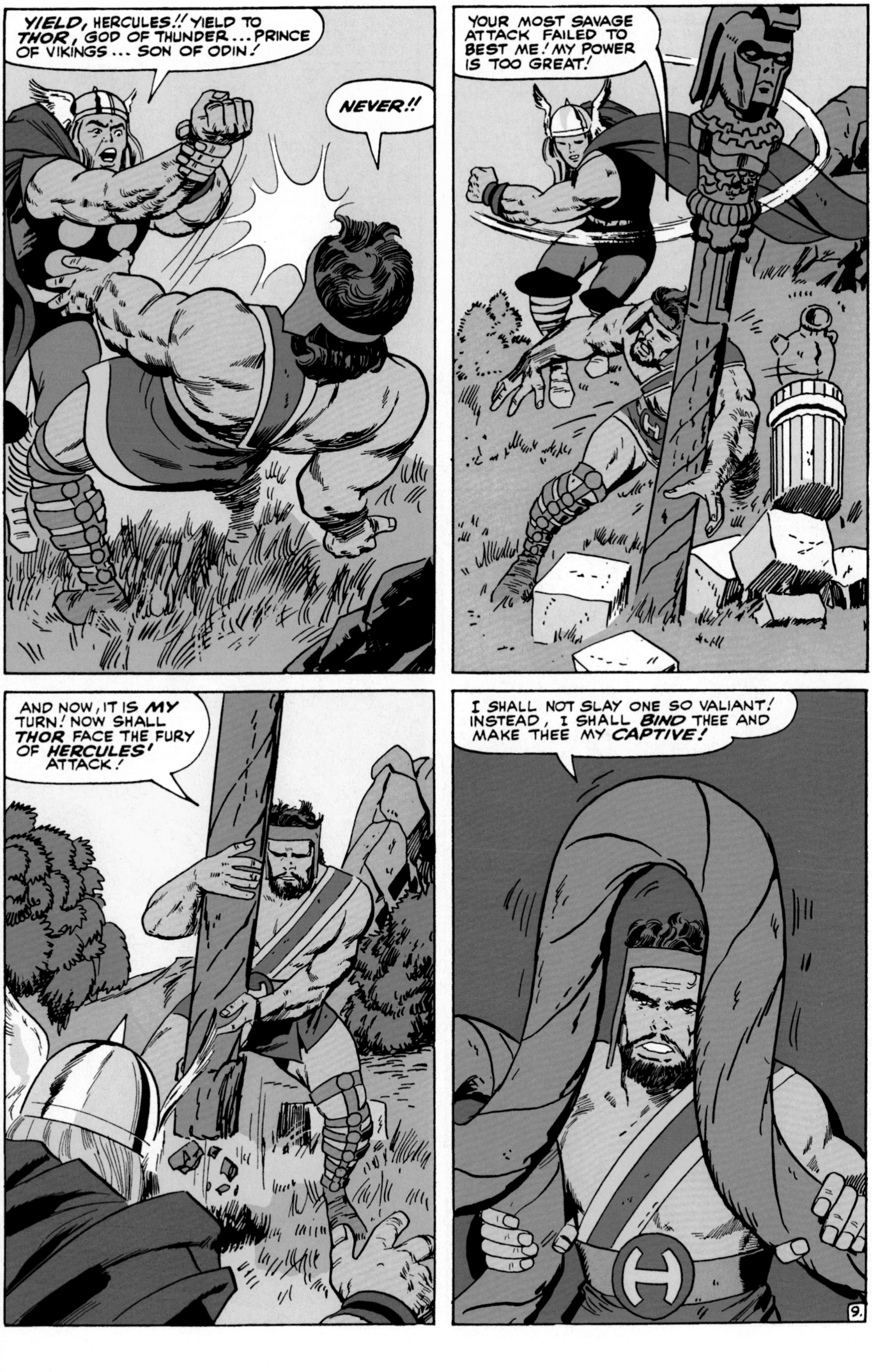
YIELD, HERCULES!! YIELD TO THOR, GOD OF THUNDER... PRINCE OF VIKINGS... SON OF ODIN!
NEVER!!
YOUR MOST SAVAGE ATTACK FAILED TO BEST ME! MY POWER IS TOO GREAT!
AND NOW, IT IS MY TURN! NOW SHALL THOR FACE THE FURY OF HERCULES' ATTACK!
I SHALL NOT SLAY ONE SO VALIANT! INSTEAD, I SHALL BIND THEE AND MAKE THEE MY CAPTIVE!
9.

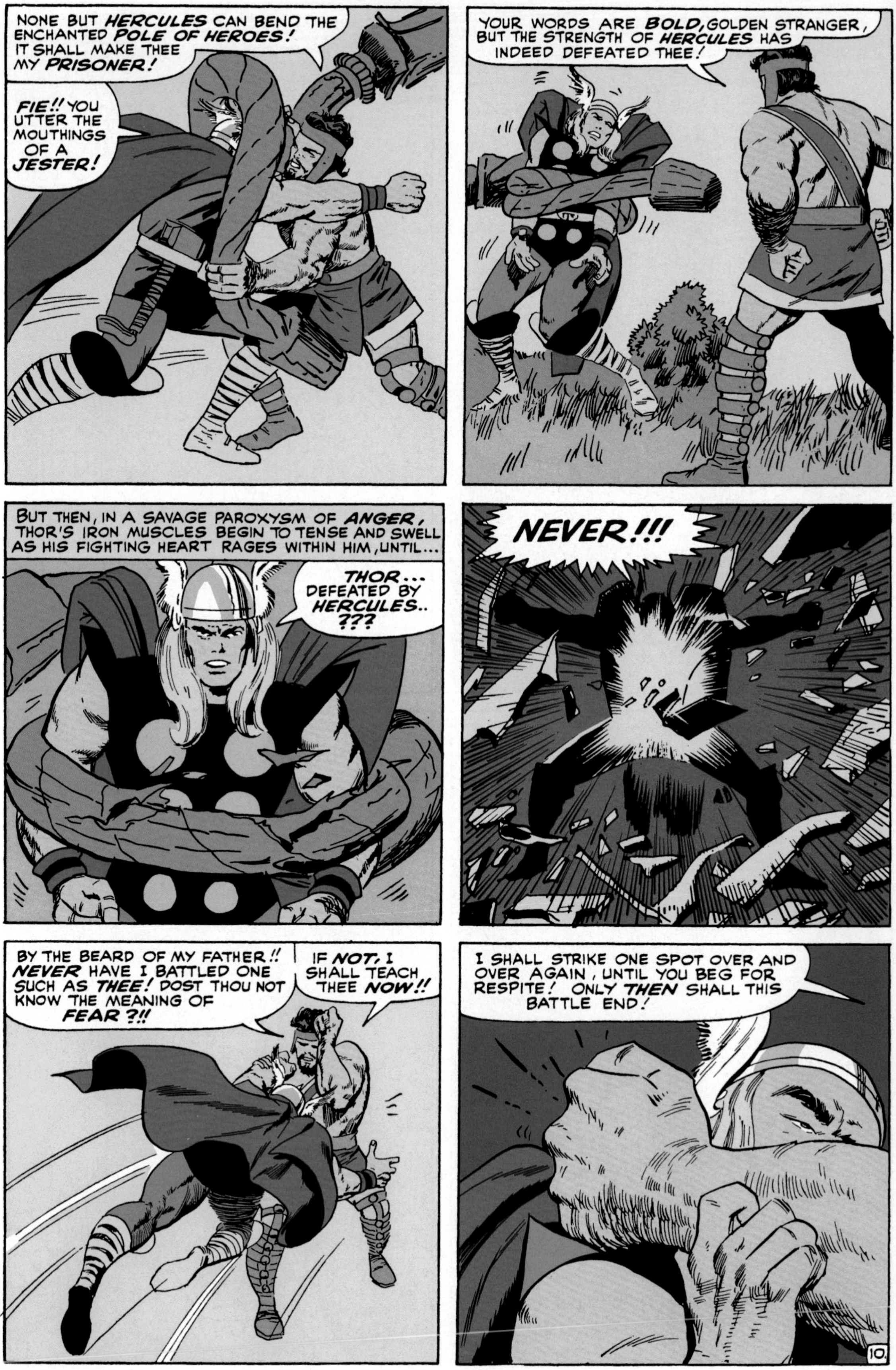
NONE BUT HERCULES CAN BEND THE ENCHANTED POLE OF HEROES! IT SHALL MAKE THEE MY PRISONER!
FIE!! YOU UTTER THE MOUTHINGS OF A JESTER!
YOUR WORDS ARE BOLD, GOLDEN STRANGER, BUT THE STRENGTH OF HERCULES HAS INDEED DEFEATED THEE!
BUT THEN, IN A SAVAGE PAROXYSM OF ANGER, THOR'S IRON MUSCLES BEGIN TO TENSE AND SWELL AS HIS FIGHTING HEART RAGES WITHIN HIM, UNTIL...
THOR... DEFEATED BY HERCULES.. ???
NEVER!!!
BY THE BEARD OF MY FATHER!! NEVER HAVE I BATTLED ONE SUCH AS THEE! DOST THOU NOT KNOW THE MEANING OF FEAR?!!
IF NOT, I SHALL TEACH THEE NOW!!
I SHALL STRIKE ONE SPOT OVER AND OVER AGAIN, UNTIL YOU BEG FOR RESPITE! ONLY THEN SHALL THIS BATTLE END!
10.

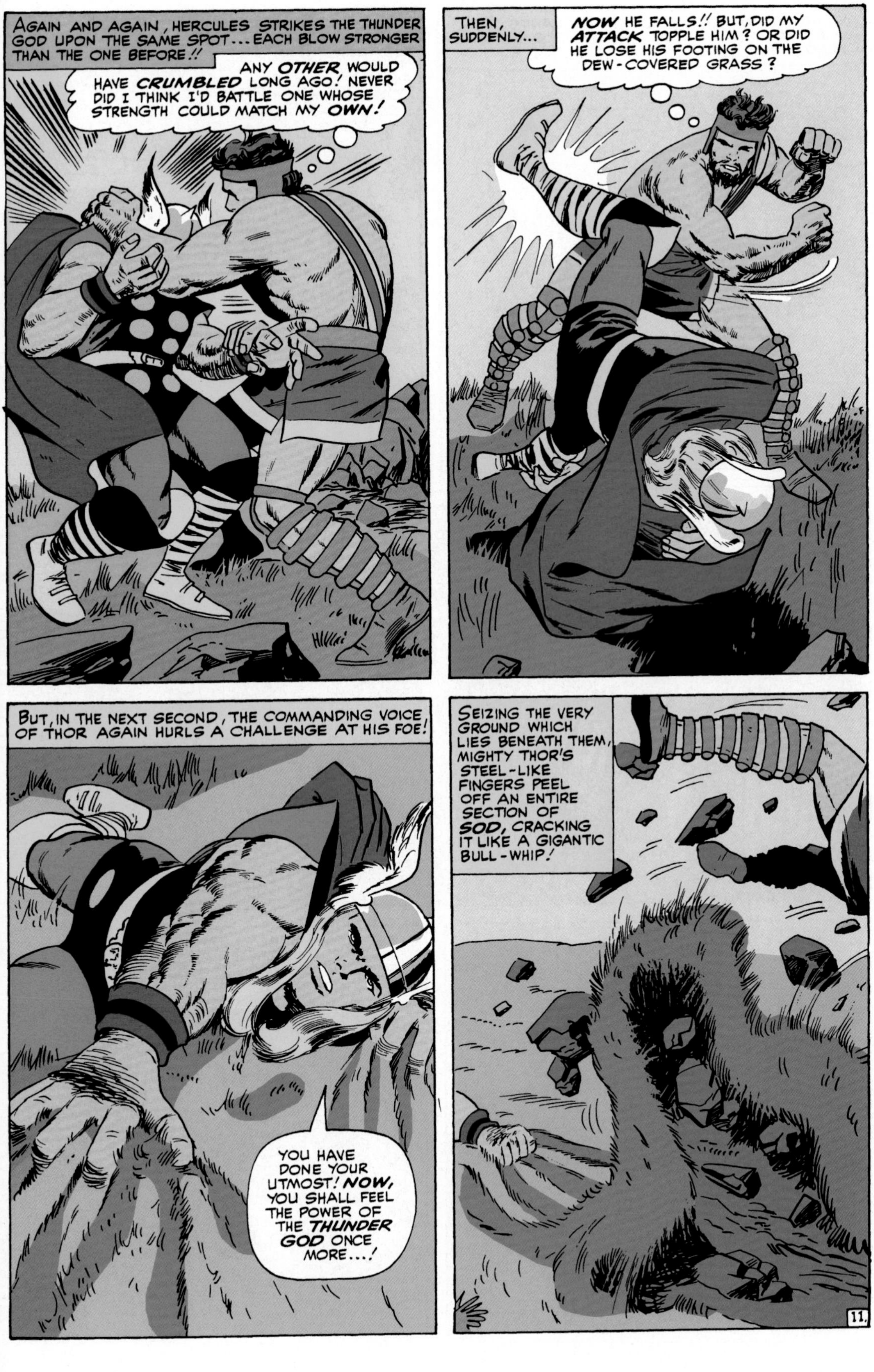

AGAIN AND AGAIN, HERCULES STRIKES THE THUNDER GOD UPON THE SAME SPOT... EACH BLOW STRONGER THAN THE ONE BEFORE!!
ANY OTHER WOULD HAVE CRUMBLED LONG AGO! NEVER DID I THINK I'D BATTLE ONE WHOSE STRENGTH COULD MATCH MY OWN!
THEN, SUDDENLY...
NOW HE FALLS!! BUT, DID MY ATTACK TOPPLE HIM? OR DID HE LOSE HIS FOOTING ON THE DEW-COVERED GRASS?
BUT, IN THE NEXT SECOND, THE COMMANDING VOICE OF THOR AGAIN HURLS A CHALLENGE AT HIS FOE!
YOU HAVE DONE YOUR UTMOST! NOW, YOU SHALL FEEL THE POWER OF THE THUNDER GOD ONCE MORE...!
SEIZING THE VERY GROUND WHICH LIES BENEATH THEM, MIGHTY THOR'S STEEL-LIKE FINGERS PEEL OFF AN ENTIRE SECTION OF SOD, CRACKING IT LIKE A GIGANTIC BULL-WHIP!
11

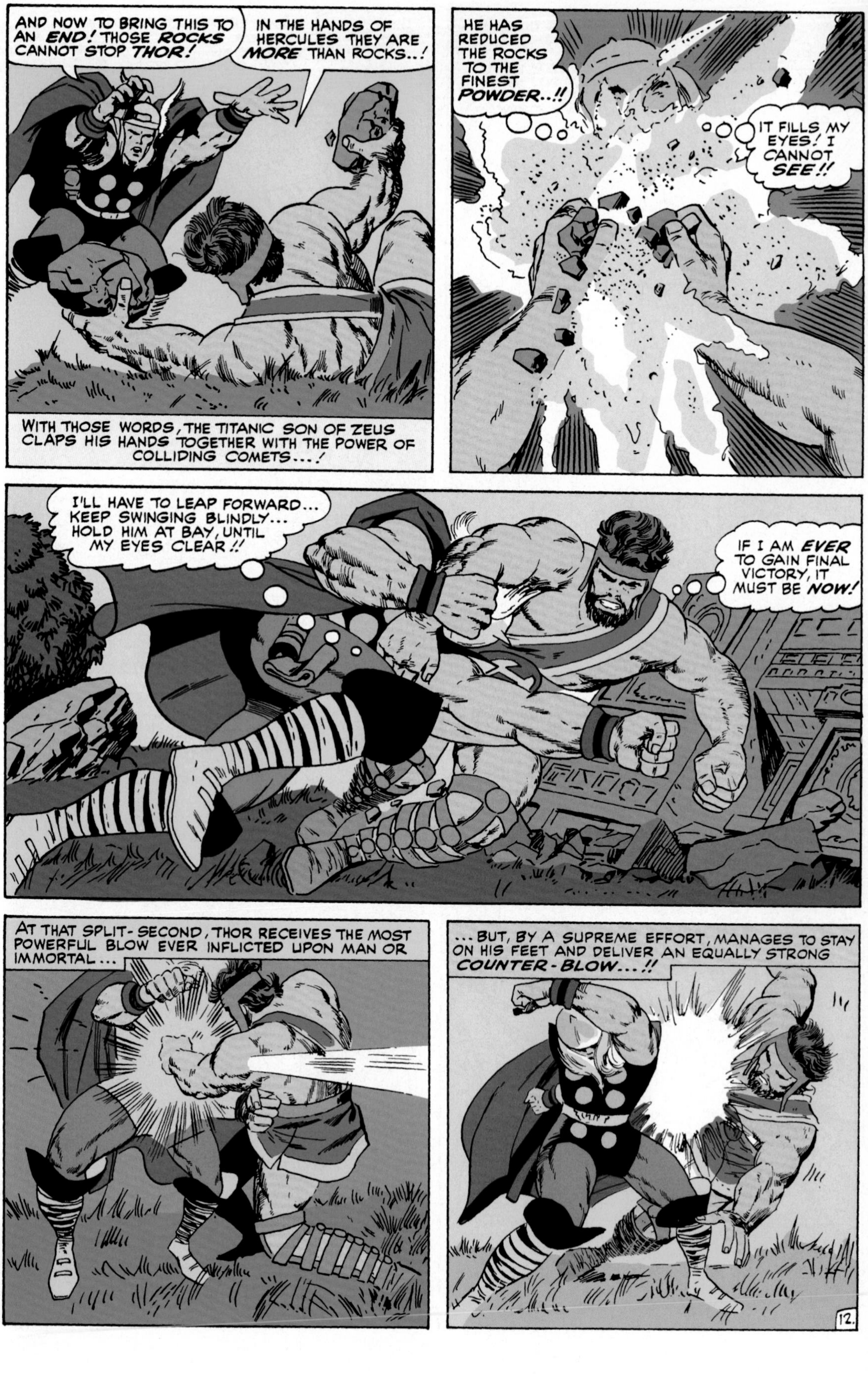

AND NOW TO BRING THIS TO AN *END!* THOSE *ROCKS* CANNOT STOP *THOR!*
IN THE HANDS OF HERCULES THEY ARE *MORE* THAN ROCKS..!
WITH THOSE WORDS, THE TITANIC SON OF ZEUS CLAPS HIS HANDS TOGETHER WITH THE POWER OF COLLIDING COMETS...!
HE HAS REDUCED THE ROCKS TO THE FINEST *POWDER*..!!
IT FILLS MY EYES! I CANNOT *SEE!!*
I'LL HAVE TO LEAP FORWARD... KEEP SWINGING BLINDLY... HOLD HIM AT BAY, UNTIL MY EYES CLEAR!!
IF I AM *EVER* TO GAIN FINAL VICTORY, IT MUST BE *NOW!*
AT THAT SPLIT-SECOND, THOR RECEIVES THE MOST POWERFUL BLOW EVER INFLICTED UPON MAN OR IMMORTAL...
...BUT, BY A SUPREME EFFORT, MANAGES TO STAY ON HIS FEET AND DELIVER AN EQUALLY STRONG *COUNTER-BLOW*...!!
12.

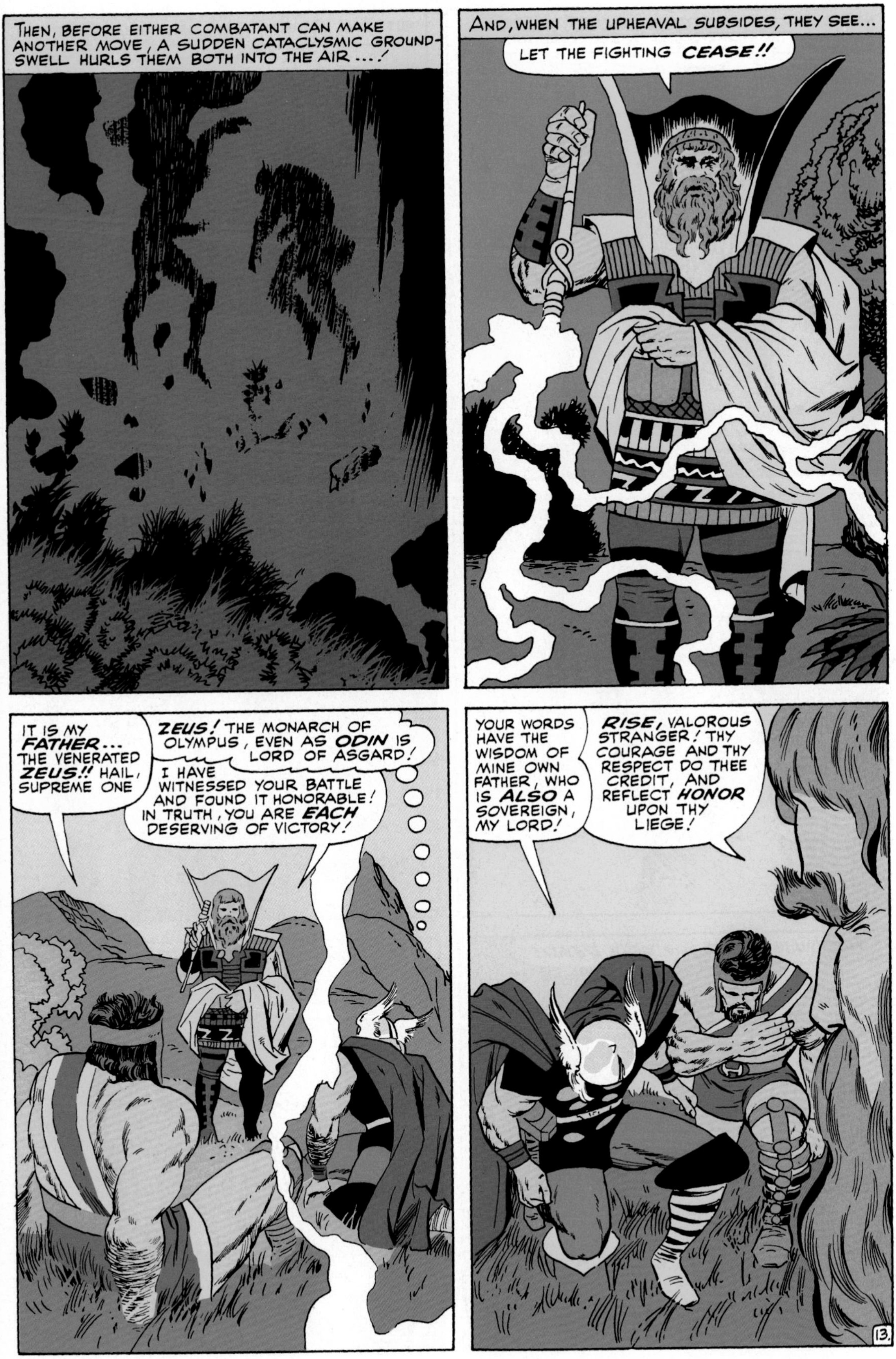

THEN, BEFORE EITHER COMBATANT CAN MAKE ANOTHER MOVE, A SUDDEN CATACLYSMIC GROUND-SWELL HURLS THEM BOTH INTO THE AIR...!
AND, WHEN THE UPHEAVAL SUBSIDES, THEY SEE...
LET THE FIGHTING CEASE!!
IT IS MY FATHER... THE VENERATED ZEUS!! HAIL, SUPREME ONE
ZEUS! THE MONARCH OF OLYMPUS, EVEN AS ODIN IS LORD OF ASGARD!
I HAVE WITNESSED YOUR BATTLE AND FOUND IT HONORABLE! IN TRUTH, YOU ARE EACH DESERVING OF VICTORY!
YOUR WORDS HAVE THE WISDOM OF MINE OWN FATHER, WHO IS ALSO A SOVEREIGN, MY LORD!
RISE, VALOROUS STRANGER! THY COURAGE AND THY RESPECT DO THEE CREDIT, AND REFLECT HONOR UPON THY LIEGE!
13.

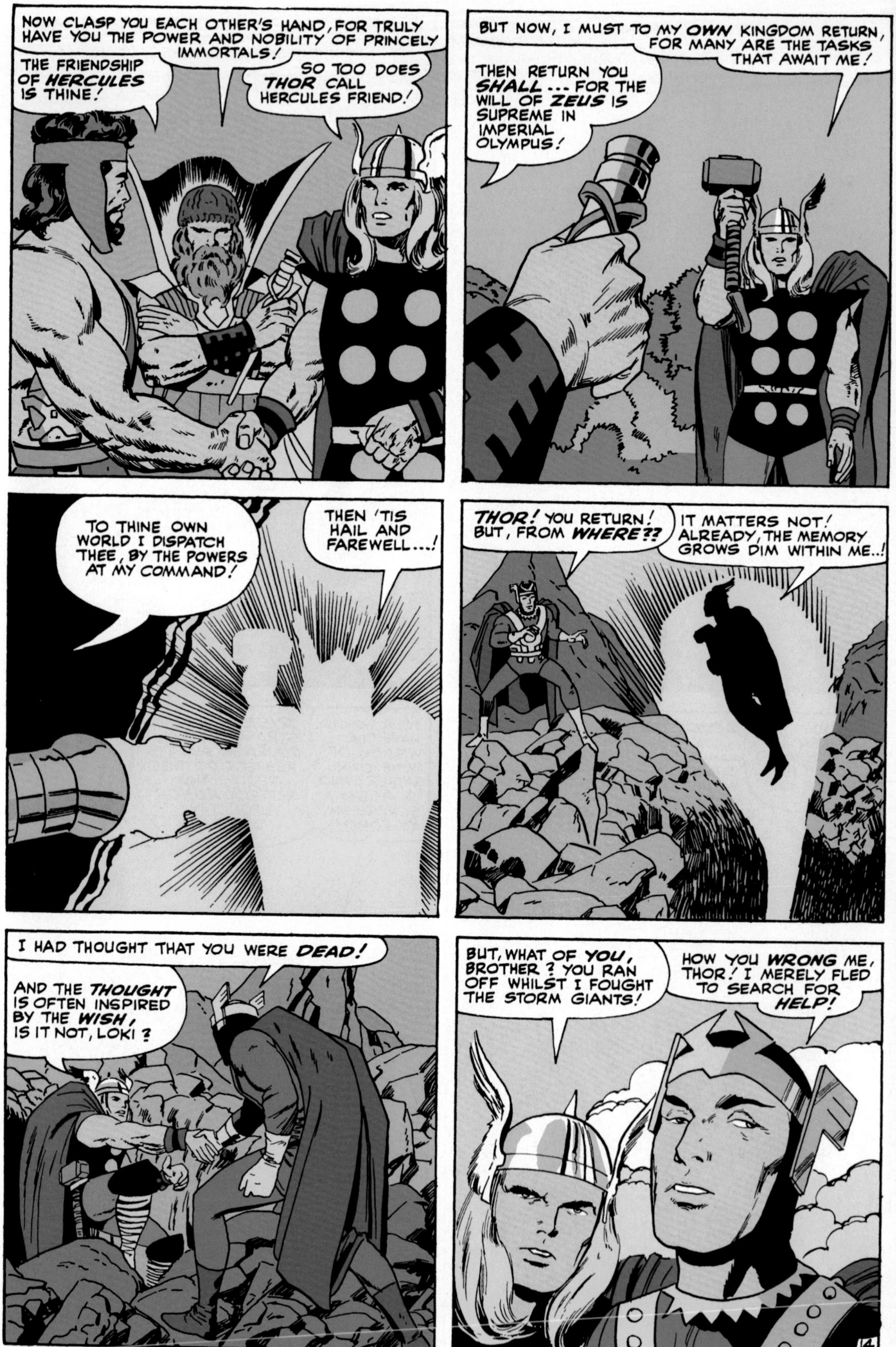
NOW CLASP YOU EACH OTHER'S HAND, FOR TRULY HAVE YOU THE POWER AND NOBILITY OF PRINCELY IMMORTALS!
THE FRIENDSHIP OF HERCULES IS THINE!
SO TOO DOES THOR CALL HERCULES FRIEND!
BUT NOW, I MUST TO MY OWN KINGDOM RETURN, FOR MANY ARE THE TASKS THAT AWAIT ME!
THEN RETURN YOU SHALL... FOR THE WILL OF ZEUS IS SUPREME IN IMPERIAL OLYMPUS!
TO THINE OWN WORLD I DISPATCH THEE, BY THE POWERS AT MY COMMAND!
THEN 'TIS HAIL AND FAREWELL...!
THOR! YOU RETURN! BUT, FROM WHERE??
IT MATTERS NOT! ALREADY, THE MEMORY GROWS DIM WITHIN ME..!
I HAD THOUGHT THAT YOU WERE DEAD!
AND THE THOUGHT IS OFTEN INSPIRED BY THE WISH, IS IT NOT, LOKI?
BUT, WHAT OF YOU, BROTHER? YOU RAN OFF WHILST I FOUGHT THE STORM GIANTS!
HOW YOU WRONG ME, THOR! I MERELY FLED TO SEARCH FOR HELP!

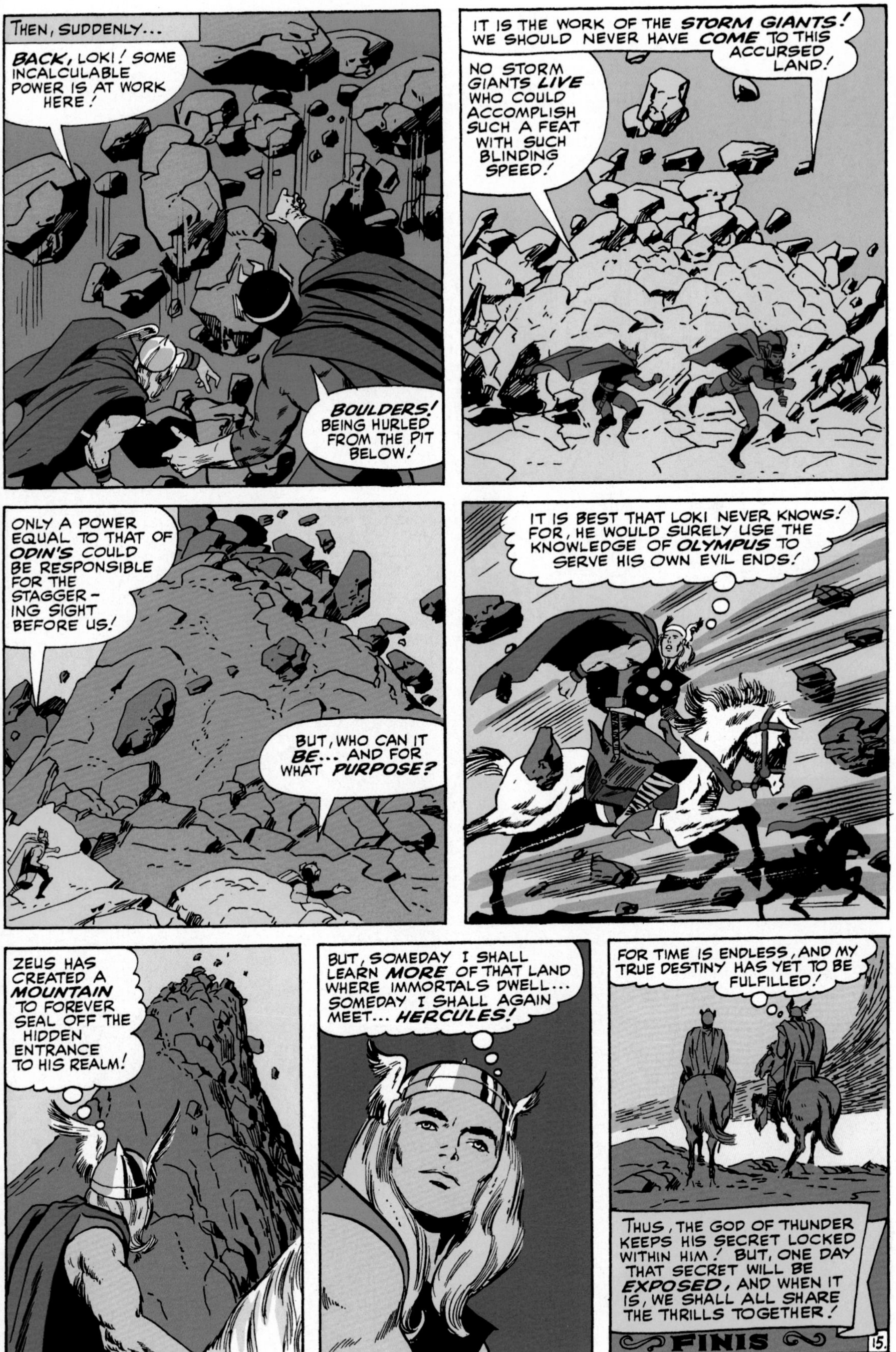
THEN, SUDDENLY...
BACK, LOKI! SOME INCALCULABLE POWER IS AT WORK HERE!
BOULDERS! BEING HURLED FROM THE PIT BELOW!
IT IS THE WORK OF THE STORM GIANTS! WE SHOULD NEVER HAVE COME TO THIS ACCURSED LAND!
NO STORM GIANTS LIVE WHO COULD ACCOMPLISH SUCH A FEAT WITH SUCH BLINDING SPEED!
ONLY A POWER EQUAL TO THAT OF ODIN'S COULD BE RESPONSIBLE FOR THE STAGGER-ING SIGHT BEFORE US!
BUT, WHO CAN IT BE... AND FOR WHAT PURPOSE?
IT IS BEST THAT LOKI NEVER KNOWS! FOR, HE WOULD SURELY USE THE KNOWLEDGE OF OLYMPUS TO SERVE HIS OWN EVIL ENDS!
ZEUS HAS CREATED A MOUNTAIN TO FOREVER SEAL OFF THE HIDDEN ENTRANCE TO HIS REALM!
BUT, SOMEDAY I SHALL LEARN MORE OF THAT LAND WHERE IMMORTALS DWELL... SOMEDAY I SHALL AGAIN MEET... HERCULES!
FOR TIME IS ENDLESS, AND MY TRUE DESTINY HAS YET TO BE FULFILLED!
THUS, THE GOD OF THUNDER KEEPS HIS SECRET LOCKED WITHIN HIM! BUT, ONE DAY THAT SECRET WILL BE EXPOSED, AND WHEN IT IS, WE SHALL ALL SHARE THE THRILLS TOGETHER!
FINIS
15.

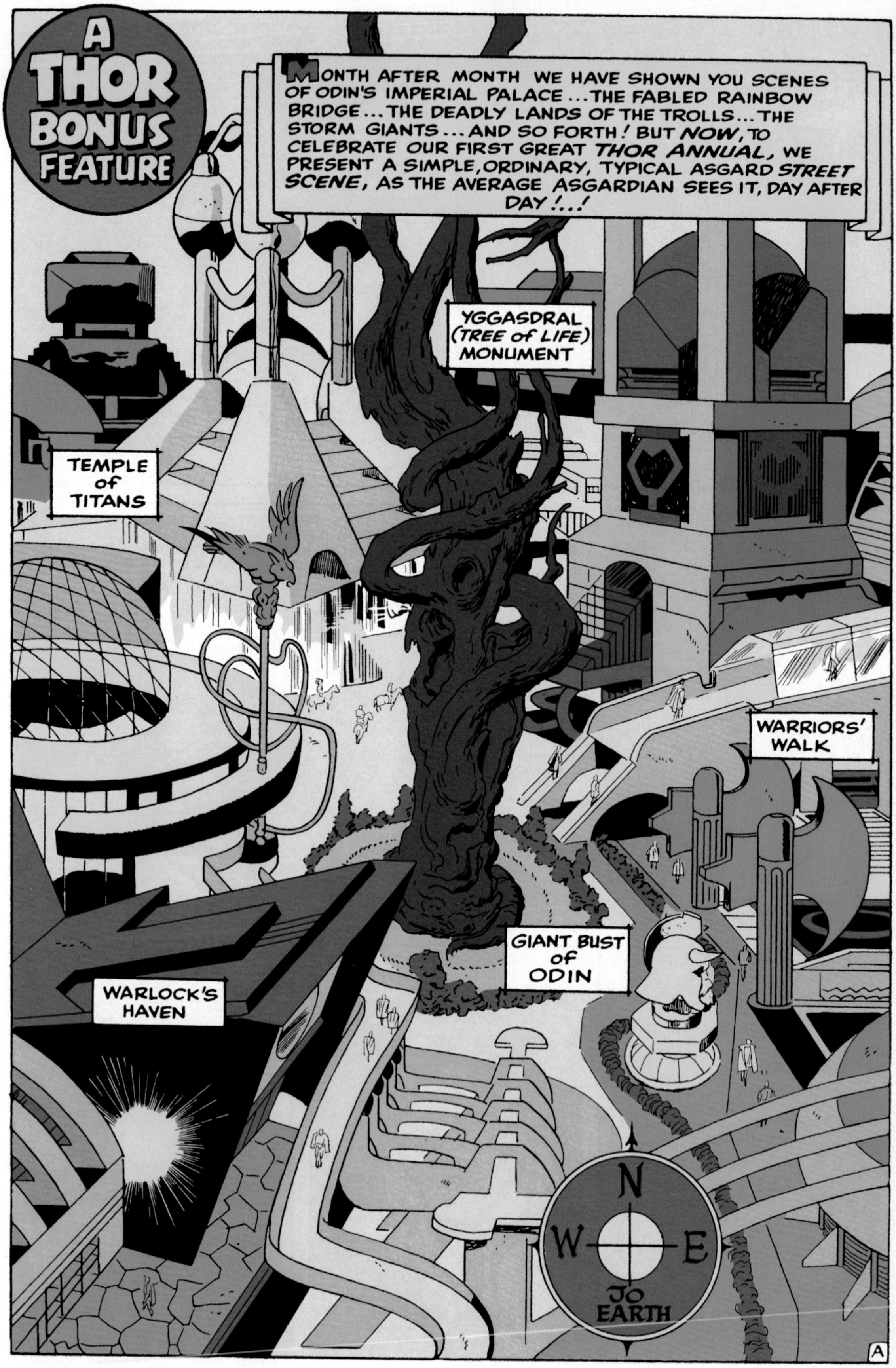
A THOR BONUS FEATURE
MONTH AFTER MONTH WE HAVE SHOWN YOU SCENES OF ODIN'S IMPERIAL PALACE... THE FABLED RAINBOW BRIDGE... THE DEADLY LANDS OF THE TROLLS... THE STORM GIANTS... AND SO FORTH! BUT NOW, TO CELEBRATE OUR FIRST GREAT THOR ANNUAL, WE PRESENT A SIMPLE, ORDINARY, TYPICAL ASGARD STREET SCENE, AS THE AVERAGE ASGARDIAN SEES IT, DAY AFTER DAY!..!
YGGASDRAL (TREE of LIFE) MONUMENT
TEMPLE of TITANS
WARRIORS' WALK
GIANT BUST of ODIN
WARLOCK'S HAVEN
N
W
E
TO EARTH
A

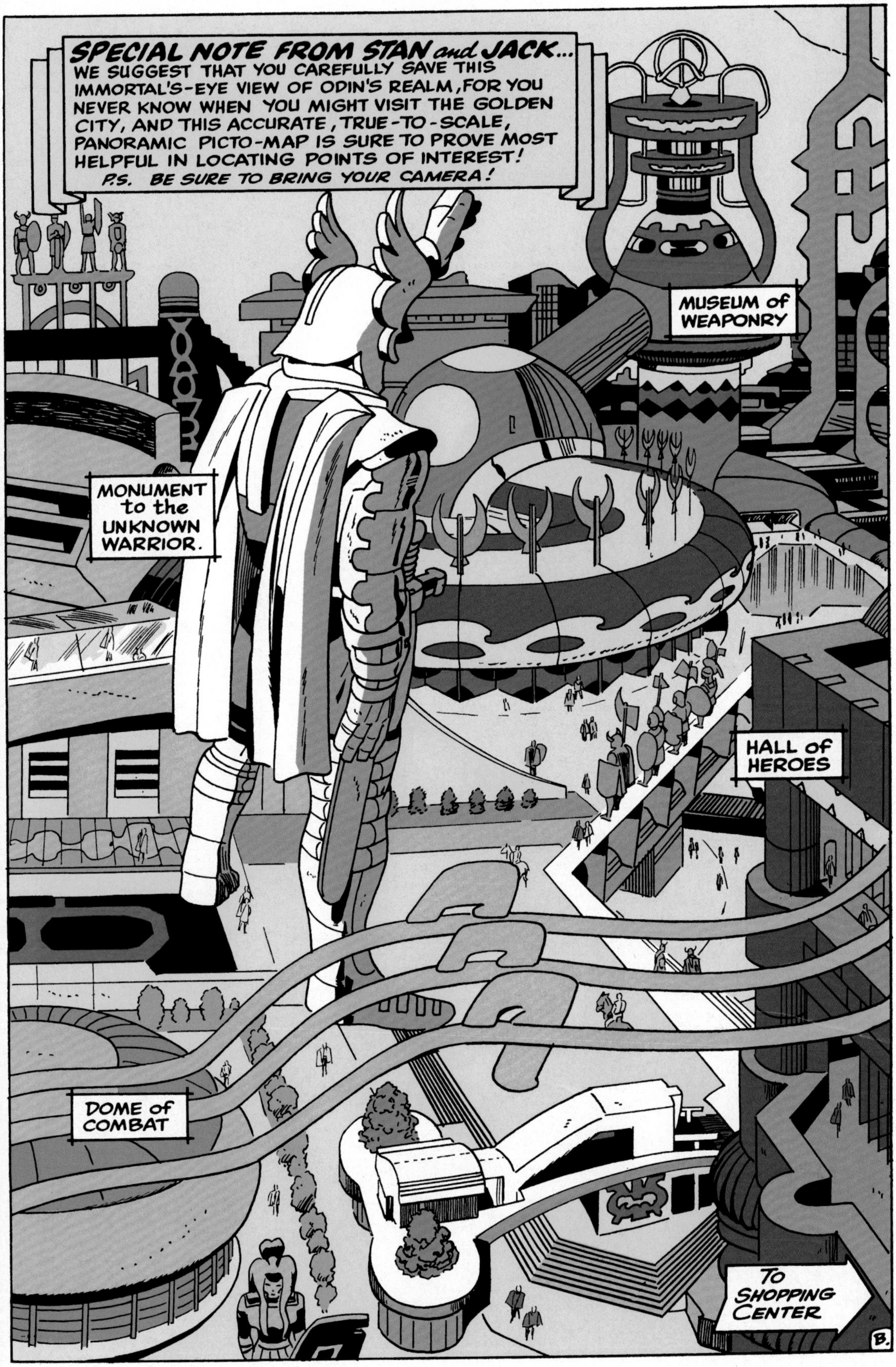
SPECIAL NOTE FROM STAN and JACK...
WE SUGGEST THAT YOU CAREFULLY SAVE THIS IMMORTAL'S-EYE VIEW OF ODIN'S REALM, FOR YOU NEVER KNOW WHEN YOU MIGHT VISIT THE GOLDEN CITY, AND THIS ACCURATE, TRUE-TO-SCALE, PANORAMIC PICTO-MAP IS SURE TO PROVE MOST HELPFUL IN LOCATING POINTS OF INTEREST!
P.S. BE SURE TO BRING YOUR CAMERA!
MUSEUM of WEAPONRY
MONUMENT to the UNKNOWN WARRIOR.
HALL of HEROES
DOME of COMBAT
TO SHOPPING CENTER
B.

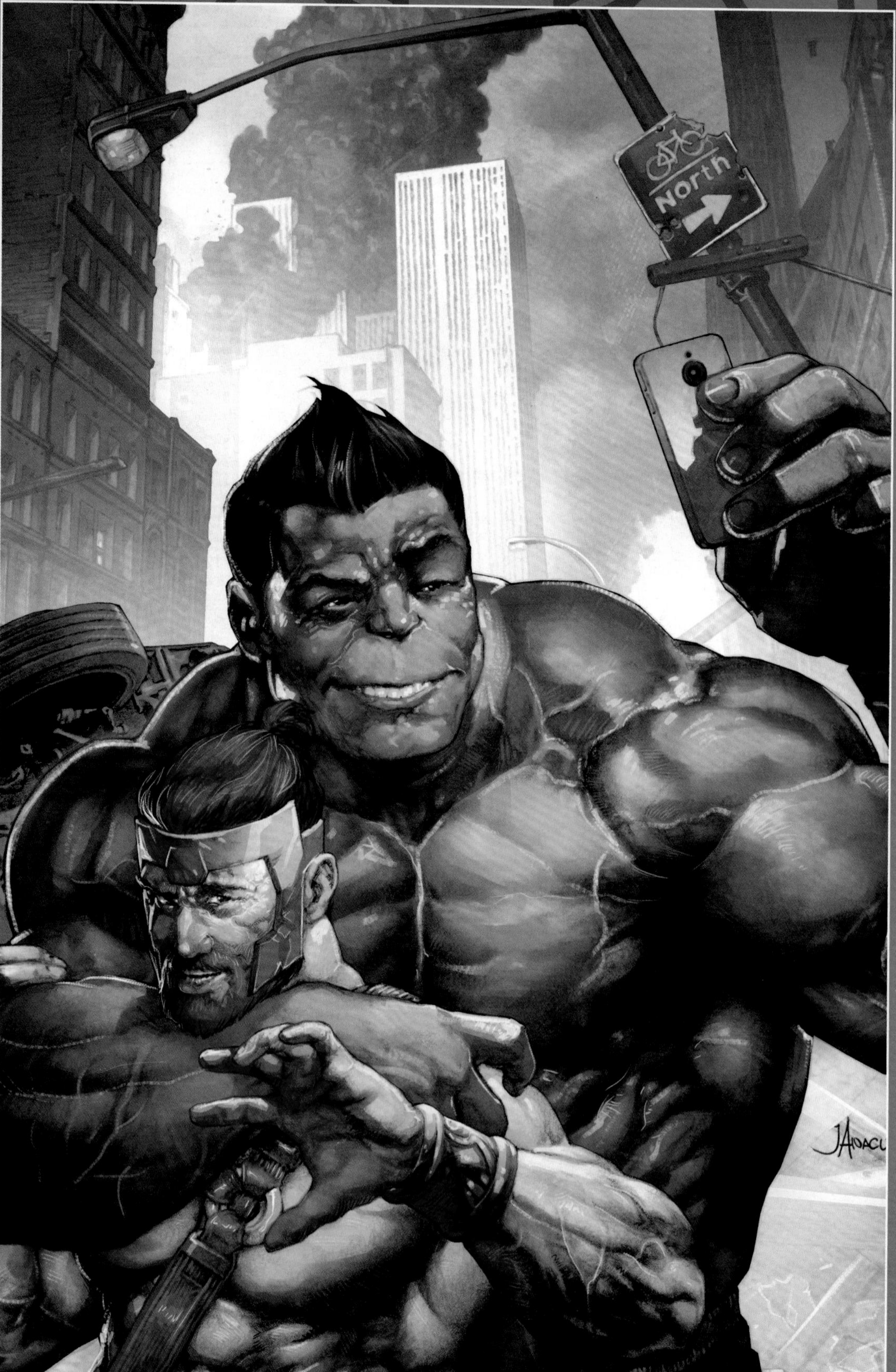
North

#1 VARIANT BY JAY ANACLETO & ROMULO FAJARDO JR.

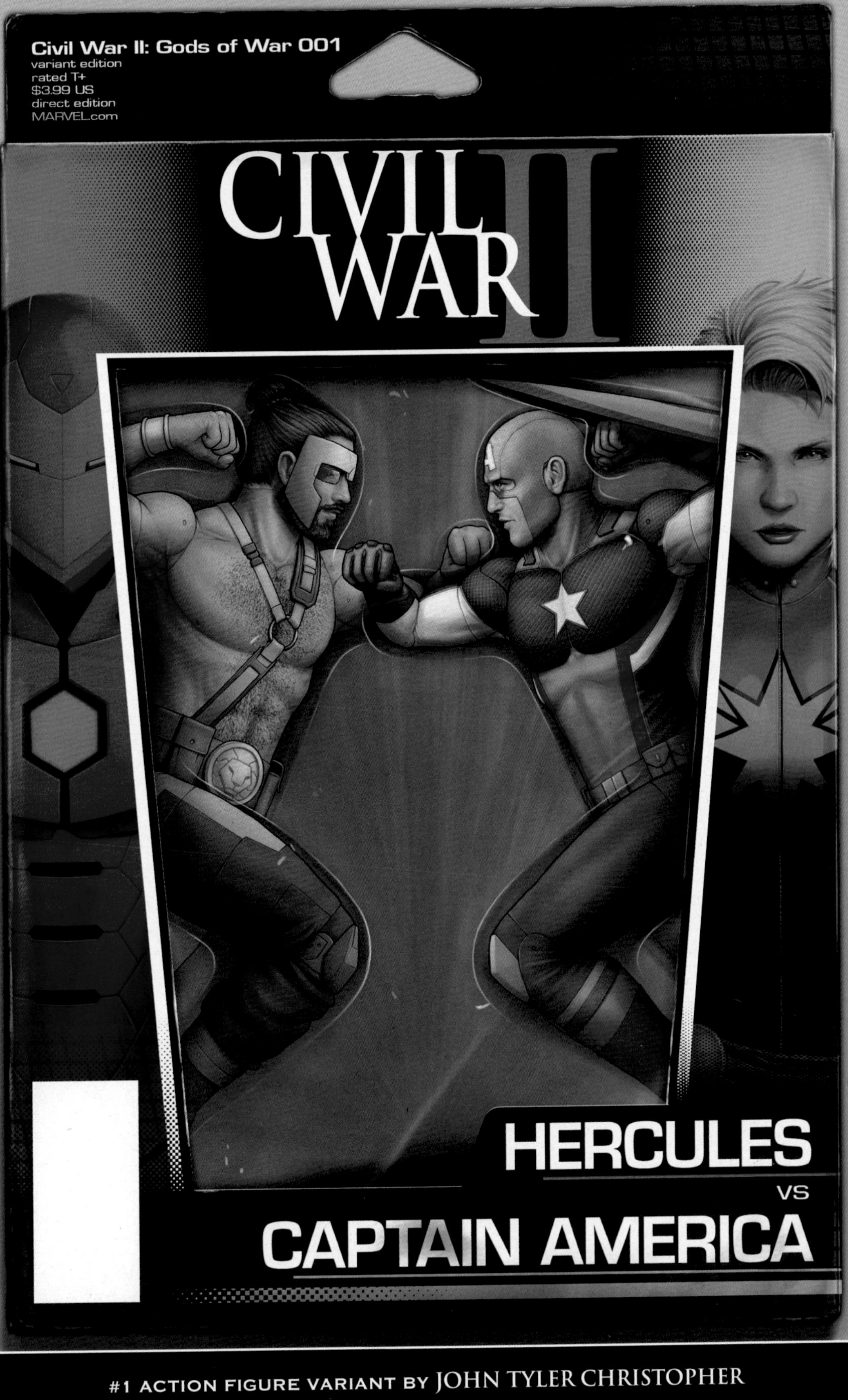

Civil War II: Gods of War 001
variant edition
rated T+
$3.99 US
direct edition
MARVEL.com

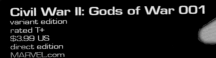

CIVIL WAR II

HERCULES

vs

CAPTAIN AMERICA

#1 ACTION FIGURE VARIANT BY JOHN TYLER CHRISTOPHER

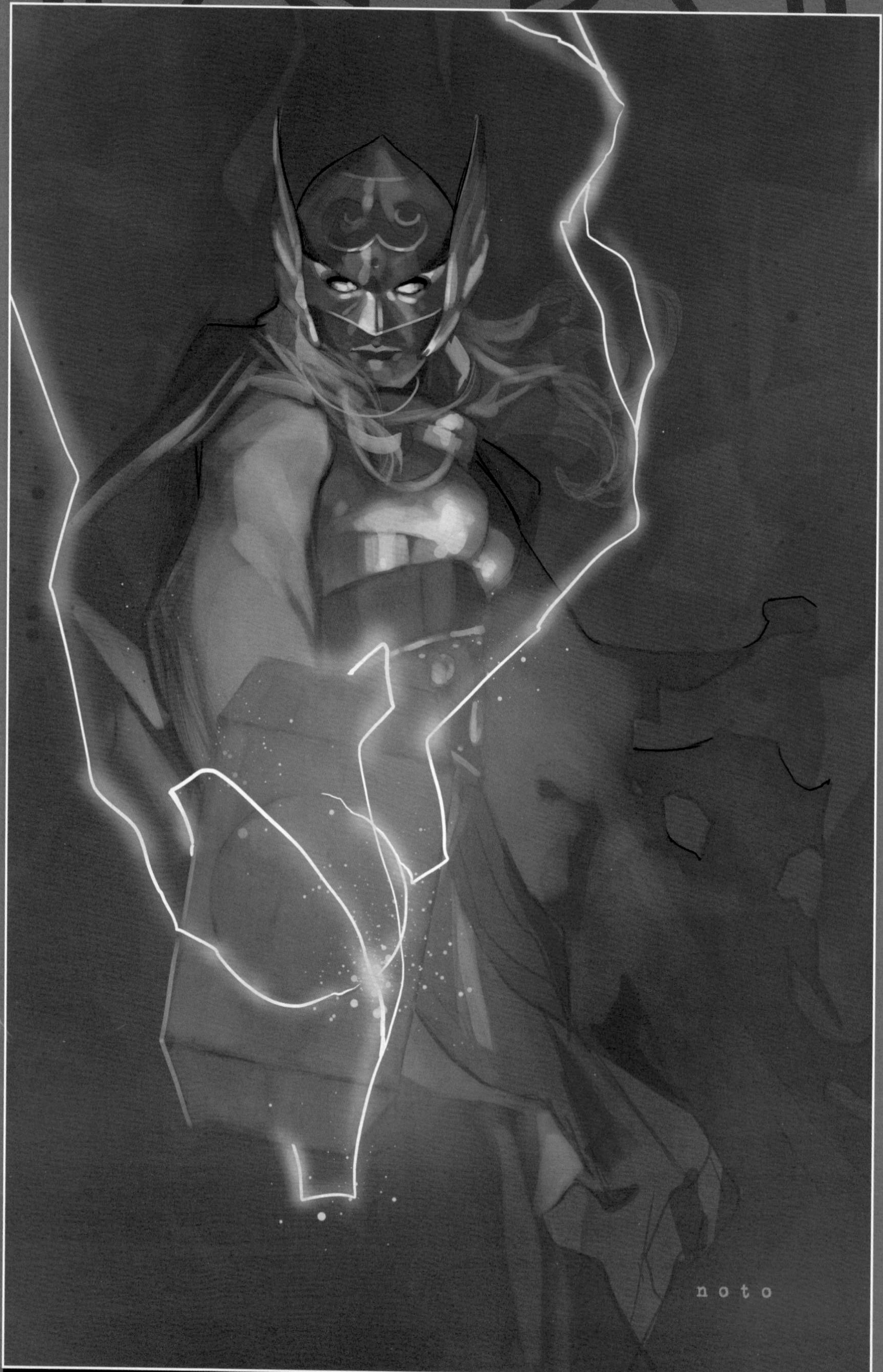
noto

#1 THOR VARIANT BY PHIL NOTO

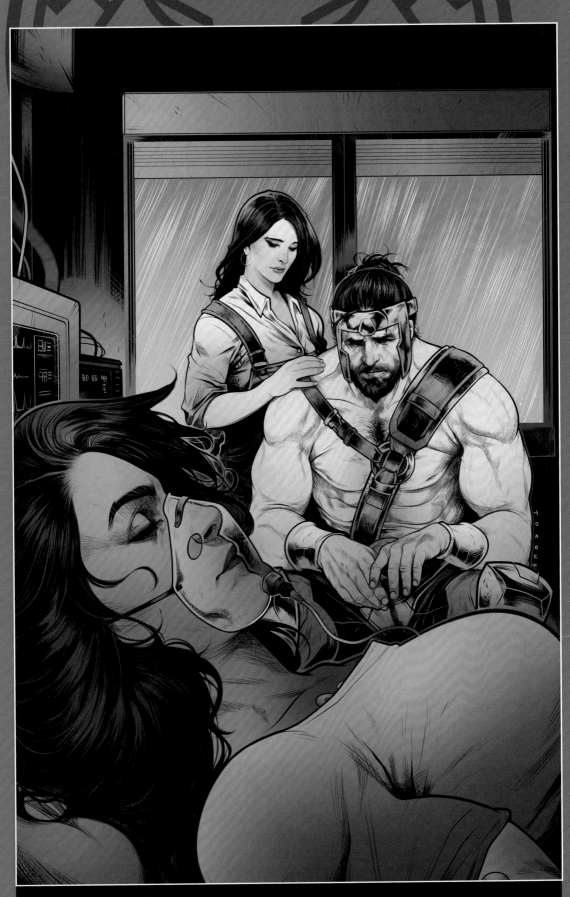

#2 VARIANT BY ELIZABETH TORQUE

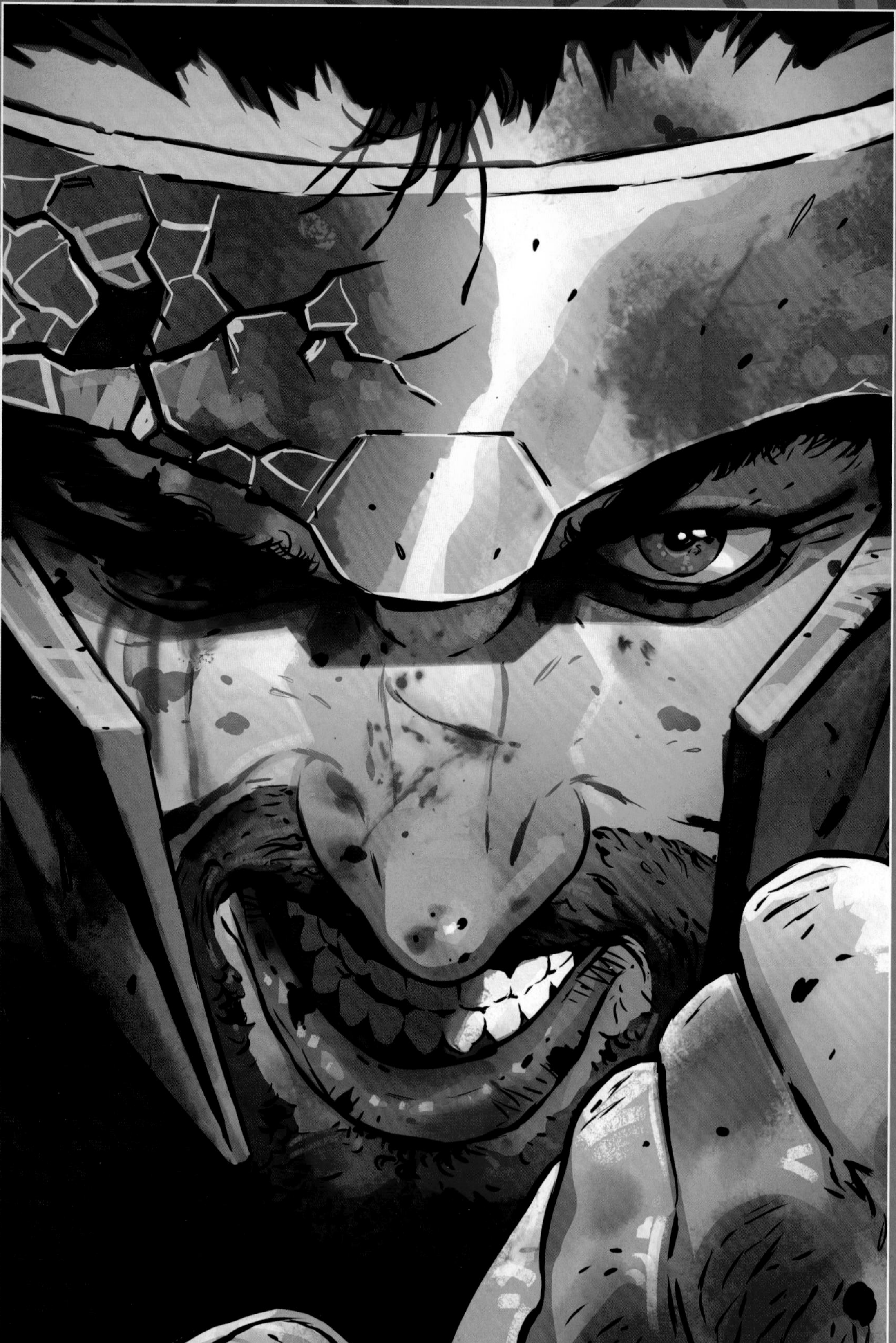

#3 VARIANT BY ACO & ROMULO FAJARDO JR.

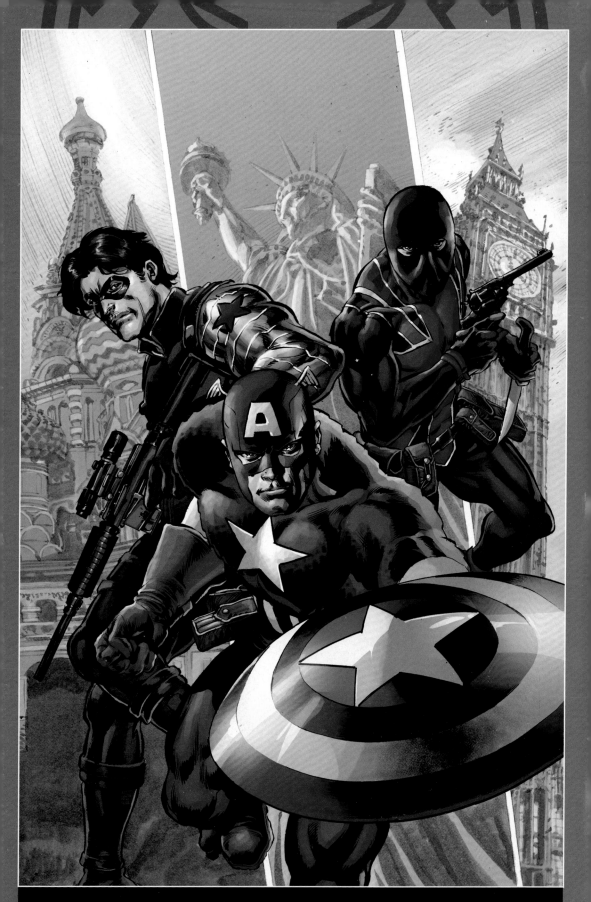

#4 CAPTAIN AMERICA 75TH ANNIVERSARY VARIANT BY
MIKE PERKINS & ANDY TROY

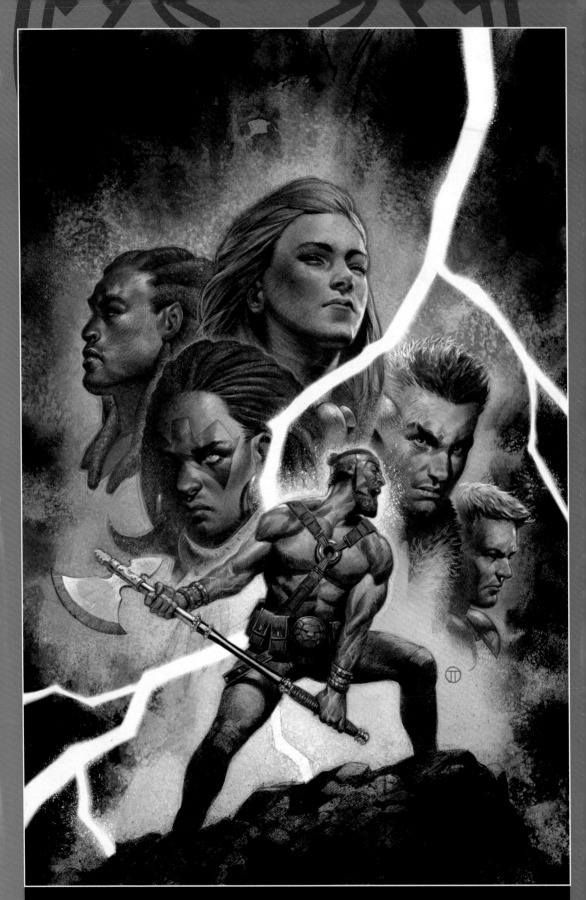

#4 VARIANT BY JULIAN TOTINO TEDESCO